...ease remember that thi... ☑ **P9-CEN-564**
and that it belongs only temporarily to each
person who uses it. Be considerate. Do
not write in this, or any, library book.

GARY LIBRARY
VERMONT COLLEGE
36 COLLEGE STREET
MONTPELIER, VT 05602
WITHDRAWN

Making It in the "Free World"

SUNY series in

WOMEN, CRIME, AND CRIMINOLOGY

———————————————

Meda Chesney-Lind and Russ Immarigeon, editors

MAKING IT IN THE
"FREE WORLD"

Women in Transition from Prison

Patricia O'Brien

State University of New York Press

364.374
O137m
2001

Published by
STATE UNIVERSITY OF NEW YORK PRESS
Albany

© 2001 State University of New York

All rights reserved

Printed in the United States of America

No part of this book may be used or reproduced in any manner whatsoever without written permission.
No part of this book may be stored in a retrieval system or transmitted in any form or by any means
including electronic, electrostatic, magnetic tape, mechanical, photocopying, recording, or otherwise
without the prior permission in writing of the publisher.

For information, address
State University of New York Press,
90 State Street, Suite 700, Albany, NY 12207

Production, Laurie Searl
Marketing, Dana E. Yanulavich

Library of Congress Cataloging-in-Publication Data

O'Brien, Patricia, 1955–
    Making it in the free world : women in transition from prison / Patricia O'Brien.
        p. cm. — (SUNY series in women, crime, and criminology)
    Includes bibliographical references and indexes.
    ISBN 0-7914-4861-4 (hardcover : alk. paper) — ISBN 0-7914-4862-2 (pbk. : alk. paper)
        1. Women ex-convicts—Services for—United States.   2. Women
    ex-convicts—Rehabilitation—United States.   3. Prison psychology—United States.   4.
    Minority women—United States—Psychology.   5. Demographic transition—United States.
    I. Title.   II. Series.

HV9304 .O145 2001
364.3'74—dc21   00-036566

10   9   8   7   6   5   4   3   2   1

To the eighteen women whose stories created this book,

and to every ex-incarcerated woman making it in the free world.

In memory of my beloved sister,

Genevieve Sue Freeman

CONTENTS

Please remember that this is a library book,
and that it belongs only temporarily to each
person who uses it. Be considerate. Do
not write in this, or any, library book.

FOREWORD

The criminal justice policies that have created the rapidly increasing U.S. female prison population are fraught with controversy. While "get tough on crime" politicians continue to vote for stronger and harsher penalties, women's advocates argue that there have to be better and more humane approaches than prison terms for dealing with problems of drugs and poverty and the types of crime that most women commit. Although there is a lack of agreement about the wisdom of prison confinement as the major public response for women convicted of criminal acts, there is general public sentiment that escalation of criminal activity, permanent psychological damage, and severed family ties are not the intent or purpose of prison sentences.

Prisons, however, are not effective in helping women lead more productive, crime-free lives. The behaviors required by prison rules and informal inmate cultures bear little resemblance to those needed for successful community living. When women leave prison, they are seldom better prepared to address the problems that led to their involvement in illegal activities and their emotional, family, and economic situations are often worse than they were prior to imprisonment. For far too many women, the exit from prison is merely a revolving door. For far too many women, the expectation that their future can and will entail a lot more than what prison offers is not even a dream, let alone a reality.

Despite many obstacles, and probably against all odds as well, some formerly incarcerated women take or make paths away from, rather than back to, prison. They manage to not only "pick up the pieces" but to also move forward with their lives in ways that are both socially acceptable and personally satisfying. Occasionally, we hear their stories—at a conference on women offenders, in a newspaper article on prisons, or on a television special. For those of us who count among our friends or families a woman who has survived a prison sentence, we know their stories, or at least parts of them, on a more personal level. Their stories may even be our stories.

Making It in the "Free World" gives us more stories, but with a combined intensity of feeling and caring and level of thoughts and analysis that are rare in the literature on persons in conflict with the law. Using an empowerment framework, it tells the stories of eighteen women, from racially diverse backgrounds, who are successfully making it in the community after having served a prison term. The women speak to us in their own voices and in their own ways about life after prison. From them we get an up close look at the day-to-day challenges involved in obtaining and maintaining employment, reestablishing close personal relationships, and meeting the requirements of parole and other social control systems. We hear the frustrations, and sometimes fear, involved in encounters with those who control the resources they need, and learn how they manage to obtain the things they need and use their internal strengths to survive and grow. We see them making it on the outside despite the fact that they can't put prison behind them and that the stigma of a prison sentence permeates life options long after the "official" time has been served. The women's voices are compelling: O'Brien's analysis and interpretations are insightful. The implications for social work and criminal justice are challenging and practical.

This book reaffirms our need to reframe the nature of the current discourse about prison policies and operations and about community reentry and long-term success. Neither an exclusive research focus on individual deviance, nor a narrow one on recidivism rates is likely to provide the knowledge and understanding we need to support post-release success. Similarly, public policies and procedures that institutionalize and "beat people down" in prison and continue to punish former prisoners by denying them rights and resources once they are released impede, rather than facilitate, post-release success. As scholars, we have a commitment to learning and advancing the truth. As caring people, we have an obligation to use those truths to make things different and better in our homes, institutions, and communities.

CREASIE FINNEY HAIRSTON

PREFACE

In this book, I identify and theorize about the factors that support the reintegration of women to the free world, that is, the world outside of the prison facility, after they have completed their terms of incarceration. As I write, the state of Illinois, where I live, is taking bids from small towns anxious to reap a potential economic bonanza to construct a new facility to confine up to 1,800 women.[1] Currently, Illinois incarcerates more than 2,500 women in four different facilities and the state Department of Corrections estimates that the female inmate population will grow an average of 8.8 percent annually, resulting in 9,820 incarcerated women by 2007.[2]

As a society, we are determined to punish offenders. Irrespective of the type of crime committed, its context, or any other factors, the punishment for women and men is increasingly becoming time in a prison cell, cut off from friends, family, and the life of the "free world" that many of us take for granted. We must be determined, however, that if a neighbor, friend, family member, coworker, or member of our greater community does her or his time that we do everything possible to make room for their return, their restoration, their reintegration. This is not a simple process, as the stories in this book attest. But these stories also remind us that, if the internal and external conditions are in place at the right time, reintegration is possible.

This study came from my sense that what practitioners know about women offenders neither supports their movement out of prison nor helps them resist the forces that recycle them back to prison. I sought to answer the following research questions.

1. How do women exiting prison establish a home and address concrete needs?

2. How do relationships that women create or maintain facilitate their transition from prison?

3. What are the internal or individual elements that facilitate women's processes of reestablishing themselves after release from prison?

4. How do parole or supervision processes affect women's ability to renegotiate their reentry after incarceration?

5. What do female ex-inmates identify as necessary to support their post-incarceration success?

The answers to these questions, culled from the narratives of eighteen women who identified themselves as successful after serving single or multiple prison sentences, provide nitty-gritty reminders and strategies for programs, policies, and research that maximize women's possibilities for reentering society in a meaningful way.

ORGANIZATION OF THE BOOK

To facilitate the book's use and the reader's understanding of the material, I describe the methods I used in this study in Appendix A. In addition, each woman's demographic profile, descriptive narrative, and institutional history is provided in Appendix B. The first chapter establishes a background for examining the issue of women's incarceration in the United States. I briefly describe the history of women's incarceration, enumerate the increasing frequency of the use of incarceration and some of the observed reasons for it, and the characteristics of imprisoned women. Chapters 2, 3, and 4 focus on different aspects of factors that contribute to women's success: addressing concrete needs, establishing healthy relationships, and revitalizing the internal self, respectively. In these chapters, I provide a framework that introduces the focus of this volume and then draws upon the women's narratives to demonstrate its main points. Chapter 5 brings together these contributory aspects and suggests an empowerment framework for assessing women's transitions from prison. The chapter ends with a section that integrates the women's recommendations with my suggestions for making it otherwise for women we identify as "offenders." Finally, I close with a brief epilogue that describes how the women are faring two years after the study.

ASSUMPTIONS AND STANDPOINT

The passion that inspired this study evolved while I was an advocate for a woman who was convicted in the homicide of her abusive husband. After Mary had served almost five years of a twenty-year sentence, she received an early release due to a post-conviction appeal. I assumed that her freedom would assure her an easy transition from prison back home to a small, rural community in a southern state. Certainly, she was relieved to be free of the daily indignities of prison life, but she struggled with many issues when she got out, not only in reestablishing her role as mother to her two adolescent sons, but also in dealing with a multitude of decisions that she had to make about her living situation and financial support. Mary eventually served another term of incarceration before she was able to amass the internal and external resources she needed in order to reconstruct her life out of prison.

My understanding of Mary's experiences, as well as those of other women in transition from prison, has influenced this inquiry and make it value-bound in that the findings were interpreted through a lens constructed out of the methods used, the context in which the inquiry took place, and my personal and professional values and assumptions. These assumptions, explicitly discussed or implicitly embedded throughout the subtext of these chapters, are as follows:

- Recognizing that women in transition from prison have different needs than their male counterparts, due to their different experiences of incarceration and the ways that gender organizes identity.

- Adopting a rehabilitation, rather than a punitive, perspective when working with women ex-inmates, promoting a belief in women's capacity for growth and change, but without precluding expectations of accountability.

- Developing strategies that are grounded in women's lived experiences and are outcome driven, promoting women's reintegration after prison.

- Recognizing that women of color are disproportionately subjected to incarceration, increasing the importance of developing and implementing culturally rich strategies for supporting their efforts toward wholeness.

- Adopting a "continuum of care" as integral to any in-prison programming efforts based on the recognition that long-term change is nonlinear and complex by its nature.

- Establishing alternative models of sanctioning that recognize the reality of women's criminal acts and revitalize women's internal and external resources, rather than models that reinforce their separation and isolation from community.

As we see the continued escalation of women's incarceration over the last twenty years, the United States is facing an increasingly complex need to understand the relationship between criminal behaviors and other grave social problems. These problems are exacerbated by the fact that the most typical woman offender is often a single parent responsible for the care of her children or other family members. When a woman is incarcerated, a tremendous ripple effect occurs in the increasing social costs of disrupting family life, in the loss of meaningful contributions to community life, and in the massive economic costs associated with prison construction and supervision.

It could be otherwise.

ACKNOWLEDGMENTS

Completing *Making It in the "Free World"* has been a six-year effort that began as my somewhat obvious observation that a woman's exit from prison did not guarantee her freedom. The idea grew as my Ph.D. dissertation in social work, and flourished as a book with the kind encouragement of Russ Immargeon and Meda Chesney-Lind to contribute to the SUNY Series in Women, Crime, and Criminology. I have had many encounters with people, only some of whom are named here, who have shaped my thinking and provided the practical support for getting this work published. The process has reinforced my belief in the connectedness of all beings.

I am first indebted to many women both inside the prison walls and outside "making it," who have shared their journeys of challenge and hope with me. To the eighteen women whose stories of transition constitute this book, I thank you for your trust in me. Your individual lives blast apart stereotypes of women "in trouble with the law," making you models for the inherent possibilities alive in any of us who will not be stopped by stumbles along the way.

I am grateful for many good teachers. I want to thank my dissertation committee at the University of Kansas, Edith Freeman, Ed Canda, Dennis Saleebey, Alice Lieberman, and Carol Warren for their kind assistance in helping me move a conceptual idea into the focus necessary for its implementation. I especially appreciate Dennis and Alice's understanding of the importance of this topic for social work and their generous support.

My colleagues at Jane Addams College of Social Work at the University of Illinois at Chicago have taken an active interest in my work. It is a fine thing to work with people who believe they are contributing to making a positive difference in the world. I thank Dean Creasie Finney Hairston for her vigorous support. I am grateful to James Gleeson for both his intellectual honesty and the friendship that has nurtured my growth as a scholar. I also greatly appreciate my vibrant students and the passion that they bring to learning about themselves and their vision for service to others.

Liane Vida Davis has been a muse whose too-short life has inspired me at the most trying moments. As a friend and mentor, Liane often reminded me that having a chance to work hard toward something in which I believe is both a privilege and a responsibility. I hope that I reflect her clear-eyed sense of justice in this book.

Meda Chesney-Lind has done so much to bring the issue of juvenile and adult females to front and center in discussing policy within the criminal justice system and I thank her for being a long-distance mentor for many years. I thank too other scholars who have blazed the trail regarding the increasing problem of women's incarceration, especially Barbara Bloom and Beth Richie. For editorial assistance and excellent support, I am most grateful to Russ Immargeon.

This book would never have been written without the enduring love of my heartkin: Diana Capen and Merrilee Barnett. Diana and Merrilee have traveled with me through so many of life's passages and know, like the gardeners that they are, how to regenerate my soul whether with a poem, a walk, or a meal at their kitchen table. Rose Karasti brings joy to my life, gentle nudges when I feel overwhelmed by all there is to do, and a belief in my passion for social change for which I am blessed. And Medha, the world's most adorable pooch, is a source of both great distraction and companionship.

Finally, I want to acknowledge Mary, Brenda, Lori, Nora, and Brigitte,* who though they were not a part of this study, gave me early assistance by sharing their experiences of transition from prison as they lived it. If any individuals who read this book stretch their capacity for humanness, their imagination, their understanding, and their sensitivity so that they can reach out in compassion and reconciliation to women in prison, my efforts will be rewarded, as will be the women whose voices fill this book.

---

*To protect the privacy of the former prisoners mentioned or interviewed in this book, I have used pseudonyms, or when requested, actual first names.

Free?

They open wide the door

'You've done your time, you're free'

But I still feel locked and chained

deep down inside of me.

—Anonymous (1982)

CHAPTER ONE

MAKING IT IN THE "FREE WORLD"

Women in Transition from Prison

Every day in the United States, women are released from state or federal prison, having served their time, to make their way in the free world. Often they have little more than a few clothes, coveted personal items, and the good wishes of buddies they leave behind when they embark on this journey of transition from prison. Each woman's route will take her in many directions, often without guidelines or a map to help her find her way, as she claims a new identity and discovers the normality of everyday life.

In this book, I will describe this journey for eighteen women who identified themselves as successful in making it after release from prison. Here too, these women will recount who and what made it possible. In this way, we get a sense of the woman behind the label of "ex-inmate." We also gain an understanding of the necessity to use our resources to make it otherwise for the thousands of women who linger in our prison facilities.

Since the naming of the "opportunistic" (Adler 1975) or "liberated" (Simon 1975) woman offender, contemporary concerned criminology has become more about lawbreaking women[1] and the correctional response to them.[2] In recent years, we have learned a great deal about the nature and extent of female offending as well as gender differences in crime. We know, however, far less about the aftermath of women offenders' conviction, incarceration, and return to the community.

The literature in criminal justice, criminology, and sociology has produced a litany of conclusions that overgeneralize men's experiences to women's experiences of release from prison. Chief among the many differences is the fact that when a man is released from prison, he typically returns to a home and a family (Belknap 1996; Fessler 1991; Johnston 1995), and has better opportunities for securing a sufficiently income-producing and legal job by virtue of his gender alone. When a woman is released, she often must reestablish a home and her family role. She is further challenged by the lack of income-producing employment with which she can support herself and her children. Other social, economic, and emotional situations she may face include the following.

1. Regaining custody of her children and reconstructing mother-child relationships severed and damaged by her absence (Baunach 1985; Bloom and Steinhart 1993; Dressel, Porterfield, and Barnhill 1998; Fessler 1991; Johnston 1995).

2. Establishing a new relational "web of connections" that reinforces noncriminal attitudes and behaviors (Covington 1998; O'Brien 1995a).

3. Finding shelter and meeting other basic needs (Austin, Bloom, and Donahue 1992).

4. Making decisions about continuing prior intimate relationships, which many incarcerated women characterize as exploitative and sexually or physically violent (American Correctional Association (ACA) 1990; Austin et al. 1992; Gilfus 1992; Harlow 1999; Robinson 1994; Sears, 1989).

5. Securing a job that pays a sufficient income, even though she may not have a legal means for supporting herself and her children prior to her being incarcerated (ACA 1990; Pollock-Byrne 1990), and even though she did not have access while in prison to vocational and educational programs to develop her skills (Feinman 1994).

6. Fulfilling the conditions of her parole plan if she has been released under the supervisory custody of the correctional system (Harris 1993).

7. Extending her sobriety (by virtue of the reduced accessibility of intoxicating or hallucinatory substances while incarcerated) to recovery from substance addiction (Arvantes 1994; Austin et al. 1992; Fletcher, Shaver, and Moon 1993).

8. Negotiating the stigmatized perception of her by others who fail to recognize her strengths and potential for change (Hoffman 1983; O'Brien 1994).

Although some of these barriers are similar to those faced by men exiting prison, many are more difficult for women, and others may have more detrimental effects on them. At the time of release, the typical female ex-inmate lacks a home, financial support, employment, socially legitimated and rewarded skills, practical knowledge about how to secure resources, and most lack a sense of hope for their future outside of prison. Contemporary feminist research has also contributed to our understanding of female experience of incarceration by not only contrasting it to that of men but emphasizing the role of patriarchy and sexual exploitation of women and girls to offending (Chesney-Lind 1989). These theories acknowledge female criminality as a reflection of the situations of women's lives, their attempts to survive sexism and racism (Arnold 1990), and the need for gender-specific treatment and services (Bloom and Covington 1998).

HISTORY OF WOMEN'S INCARCERATION IN THE UNITED STATES

Concepts such as vengeance, retaliation, penance, confinement, and rehabilitation are found in legal writings dating back to the ancient Sumarian Code. The first American prison was authorized by the Pennsylvania state legislature in 1790 for a design by the Philadelphia Quakers. They proposed that the Walnut Street Jail, built in the 1770s, be remodeled and opened as a penitentiary for children, women, and men. When opened, it contained separate facilities for women and children. By 1860 the county jail held fifty-seven white women and twenty-four black women, a female population of about 18 percent (Meranze 1996). These "custodial" institutions, derived from men's prisons and including regimes that stressed hard labor and harsh discipline, were the only type of penal units for women until the late 1800s. The first freestanding, independent prison for women was not built until 1874 in Indiana (Friedman 1993).

At the turn of the century, stimulated by the prison tours of social reformist Dorothea Dix, a movement began to promote the idea of a different and separate type of institution for women: the reformatory. Reformatories were based on the ideals of "true womanhood" that included religious uplift, an acquisition of domestic skills, and the ability to confine women for indeterminate terms until she was judged to be morally fit to reenter society. It was male protectiveness in the form of paternalism, when women are indeterminately sentenced to prison for reform of their deviant and unfeminine behaviors, that characterized early sentencing practices (Freedman 1981; Rafter 1990).

Dobash, Dobash, and Gutteridge note, "From the very beginning, women in prison were treated differently from men, considered more morally depraved and corrupt and in need of special, closer forms of control and confinement" (1986). Women were arrested for petty crimes or offenses "against Chastity." These crimes included fornication, adultery, and lewd cohabitation as well as "common night-walking" and required that women should be reformed as much as punished for their moral lapses (Friedman 1993, 233).

The allegedly more benign treatment of women was used to justify longer and indeterminate sentences when men received a definite minimum and maximum term at the county jail for the same offense. An interesting example is *State v. Heitman* (1919). In 1919 the Supreme Court of Kansas dismissed Mrs. Heitman's appeal of her indeterminate minimum sentence to the correctional state industrial farm for women for the offense of "keeping a liquor nuisance." The court saw no grounds for Heitman's appeal based on violation of the Fourteenth Amendment, the "equal protection" clause, opining that "the definite prison term was a relic of the stone age of penological theory and practice" while the treatment of delinquent women should rest on the "definite principle of reclamation as opposed to naked punishment" (634). Heitman would have the benefit of going to a separate institution in which she would work "in the sunshine and wind and free air" (633). Presumably this pastoral work would dissuade her from her depraved (albeit profitable) former occupation. No case of sentencing women superceded this decision until in 1973 the state statute was repealed by the Kansas legislature.[3]

Some scholars doubt that black women ever benefited from favorable sentencing practices (Collins 1997; Freedman 1981; Rafter 1990). Rafter notes, for example, that black women were put in chain gangs while white females were placed in reformatories. Black women historically were disproportionately committed to custodial settings as they are today, while higher proportions of white women were once sent to reformatories or, currently, to treatment centers.

The "reform" period for incarcerated women was relatively brief. Rafter (1990) notes that between 1900 and 1935, seventeen states opened women's reformatories. However, as both a response to perceptions about women's criminal behaviors and the belief that women were not being treated "equally" by the criminal justice system, the ideas that marked the reform period were diluted and the custodial emphasis reinstated. Chesney-Lind (1992) refers to this renewed emphasis and the increasing pace of prison construction as "equality with a vengeance," emphasizing the need to treat female offenders as though they were "equal" to male offenders. Rafter (1990) notes that by the 1980s, thirty-four women's units or prisons were established. This more punitive response to women's offending has not slackened in recent years as the surge in the numbers of women being incarcerated reflects a fundamental shift in our country's approach to women's offenses.

GROWTH IN THE FEMALE INMATE POPULATION

Since 1990 the number of people in U.S. correctional custody has risen more than an average of 1,708 inmates per week, resulting by midyear 1999 in nearly 1.9 million men and women in the nation's prisons and jails. Relative to their number in the U.S. resident population, men are sixteen times more likely than women to be incarcerated. However, since 1990, the female prisoner population has nearly doubled (92 percent) as compared to men (67 percent) and in each year since 1990, the annual rate of growth of incarcerated women has surpassed that of men (8.4 percent as compared to 6.5 percent) (Beck and Mumola 1999).

By the end of 1998 almost a million women were under some form of correctional supervision. Table 1.1 summarizes the category of supervision (probation, jail, prison, and parole) for both females and males, and indicates the percent increase in these categories from 1990 to 1998.

The data indicate that by the end of 1998 almost 150,000 women were incarcerated in either jails (63,791) or state and federal prisons (84,427) (Beck and Mumola 1999). Nine percent of the women on correctional supervision were on parole (82,300), while the bulk of women (76 percent) were on probation (721,400) (Bonczar and Glaze 1999). The total number of women under correctional control increased 57 percent in the eight years between 1990 and 1998 as compared to a 34 percent increase of men under correctional control

Table 1.1

INMATES UNDER CORRECTIONAL CONTROL BY SEX, 1990 AND 1998

	1990	1998	Percent Change
Probation			
Females	480,642	721,400	50
Males	2,189,592	2,696,213	23
Jail			
Females	37,198	63,791	71
Males	365,821	520,581	42
Prison (state and federal)			
Females	44,065	84,427[a]	92
Males	729,840	1,217,592[a]	67
Parole			
Females	42,513	82,300	94
Males	488,894	622,664	27
Total (all categories)			
Females	604,418	951,918	57
Males	3,774,147	5,057,050	34

SOURCES: Beck, A. J. (2000). *Prison and Jail Inmates at Midyear 1999.*
Beck, A. J., and Mumola, C. J. (1999). *Prisoners in 1998.*
Bonczar, T. P., and Glaze, L. E. (1999). *Probation and Parole in the United States 1998.*
[a]Estimated; see Bureau of Justice Statistics publication *Prisoners in 1999* for final 1998 count.

during the same period. Population growth has occurred in each functional component of corrections since 1990—the number of women per capita under probation supervision climbed 40 percent; the jail rate grew 60 percent; the imprisonment rate increased 88 percent; and the per capita number of offenders under parole supervision was up 80 percent (Greenfeld and Snell 1999).[4] By midyear 1999, 154,686 women were in jails or under the jurisdiction of state and federal prison authorities (Beck 2000).

CHARACTERISTICS OF
INCARCERATED WOMEN

Female inmates largely resemble male inmates in terms of race, ethnicity, education, and age. Most female offenders are in their late twenties or early thirties, at least high school graduates or holders of a General Equivalency Diploma (GED), and often members of a racial or ethnic minority.

African Americans have always represented a disproportionate number in our nation's prisons. African Americans have constituted more than 50 percent of the female prison population since 1996, far exceeding the roughly 12 percent of the general population they represent. Latina women are also disproportionately incarcerated in U.S. jails and prisons, but to a much lesser extent: In 1997 they constituted 13.9 percent of the female inmate population (Gilliard and Beck 1998).[5]

Women are, however, substantially more likely than men to serve time for a drug offense and less likely to receive a sentence for a violent crime, and, as a result, they generally serve shorter sentences than men. Recent statistics indicate that drug offenders accounted for the largest sources of the total growth among female inmates, 38 percent compared to 17 percent among male inmates (Beck and Mumola 1999).

Nearly six in ten female inmates grew up in a household with at least one parent absent, and about half of these women reported that an immediate family member had also served time (Snell 1994). Forty percent of female federal prison inmates and 57 percent of female state prison inmates reported physical or sexual abuse previous to their admission (as compared to 7.2 percent of the male federal inmates and 16 percent of the male state inmates) (Harlow 1999). This self-reported rate among incarcerated women is higher than the general population estimate of 12 to 17 percent (Gorey and Leslie 1997).

In a prevalence study of mental illnesses among male and female admissions in a large urban jail, Teplin (1994, 1996) found that 8.9 percent of males and 18.5 percent of females had diagnosable serious mental illnesses (dysthymia, anxiety, schizophrenia, bipolar-manic, major depression, posttraumatic stress disorder). A national survey of prison inmates found the highest rate of mental illness was among white females—29 percent (Ditton 1999).

Nationally, the proportion of female inmates who are HIV positive/AIDS affected is increasing at a higher rate than that of men (Brien and Beck 1996). In a 1994 study of incoming inmates in New York, the rate of HIV infection among women was almost twice that of men (20.3 percent as compared to 11.5 percent) (ACE Program Members 1998). Smith and Dailard (1994) argue that the high incidence of HIV among women in prison can be explained by the similar factors that put these women at risk for contracting HIV or for being incarcerated: poverty, race, and drug use. Young (1996) found that women enter prison with a poor physical health status that derives from a combination of societal conditions and personal antecedents.

A major difference between male and female incarcerated offenders is the fact that most of the women are mothers. In 1991, more than three-fourths of the women in prison were mothers. Two-thirds of the inmates had at least one child under age eighteen. More than half of the female inmates reported their children were living with grandparents; a quarter with the child's father (Snell 1994). In a study of women in California prisons (where the largest number of incarcerated women reside), Bloom and her colleagues found that 80 percent of their respondents were mothers (Bloom, Chesney-Lind, and Owen 1994).

A conservative estimate extrapolated from the number of incarcerated women in 1998 suggests that at least 195,000 children younger than age 18 are impacted by their mother's incarceration (Young and Smith 2000). These mothers have to deal with the trauma of separation from their children that is usually compounded by the difficulties of maintaining their relationship via letters, phone calls (when available),[6] and visitation, depending on the distance of the facility from the children, the willingness of the caregiver to allow visitation, and the availability of transportation (Bloom and Steinhart 1993).

ETIOLOGY OF WOMEN'S INVOLVEMENT IN CRIME

Although researchers are currently developing an epistemology of women's criminality (Daly 1994; Leonard 1982; Smart 1977), historically women's presence in the criminal justice system was often a footnote on works distinctly about men that claimed to cover criminality in general.

The earliest sociological writing purportedly about women's criminal behavior examined women's physiological or psychological nature as causative, to the exclusion of economic, political, or social forces. These deterministic theories include those of Lombroso (1903, 1916) who examined women's physical features to identify what he described as "anthropological anomalies" that led to women's abnormality; Glueck and Glueck (1934) who correlated "body types and feeble mindedness, psychopathic personality, and marked emotional instability" (299) to sexual deviance; Thomas (1907, 1923) who concluded that adolescent girls became "unadjusted" when they were deprived from making their wishes known or addressed by "socially useful" means (1923, 232); and Pollak (1950) who argued that it was women's intrinsic ability to conceal bodily processes that allows them to successfully commit crimes in stealth.

Common to this group of classical criminological writers is their heavily stereotyped view of women. Women are defined according to domestic and sexual roles; they are assumed to be dominated by biological imperatives; they are emotional and irrational. Because these writers see criminality as an individual activity, the focus is on biological, psychological, and social factors that would turn a woman toward criminal activity. These writings had a major influence on turn-of-the century reform responses to what were considered deviant and immoral women. They also provide the backdrop to more contemporary theories on female criminality, such as Konopka (1966), Vedder and Sommerville (1970), and Cowie, Cowie and Slater (1968), all of whom attribute delinquency in varying degrees to female emotions, dependency needs and sexual frustrations. They suggest that it is maladjustment to the feminine role that causes high rates of delinquency (Klein 1973).

More contemporary theories of criminology have produced a "sociology of deviance" (Heidensohn 1985; Leonard 1982) that has increasingly moved away from viewing deviant behavior through an individualistic lens of inherent abnormality and pathology. These theories see deviance as a normal response to structural demands and insufficiencies (Merton 1956), a process of role labeling created by those with the power to make rules about behavior (Becker 1963), and as learned behavior from relationships with others who define law violation as acceptable (Sutherland 1934).

Although these theories are useful for emphasizing that criminal behavior is not psychologically or biologically determined, it is men's experience that informs the findings. In this consciously new approach to deviance, women and girls are still not visible. Leonard (1982) critically examines the major sociological theories through a gender-specific lens to look at their fit for women's commission of crimes. She concludes that the theories of anomie (Merton 1956), labeling (Becker 1963), and differential association (Sutherland 1934) are all insufficient in that women, unlike men, are generally shielded from criminal learning experiences, more likely to learn values conducive to law-abiding behavior and so be at lower risk for labeling, and have different role-socialization.

Contemporary criminologists have provided a number of explanations for the increased conviction of women for crimes. Adler (1975) and Simon (1975) brought the issue of women's putatively increasing level of crime to the forefront by theorizing that the women's liberation movement that emerged in the mid- to late 1960s served as an equalizer, enhancing women's ability and accessibility to participate in criminal behaviors. A number of other scholars have solidly refuted these theories.[7] Others have identified more stringent law enforcement and surveillance of women due to the "war on drugs" (Steffensmeier and Streifel 1993; Wilson 1993), and the significant increase in the 1980s of women's illegal and, in the case of crack cocaine, highly addictive drug use and consequent criminal activities (Mahan 1996).

Feminist theorists examine other factors that relate to women and crime including women's economic marginalization and dislocation (Carlen 1988; Carlen and Worrall 1987; Chapman 1980; Dressel 1994), the connection between victimization by abuse and criminal behavior (Browne 1987; Comack 1993; Gilfus 1992; Jones 1980; Robinson 1994), racism coupled with sexism (Daly and Stephens 1995; Hill and Crawford 1990), and adaptive resistance to victimization and/or oppression (Arnold 1990; Chesney-Lind 1992). These theories inform this study of former inmates to conceptualize the struggles that women surmount as they make the transition from prison.

Some studies (Arnold, 1990; Chesney-Lind and Rodriguez 1983; Robinson 1994; Widom 1989) have examined women's pathways into crime from early and repeated experiences of victimization. Chesney-Lind and Rodriguez described the existence of a systematic process of criminalization unique to women that magnifies the relationship between ongoing societal victimization and eventual entrapment in the criminal justice system. Widom (1989) found that both black and white women who were adjudicated abused or neglected as children had higher arrest rates as adults than women who had not suffered maltreatment as children. Robinson (1994) reported that girls' experience of sexual abuse and early sexualization produced increasing isolation and alienation from normative juvenile experiences and, hence, contributed to later criminal activities.

Structural sources of inequity play an even greater role in black than white women's crime. Chapman's research (1980) demonstrated that drug crimes are directly associated with economic need and, therefore, economic crime. Phillips and Votey (1984) analyzed participation in crime by black women who face problems common to all women in terms of unemployment, restricted labor market opportunities, and absence of a partner; however, they found that these problems are magnified for black women due to their status in society. Phillips and Votey (1984) also suggest that some crime is a consequence of disincentives created when former welfare recipients receive a less than a fair wage for their work and lose medical benefits.

Hill and Crawford (1990) found that a cluster of variables they term structural (i.e., unemployment rate and the gap between educational aspiration and achievement) more directly affected black women's lawbreaking, whereas, for white women, variables reflecting social-psychological processes (i.e., self-esteem and sex-specific goal attainment) were more influential. Dressel (1994), drawing from her work with mostly black incarcerated mothers in Georgia, described a kind of economic hopelessness in which the avenues for legitimate income-producing activities are becoming less accessible due to the interplay of racism, classism, and sexism.

Arnold (1990) suggests that this trajectory for young black girls from lower socioeconomic classes starts with precriminal behavior (i.e., runaway offenses) that in many cases represents resistance to victimization. These runaway girls are then labeled as "status offenders," and institutionalized in girls' homes, or imprisoned for vagrancy and other nonviolent crimes. Common to the girls' experience is a structural dislocation from the family, education, and legitimate and sufficient occupations. Arnold observes that once this process of criminalization is set in motion, "sustained criminal involvement becomes the norm as well as a rational coping strategy" (153). From interviews that Arnold conducted with fifty black women in jail, she concluded, "When not in prison, these women can be counted among the hard-core unemployed, the homeless, the drug addicted, and the sexually abused" (163).

Collins (1997) suggests that there are recurring variables in black women's lives that might in part account for the overrepresentation of blacks in the prison system. She contends that these variables constitute a "wheel of misfortune," including racism, sexism, poverty, and miseducation (37). Richie's work (1996) extends this contextual examination. Borrowing from the legal notion of "gender entrapment," she describes a cycle of vulnerability to men's violence and desperation that propels black women into a repressive criminal justice system.

The proportionately small number of women in the total inmate population can be best explained by the fact that historically and contemporarily, they commit fewer illegal acts (Simon and Landis 1991). Chivalry has also been discussed as a factor that has resulted in the lower representation of women among those convicted of crimes. The "chivalry" factor, defined by Raeder (1993) as protectiveness by male judges who wish to save women from the harsh reality of prison, has been thought to contribute to disparate and less severe sentencing of women. Research results are inconclusive about the extent to which chivalry has ever existed for women (Odubekun 1992; Visher 1983).

TRENDS IN WOMEN'S OFFENSES

Nearly one in three female inmates was serving a sentence for drug offenses in 1991, compared to one in eight in 1986. This increase in sentenced drug offenders accounts for 55 percent of the increase in the female prison population between 1986 and 1991 (Snell 1994) and 45 percent of the increase in the female prison population from 1990 to 1996 (Gilliard and Beck 1998). Uniform Crime Reports show a substantial increase of 176 percent between 1980 and 1989 of women arrested for narcotics and drug-related offenses from the previous decade (Durant 1993). Inciardi, Lockwood, and Pottieger (1993) related women's use of highly addictive crack cocaine to the commission of illegal crimes to purchase the drug and to the fact that many women are convicted for drug offenses committed in the context of intimate relationships. Pottieger (in Feinman 1994) reported from her study that 29.6 percent of female heroin addicts relied on criminal activities, primarily prostitution, drug sales, and shoplifting, as their major sources of income. Pottieger also noted that "fewer women than men had steady employment and income, which might explain why more women than men relied on illegal means of getting money for narcotics" (Feinman 1994, 23). Women in state prisons (62 percent) were more likely than men (56 percent) to have used drugs in the month before the offense and to have committed their offense while under the influence of drugs (40 percent, compared to 32 percent) (Beck and Mumola 1999).

For every category of major crime for the period 1990–96—violent, property, drugs, and other felonies—the rate of increase in the number of convicted female defendants has outpaced the changes in the number of convicted male defendants. Property felonies, in particular, have evidenced a large disparity in rates of change; from 1990 to 1996, the number of males convicted of property crimes decreased about two percent while convicted female defendants increased 44 percent. The amount of violence committed by female offenders has attracted a great deal of attention over the past twenty years especially in media and popular culture depictions. Many assume that women are committing more violent and aggressive crimes than in the past but national statistics suggest otherwise. In 1998, 22 percent of women incarcerated in jails or prisons were convicted for violent offenses (Greenfeld and Snell 1999), compared to 32.2 percent in 1991, 41 percent in 1986, and 49 percent in 1979 (Snell, 1994). Table 1.2 provides the most recently reported numbers and percentages in each category.[8]

Table 1.2
OFFENSES OF WOMEN IN JAIL OR PRISON, 1998

	Jails	State Prison	Federal Prison
Violent Offenses	7,655 (12%)	21,056 (28%)	644 (7%)
Property Offenses	21,689 (34%)	20,304 (27%)	1,104 (12%)
Drug Offenses	19,137 (30%)	25,568 (34%)	6,624 (72%)
Public-order Offenses	15,310 (24%)	8,272 (11%)	736 (8%)
Total	63,791	75,200	9,108

SOURCE: Greenfeld, L. A. and Snell, T. L. (1999). *Women Offenders.*

Murder accounted for about 30 percent of the women incarcerated for violent offenses in 1997. The victim–offender relationship differed substantially between female and male murderers. Of the 60,000 murders committed by women between 1976 and 1997, just over 60 percent were against an intimate or family member; among the 400,000 murders committed by men over the same period, 20 percent were against family members or intimates (Beck and Mumola 1999).

From 1990 to 1997 the number of female inmates serving time for drug offenses nearly doubled (99 percent) while the number of male inmates in for drug offenses rose 48 percent. Drug offenders accounted for the largest source of the total growth among female inmates (38 percent), compared to 17 percent among male inmates (Beck and Mumola 1999).

Steffensmeir and Allan (1998) propose a gendered theory of female offending that takes into account gender differences that "inhibit female crime and encourage male crime." These include: gender norms, moral development and relational concerns, social control, physical strength and aggressiveness, and sexuality. They argue that women's criminal lawbreaking parallels their economic marginality and different social context.

SENTENCING POLICIES

Despite the fact that every major type of crime measured has decreased significantly since 1993 (Rennison 1999), the general American fear of crime has remained. For example, in 1994, a Louis Harris poll found that 46 percent of a national random sample identified crime as the number one "serious problem facing the country" (Kagay 1994, 24). In 1997, an ABC poll found that 51 percent of respondents were more afraid of crime than five years before (Fear of Crime 1998).

This fear has fed a continuing "get tough on crime" campaign that has produced more punitive policies and more prison beds (Chesney-Lind 1991; Dressel 1994; Klein 1995). These policies are meant to make all of "us" feel more secure when "they" are removed from our midst. Rehabilitation efforts, as represented by programming within the institution for the offender, are eliminated by the competing (and growing) cost of putting people away for longer incarcerations, which have not been proven effective at deterring repeat offenses (Clarke and Harrison 1992).

State and federal jurisdictions have engaged in three decades of sentencing reform beginning with "indeterminate sentencing" in the early 1970s that empowered parole boards to determine an individual's release from prison up to "truth-in-sentencing" laws first enacted in 1984 that require offenders to serve a substantial portion of their prison sentences (50–85 percent depending on the state). Chesney-Lind (1991) has argued that the increases in women's imprisonment can be attributed to three major policy shifts: the "war on drugs," the implementation of mandatory minimum sentencing guidelines, and the "get tough on crime" attitude that has widened the net as a consequence of changes in laws and enforcement of penalties for less serious forms of lawbreaking.

These combined reforms have strongly influenced a nationwide response from that of rehabilitation of offenders to one that is almost exclusively punitive. Various state studies that indicate a sharp increase in women's incarceration rates for possession of drugs, as well as overlapping charges related to trafficking, support the contention that the putative war on drugs is a war on women that has clearly contributed to the explosion in the women's prison population (Bloom, Leonard, and Owen 1994; Chesney-Lind 1991; Gilliard and Beck 1998). In addition, Steffensmeier and Allan (1998), and Wilson (1993) argue that more stringent law enforcement and increased surveillance of women to gain information against associates in the drug-dealing network also results in their increasing conviction for drug-related crimes.

Mandatory sentencing for offenses at both state and federal levels also has affected women's increasing incarceration. Sentencing reforms were implemented to address race, social class, and other unwarranted disparities in the sentencing of men, but those reforms have operated in ways that distinctly disadvantage women, particularly in the federal system. Raeder (1993) found that in 1989, 44.5 percent of the women incarcerated in federal institutions were being held for drug offenses, and that two years later, this figure had increased to 68 percent. She also found that in 1991 only 28 percent of the women convicted of federal felonies were granted probation as compared to about two-thirds twenty years ago.

Judges in the gender-free world of federal sentencing guidelines have eliminated women's care for others as a relevant consideration for departing from the guidelines. In the past, these family responsibilities may have kept women out of prison. In 1988, before full implementation of sentencing guidelines, women constituted 6.5 percent of those in federal institutions; by year-end 1997, this figure had increased to 7.4 percent (Gilliard and Beck 1998). Not only do the guidelines contribute to the increased numbers of incarcerated women, they also ensure that women who are incarcerated spend more time in prison. For example, the mean federal prison sentence for drug offenders increased from thirty months in 1986 to a startling sixty-six months by 1997, after sentencing guidelines went into effect (Sabol and McGready 1999).

Finally, the proliferation of prison facilities for women as part of a "get tough on crime" public response may also contribute to the increasing use of facilities by judges and juries. When prisons are built, they tend to be filled, regardless of need as the net of social control widens (Chesney-Lind 1991; Harris 1987; Pollock-Byrne 1990).

EFFECTS OF INCARCERATION ON WOMEN

Jo Ann Brown is a young African-American woman who was accused, convicted, and sentenced to life imprisonment for a murder she did not commit. Although she regained her freedom after nine years of imprisonment, her autobiography addresses the major "pains of imprisonment" that Sykes (1958) describes, such as loss of identity and separation from family and community. Brown summarizes some of these losses in the following statement from her book (1990):

> Remember that when you enter prison your individuality is immediately
> surrendered. From day one, you cease to be a person. You are a number,
> another head of cattle. All rights, privileges, and possessions belong to the
> prison administrators and, by their dictates, are doled out by their officers
> (119).

Goffman's (1961) observations of the daily regime in the "total institution" of the mental hospital have been used as an analog for the controlling features of prisons that effectively reduce to survival the inmate's exercise of personal agency and autonomy. These adaptive strategies usually do not address the personal and structural challenges of moving toward noncriminalized behaviors upon release. Jose-Kampfner (1990) notes, in a study of long-term incarcerated women, that they have to give up their concerns and relationships in the free world to a certain extent, so that they will not expose their vulnerability to feelings of grief and loss. She believes that exposure to external crises that the women have no power to manage could be counterproductive to learning what it takes to survive while incarcerated.

In the current climate, which has seen a huge influx of people incarcerated in state and federal prisons, there is little attention paid to the turn-of-the-century North American penitentiary ideal of rehabilitation or reform of the inmate's behavior (Faith 1993; Freedman 1981; Rafter 1990). Instead, the criminal justice system has two major purposes: protection of society by incapacitating the offender, and punishment of the offender.

Although lip service may be given to the ideal of rehabilitation, incarceration practices reflect the former view. For example, the implementation of sentencing guidelines, which standardize time served for all felony crimes, has effectively removed a powerful incentive for inmate participation in prison programs and avoidance of disciplinary problems, since there is no possibility of earning "good time" that might lead to early release from prison. Ultimately, the viability of the notion of rehabilitation is compromised both by the reality that most prisoners will return to the same social conditions that generated undesirable behaviors, and by the indisputably punitive nature of prisons as a measure and expression of power relations within society. Foucault (1977) reflected this characterization of prisons as "the only place where power is manifested in its naked state, in its most excessive form, and where it is justified as moral force" (210).

Women who are incarcerated in the U.S. prison system have a variety of complex cognitive, emotional, and behavioral reactions to the constraints of the correctional environment (Baunach 1985; Burkhart 1973; Feinman 1994; Pollock-Byrne 1990; Watterson 1996).

Research shows that women, many of whom enter prison in poor health, experience more medical and health problems than male inmates (General Accounting Office 1979; Pollock-Byrne 1990; Sobel 1982; Young 1996). Women are more likely than men to seek health care in society at large and are no different in prison. Women have more medical problems related to their reproductive systems than do men. Women in prison also have a profusion of health problems related to their lives on the street. They may be pregnant on entering prison, increasing their need for medical services. They might also be suffering from sexually transmitted disease; they might be substance abusers, with all the medical problems associated with those addictions.

Comparatively, a smaller percentage of incarcerated men had children (63.9 percent versus 78.1 percent) and while only 25.4 percent of the incarcerated women's minor children lived with their father, 89.7 percent of the incarcerated men's children lived with the children's mother (Snell 1994). Because current demographics reflect a shift of the exclusive burden of responsibility of childcare onto a larger proportion of single women, a major source of trauma for women in prison relates to the effects of their separation from children, visitation with children, and custody during and after incarceration (Beckerman 1989; Bloom and Steinhart 1993; Dressel, Porterfield, and Barnhill 1998; Gaudin 1984; Johnston 1995; Ward and Kassebaum 1965).

Fessler (1991) found, in her study of both incarcerated women and women on parole, that long substance abuse histories had an effect on their reunification with their children after incarceration. Related to the needs of addicted women is the lack of drug-addiction treatment programs that allow women to have their children with them while in treatment. This policy sets up the woman to choose between continued separation from her children or her own recovery. Bloom et al. concluded from their evaluation of programs in women's facilities in California that even though 80 percent of the women prisoners are mothers, "There is a dearth of programs which address the critical parenting and family reunification needs of inmate mothers and their children" (1994, 14).

Turn-of-the-century prison reformers built women's state prison facilities in rural areas. The reasoning behind the choice of these pastoral settings is that they would inspire a sense of tranquillity and remove women from the corruption of the cities (Freedman 1981). The rural locations of prison facilities have also removed women from access to schools, training programs, and work-release opportunities usually found in cities (Pollock-Byrne 1990).

Educational programs for all inmates stop at the secondary level with the completion of the General Equivalency Diploma (GED) unless the inmate is able to independently pay for additional academic courses. A national study of prison programs by Glick and Neto (1977), as well as more recent surveys cited by Sobel (1982) and Pollock-Byrne (1990), indicate that women do not have vocational and programming opportunities equal to those of men, and that the available programs are limited to sex-typed, low-paying careers.

The lack of programs designed to prepare women for the transition from prison further exacerbates women's reentry challenges. Pre-release centers that provided support for male offenders proliferated in the 1970s, when federal funds were plentiful and faith in the rehabilitative ideal was strong. Although there is an insufficient quantity of pre-release programs and halfway houses for the men who need them, such services seldom even exist for incarcerated women, due to their smaller population.

A nationwide descriptive evaluation of 100 model programs that focus on women offenders in community settings found that the programs assisted participants in gaining self-confidence and successfully functioning within their communities (Austin et al. 1992). The effectiveness of the transition programs assessed in this study was strongly related to the individual program's attention to the participants' substance addictions, prior physical and sexual abuse, employment skills and aspirations, and familial relationships. Although the authors of the evaluation called for more commitment to funding such programs for addressing the "multidimensional problems of women offenders" (33), that commitment has not been forthcoming, except on a very limited and inconsistent state-by-state basis. When the necessary supports and resources are not made available to women leaving prison, the multitude of crushing realities and expectations for reestablishing their lives drug-free may send them straight to the corner dealer to begin the cycle again.

Although there have been improvements in the number and variety of programs offered in women's prison facilities, mostly due to litigation brought by women prisoners and their advocates (Pollock-Byrne 1990), meaningful and realistic programs designed to foster women's efficacy upon release are most notable for their scarcity. This significant lack of services for incarcerated women reinforces their relative powerlessness and economic marginalization in the free world.

Early studies of incarcerated women focused on their roles in prison and their development of "pseudofamilies" to compensate for their isolation from their "free world" families and intimate partners (Burkhart 1973; Giallombardo 1966; Heffernan 1972; Pollock-Byrne 1990). Each of these researchers found a system of kinship prison ties emanating from a dyad configuration of "mom" and "dad" and extending to a large network of loosely structured families. Gilfus (1988) found in her study of incarcerated women that these informal prison family systems are a gender-related response to the loneliness and deprivations of prison life and the loss of social status and roles; she also found that these families fulfill economic, relational, and protective purposes.

Although the dyadic relationships may or may not involve sexual activity, Pollock-Byrne (1990) discusses early investigators' overconcern with the "subcultural adaptation" of homosexuality in the women's institution (144). Robson (1992) notes prison administrators' fear of lesbian relationships within correctional facilities and the consequent discouragement and control of relationships by the "no-contact" rule (108). Men may also develop affiliations and relationships in prison as a subcultural adaptation to the prison experience. What is different about women's affiliations is that they intentionally replicate the family system from which they are separated, and seem to fulfill expressive rather than instrumental needs (Pollock-Byrne 1990).

The type and quality of relationships that women create with other inmates may be important for helping them survive the pains of incarceration. More important, the relationships may help model for them the possibilities and power that can be found in shared hopes. Ironically, a common parole condition mandates that former inmates not associate with other current or former inmates, even though other formerly or currently incarcerated women may have composed a former inmate's primary support system.

Finally, Jose-Kampfner (1990) provides eloquent testimony, from her qualitative study of seventy women serving long sentences, to the "existential death" that women experience from the day-to-day losses of self and their separation from the world outside the prison institution. Jose-Kampfner found that women who receive life sentences go through several stages of adaptation and response to the meaning of their own incarceration and, in order to cope with their sentences, experience an existential death that is similar to the stages of grief and loss described by Kubler-Ross (1969). If Jose-Kampfner's theory holds, women who are in transition from prison may need a process of rebirthing while they are still in prison. In other words, a woman who has experienced existential death would need to identify the parts of her former life she wants to resume as she prepares to resurrect into a world that has evolved in her absence (1990, 123).

FACTORS CONTRIBUTING TO WOMEN'S RECIDIVISM

There are various definitions for recidivism that often make it complicated to measure (Maltz 1984). One common definition is the resumption of an illegal pattern of behavior. Each recidivistic event or, more accurately, process reflects a combination of shifts in attitudes, thoughts, and behaviors that may culminate in eventual reincarceration, or some lesser sentence, (e.g., fines, additional parole conditions, jail time, changes in parole supervision from less intensive to more intensive, or other forms of community sanctions or monitoring). As represented by rates of recidivism, neither failure nor success are fixed outcomes.

Recidivism is the consequence of becoming reinvolved in a criminal activity that is reported and acted upon by law enforcement. While remaining uninvolved with the law is an achievement for a former inmate, it is only one criterion of community reintegration. Measures of success should be based on positive accomplishments, not simply on the absence of negative findings. From that perspective, the literature that describes how women make it in the community after release from prison is even scarcer than the literature identifying predictors of failure for women.

Very little research has focused on the identifying predictive factors for female reoffending and/or whether they differ from those that are predictive for male offenders. Recidivism is one of the most important issues facing those who formulate and administer sanctioning policies. Rates of recidivism are analyzed as an indicator of the effectiveness of correctional interventions to deter offenders from the commission of further crimes in the pursuit of public safety and optimally, to rehabilitate and restore individuals to the community.

A national report from a survey of adult releases in 1983 (Beck and Shipley 1989) identifies a number of variables that correlated with recidivism, including gender: men are more likely than women to be rearrested, reconvicted, and reincarcerated after their release from prison—the rate of rearrest is 11 percent higher among men than among women. Other findings indicated that recidivism rates are highest in the first year (25 percent are rearrested in the first six months and 65 percent within the first year); older prisoners have lower rates of recidivism; the more extensive a prisoner's prior arrest record, the higher the rate of recidivism and in the case of prior arrests, females with more than six prior arrests are just as likely to be rearrested within three years of release as are men; those who serve five years or more have lower rates of rearrest; and those released for property offense are most likely to be rearrested (Beck and Shipley 1989).

My analysis of the literature with male samples has produced sixteen variables in five categories that are associated with recidivism. Table 1.3 summarizes them.

Many of the state, county, and large city studies are consistent with Beck and Shipley's (1989) study. The single most salient variable for predicting recidivism among males is offense history, particularly the number of arrests prior to incarceration and the age when first charged with a crime as an adult.

In comparison to the studies on recidivism with men, there are fewer studies that have examined specific factors contributing to women's recidivism. Five prospective studies have identified several correlates of women's

Table 1.3
VARIABLES ASSOCIATED WITH
RECIDIVISM ON MALE SAMPLES

Demographics

1.1 Age (Black and Gregson 1973; Blumstein, Cohen, Roth, and Visher 1989; Boudouris 1984; Carney 1967; Hoffman and Beck 1984; Ozawa 1994)

1.2 Minority status (Piper 1985; Beck and Shipley 1989)

1.3 Marital status (Curtis and Schulman 1984; Gunn, Nicol, Gristwoon, and Foggitt 1973)

1.4 Educational levels (Denver Anti-Crime Council 1974)

Family Dynamics

2.1 Victim of child abuse (Petersilia, Greenwood, and Lavin 1978)

2.2 Family criminality/incarceration (Blackler 1968)

Institutional Experiences

3.1 Education/Vocational Training (Boudouris 1984; Buttram and Dusewicz 1977; Cogburn 1988; Ducan 1977; Hassel 1988; Holloway and Moke 1986; Linden, Perry, Ayers, and Parlett 1984)

3.2 Maintenance of family contacts during incarceration (Adams and Fischer 1976; Glaser 1969; Holt and Miller 1972)

3.3 Relationships in prison (Adams 1979; Carney 1967)

3.4 Psychotherapeutic interventions (Carney 1971; Lindforss and Magnussen 1997)

3.5 Substance abuse treatment (Field 1989; Rouse 1991)

Life Contingencies

4.1 Employment stability (Curtis and Schulman 1984; Gunn et al. 1973; Petersilia et al. 1978)

4.2 Substance abuse (Petersilia et al. 1978)

Offense History

5.1 Juvenile record (Blumstein et al. 1989; Petersilia et al. 1978;

5.2 Younger at first adult arrest (Petersilia et al. 1978)

5.3 Previous arrests (Beck and Shipley 1989; Illinois Criminal Justice Information Authority 1985)

---

post-incarceration recidivism (Bonta, Pang, and Wallace-Capretta 1995; Jurik 1983; Lambert and Madden 1976; Martin, Cloninger, Guze 1978; Robinson 1971). Other retrospective studies have examined factors contributing to recidivism after reincarceration. Table 1.3 summarizes the studies generated by research with female samples.

The demographics for women recidivists are similar to those of men: they tend to be undereducated, low income, and unmarried. However, the studies indicate mixed findings for age and race. Jurik (1983) reports in her experimental study of female ex-offenders that older women have about the same probability

Table 1.4
VARIABLES ASSOCIATED WITH
RECIDIVISM ON FEMALE SAMPLES

Demographics

1.1   Age (Jurik 1983; Robinson 1971)
1.2[1] Minority status (Warren and Rosenbaum 1986)
1.3   Marital status (Long et al. 1984; Martin, Cloninger, and Guze 1978)
1.4   Socioeconomic status (Warren and Rosenbaum 1986)
1.5   Educational levels (Martin, Cloninger, and Guze 1978)

Family Dynamics
2.1   Victim of child abuse (Long et al. 1984)
2.2[1] Involved in spouse abuse (Bonta et al. 1995; Danner et al. 1995)
2.3   Family criminality/incarceration (Danner et al. 1995)
2.4[1] Broken home (Danner et al. 1995)

Institutional Experiences
3.1[1] Education (GED only) (Johnson, Shearon, and Britton 1974)
3.2   Maintenance of family contacts during incarceration (Bloom 1987)
3.3[1] Relationships in prison (Larson and Nelson 1984; Robinson 1971)
3.4   Psychotherapy (Banks and Ackerman 1983)
3.5   Substance abuse treatment (Fletcher et al. 1993)

Life Contingencies
4.1   Employment stability (Danner et al. 1995; Lambert and Madden 1976; Jurik 1983)
4.2   Substance abuse (Danner et al. 1995; Inciardi and Pottieger 1986; Lambert and Madden 1976; Lindstrom and Hallet 1992; Martin, Cloninger, and Guze 1978)

Offense History
5.1   Juvenile Record (Hamparian et al. 1985; Lindstrom and Hallet 1992; Warren and Rosenbaum 1986)
5.2   Age at first adult arrest (Beck and Shipley 1989; Danner et al. 1995)
5.3   Previous arrests (Beck and Shipley 1989; Bonta et al. 1995; Fletcher et al. 1993)

[1]Indicates inconclusive findings or findings that are inconsistent with those of men.

for rearrest as younger women and Robinson (1971) found in her sample of former inmates that black women are less likely to recidivate than white women.

These studies also indicate that family dynamics have more of an effect on recidivism for women. For example, women's involvement in spouse abuse is a factor in several studies (Bonta et al. 1995; Danner et al. 1995). This is consistent with studies that estimate the incidence of spouse abuse to be much higher among women offenders than among women generally (Snell 1994; Harlow 1999) or among male prisoners (Snell 1994). Another unexamined area relating to family dynamics and possibly spouse abuse is the proportion of women who are convicted with a co-defendant or who commit a crime for, with, or because of a male intimate partner (see, e.g., Sears 1989 and Wilson 1993). Other relationships that women have while in prison seem to have mixed effects on recidivism: Robinson (1971) found that interpersonal competence in relationships reduces recidivism, while Larson and Nelson (1984) report that in-prison friendships lead to what they describe as a "criminal mind set."

Other differences in the findings (in comparison to studies of male recidivists) indicate that women who came from a broken home are more likely to recidivate. Surprisingly, women who completed their GED while in prison are only slightly less likely to recidivate than those who did not (Johnson et al. 1974). A follow-up study that tested the effects of a group psychotherapeutic approach during incarceration found a one-third drop in the recidivism rate among this small sample (Banks and Ackerman 1983).

A number of other studies that examine recidivism after the fact provide impressionistic findings that positive relationships (Schulke 1993), family support (Lambert and Madden 1976), and substance abuse treatment (Fletcher et al. 1993) may adversely effect recidivism. Only one experimental study tested whether economic support related to recidivism (Jurik 1983). In this controlled design with a subsample from the larger Transitional Aid Research Project (TARP), Jurik found a causal and negative relationship between economic support and rearrest for property offenses: as the women's income increased, the rate of arrest for property crimes diminished. In addition to the scarcity of prospective studies examining women's recidivism, many of the cited studies are methodologically weak using, for instance, nonrandom samples and retrospective impressionistic data.

INDICATORS OF SUCCESS FOR FORMER INMATES

Categories of findings were initially derived from the studies that have examined indicators of post-incarceration success for men, including family stability (Adams and Fischer 1976; Clarke and Crum 1985; DeVine 1974) and marital relationships (Burstein 1977; Curtis and Schulman 1984; Fishman 1986; Holt 1986). Table 1.4 summarizes the studies that have identified indicators of post-incarceration success or reintegration for women.

Table 1.5
SUMMARY OF FINDINGS RELATED TO WOMEN'S POST-INCARCERATION REINTEGRATION

Category	Author/Year	Findings
Employment	Lambert and Madden 1976 Schulke 1993	Greater life-satisfaction and well-being found among former offenders with employment success.
	Koons et al. 1997	Acquisition of needed skills.
Family stability	Lambert and Madden 1976 Bloom 1987 Hairston 1991	Quality of life improved for women with close family ties; maintaining family ties of incarcerated women with children essential to post-release reunification.
Relationships	Schulke 1993	Relationships established during prison support post-incarceration efforts.
	Koons et al. 1997	Positive peer influences.
Self-efficacy	Hardesty, Hardwick, and Thompson 1993	Self-esteem related to perceptions of post-prison adjustment

These studies provide a starting place for identifying some of the elements that contribute to women's well-being after prison. Evaluations of community reintegration programs are also useful. For example, Banks and Ackerman (1983) suggest that important characteristics of a therapeutic program aimed at helping women make the transition from prison to the community include the development of socially appropriate coping skills, learning about community resources, and gaining a perspective on family and community roles. Gendreau (1996) notes that successful reentry programs emphasize teaching prosocial activities, utilizing cognitive and behavioral strategies, and facilitation of programs by sensitive and well-trained therapists. Bloom (1987) believes that increasing linkages with community resources and ameliorating negative factors in the social environments of former inmates are keys to the women's successful reintegration.

Internal perceptions about one's ability to manage daily life are related to the notion of self-esteem. High self-esteem has been found to be inversely related to recidivism (Fletcher, Shaver, and Moon 1993; Gendreau, Grant, and Leipciger 1979). However, Widom (1979), in her empirical study of incarcerated and non-incarcerated women, found that the assumption about offenders' lower self-esteem did not hold.

A review of these empirically derived findings indicate that successful reintegration is conditionally defined as: the former inmate's acceptance of adult role responsibilities according to her capabilities (i.e., economic sufficiency, parenting), the individual's perceptions of acceptance by the community despite what is often a stigmatized status, and the woman's sense of self-esteem or self-efficacy.[9]

Any complete effort to understand the causes of criminal behavior, and therefore to develop a helpful means of intervening and supporting behavioral and social change, has to examine all possible variables and individuals involved in the phenomenon, including both genders, all ages, all classes, and all ethnic groups. However, since the inception of the criminology field, research and correctional practices have focused almost exclusively on men, and much remains to be discovered about the impact of gender relations on social life, particularly in a field in which women's voices have not been privileged. As Daly and Chesney-Lind (1988) emphasize, feminist scholarship is not only about women; it is meant "to describe and change both men's and women's lives" (501). Perhaps as more is known about women and their needs, especially as they attempt to create a path for themselves out of crime, multiple perspectives can create a model of justice that is dignifying for all (Harris 1987).

As little as we know about women's pathways into prison, we understand even less about what happens to them after they are released from prison. The focus of this study is the discovery of those elements that support women as they reestablish their lives outside prison through legal means. Rather than measuring failure, I was interested in learning what contributed to the measurement of success as described by women who had served various sentences in prison facilities. The focus does not preclude the possibility that women will stumble along the way, that they will face barriers that they cannot surmount, or that they may in fact identify themselves as less than successful. However, there are women who make it in the free world despite these observed obstacles.

At the time that rehabilitation was recognized as a viable goal of incarceration (Maltz 1984), many studies examined the concept of recidivism and how to prevent it. Recidivism rates are a major, and usually the only, empirical demonstration of the effectiveness of the correction. However, for the most part, studies on recidivism have been conducted on all-male groups or mixed gender groups having a small female sample. Studies of women after incarceration have focused more on the cause of their previous criminal behaviors rather than on how they perceive the effect of incarceration on their current lives or the process of their reintegration.

Identifying at what point a person is determined to have recidivated is difficult when comparing findings across studies due to differing and overlapping definitions and inconsistent measurement.[10] In addition, there are a number of variations in post-release failure that relate to whether former inmates will become immediate or eventual recidivists (Glaser 1969). Maltz (1984) used statistical modeling to identify that a higher percentage of the sample "failed" within the first six months than in the following one-year and two-year observation periods. Reasons that have been given for early failure for women after release include family troubles, lack of employment or economic support, and drug abuse/addiction (Jurik 1983; Lambert and Madden 1976).

One national survey of women in state facilities that included juvenile history found that about 71 percent of all state female prisoners had served a prior sentence of probation or incarceration as a juvenile (Snell 1994). In Oklahoma, where more women are incarcerated per capita than in any other state in the country, 46 percent of a sample of incarcerated women had been imprisoned at least once previously (Fletcher et al. 1993). A study of jailed inmates in Ohio found that the average number of previous incarcerations among the women in the sample was 3.9 (Singer, Bussey, Song, and Lunghofer 1995). These high rates suggest that the previous methods of incarceration are not effective for ending women's criminal behavior. It is likely that many former inmates return to the streets facing the same issues they faced when they were sentenced, and with little choice but to use the same survival tactics that precipitated their incarceration.

A diverse sample of eighteen women in a midwestern area of the United States, who have been out of prison for at least six months, formed the basis of analysis in this study. The first six months of release from prison are crucial for the former inmate to reestablish her life, her relationships, and her well-being. The study provided an opportunity for each participant to reflect on what she had learned and experienced as she moved through the process of transition. In addition, the study facilitated each woman's examining future goals and needed resources to meet those goals. This study was significant in that no other work enabled former incarcerated women to discuss their perceptions of the process of reintegration as they moved from prison to the free world.

CHAPTER TWO

ESTABLISHING HOME

There's no place like home.

—Dorothy, in the Land of Oz

I got my place, and I slept on the floor. I had one blanket. I didn't have anything, but I was so happy. Just me and my daughter. We didn't have nothin', but we was just so happy to be together. I mean, I feel good sleepin' on that floor. I was free.

—Deeni

Home, for most of us, is a complex blend of both finding a literal place to lay our head where we can be assured of warmth and security and creating a figurative place where we feel comforted and nurtured, sexy and alive. The concrete structure often influences the abstract feeling of well-being. Family also makes a home, either as in the home of origin or in the family we choose as we move into adulthood.

The women in this study confronted major challenges in finding the places they could call "home." Their success in establishing a home in all its concrete and metaphorical possibilities provided the foundation for other experiences of "making it" after being released from prison. The set of needs that women identified included not only housing but also education, job skills, and other concrete supports that address the economic conditions of their lives and their role in how they managed their lives.

Exiting prison is not a smooth process for most women. Embedded in the process is a complex interplay of internal challenges and strengths and external constraints and protective factors. One of the most egregious psychological harms that the prison institution fosters is the repression and control of individuals who violate societal norms. Goffman (1963) has described the characteristics of the institution and the dependency it produces among its inmates. Given that criminal behavior is most often perceived as a male bastion, women who break the law suffer the double impact of not only violating a given social norm, but of violating sex role expectations as well. This double violation helps to determine the nature of women's prisons, the internalization of disciplinary surveillance (Foucault 1977), and the additional challenges women face in attempting to resume power once they are released.

My review of the literature found that conceptual formulations and studies regarding women's reintegration after prison are few and limited in their observations of the factors relating to their outcomes, mostly of failure or recidivism. As noted in the first chapter's discussion of the use of power to control the daily life of inmates and the particular ways in which that affects women, the central organizing theme for an understanding of women's emancipatory process is how they are able to resurrect to a life that includes reclaiming their identity and power. I used an empowerment framework to organize the factors that are associated with women's successful transition from prison.

A framework that has salience for changing practice or policy has at its foundation a dual focus on person and environment that evolves from a historical understanding of a concomitant need for simultaneously aiding people in need and attacking the social ills that relate to individual behaviors. In this paradigm, the welfare of individuals and their families is linked inextricably with the life-promoting qualities of their social contexts. Similarly, feminist theorists have pointed to the necessarily intertwined nature of the personal and the political realities of women's lives.[1]

EMPOWERMENT

Empowerment, as an ideal, a goal, and/or a process, is a term that is used repeatedly in today's cultural and political lexicon, with multiple meanings and intentions. As a step toward developing a definition for its use in this study, it is helpful to conceptualize power. Pinderhughes (1994) describes power as "the capacity to have some control over the forces that affect one's life, the capacity to produce desired effects on others, and to demonstrate mastery over self" (22). A sense of power is critical to mental health, and human beings strive naturally toward this sense of controlling one's destiny. Power is a dynamic that exists in the interaction between and among people whether characterized by dominance, subordination, or equality. In addition, one may be personally powerful but have virtually no legitimate socially derived power to determine one's own economic, social, or political fate. Thus, to become empowered means to gain intrapersonal, interpersonal, and social power that enables one to make efficacious choices for everyday life.

Empowerment theory posits individual problems as arising not from personal deficits, but from the failure of society to meet the needs of all people. The theory assumes that the potential for positive change exists within every individual, but acknowledges that negative personal behavioral patterns can emerge from attempts to cope with a hostile world, particularly when related to an individual's membership in an oppressed group (Pinderhughes 1994). Although individuals can develop less personally destructive coping strategies, changes in the power structure of society to assure equal access to environmental supports are considered crucial if individual problems are to be prevented or rectified (Rose and Black 1985; Solomon 1982)

Within the last twenty years, empowerment has emerged as an approach for working with women, people of color, poor people, and other socially oppressed groups. A feminist perspective on empowerment focuses specifically on how individual women have been affected by forces such as racism and sexism, and on ways in which social structures must be challenged. Gaining a sense of personal power is viewed as only the first step toward the ultimate goal of changing oppressive structures (Bricker-Jenkins and Hooyman 1986).

In the following section, I describe some of the social, political, and cultural resources that facilitate women being able to reestablish their home. I then discuss how the women I interviewed were able to draw the resources together that enabled them to find a start toward making it in the free world after incarceration.

ENVIRONMENTAL SUFFICIENCIES

The welfare of ex-incarcerated women and their families is linked inextricably with the quality of their social contexts. Pinderhughes (1983) asserts, "When the environment in which people live is nutritive, they flourish. There is a goodness-of-fit which facilitates growth, development, and realization of potential" (332). Thus, the discussion on environmental sufficiencies focuses on the array of social supports and the opportunities that empower women's transition from prison.

Inmates, before entering prison, during their stay, and after release, have basic concrete needs to address: satisfactory income, adequate and safe housing, nutritious food, clothing, legal protection, and the possibility to participate in socially meaningful interaction with others. Lack of sufficient income limits people's abilities to manage their lives regardless of where they have been. Often, this factor is not recognized as a major challenge for women exiting prison. When a woman leaves the institution, she is required to identify the address to which she is going. However, there is no formalized process to assist a woman with finding and maintaining her own residence, or to explore whether a woman's parole plan is a set up for failure because she has no income supports in place.

As a corollary to meeting basic needs, Simon (1995) specifies that an op-
erating assumption for empowerment practice is a belief that people, regardless
of a stigmatized status, have a constellation of rights to which they are entitled
as members of society. No fixed definition of rights is possible since a claim to
rights is complicated by both historical contingency and the willingness of the
state to acknowledge the claimant, based on membership in claimant groups. A
woman who is a convicted felon, for example, has far fewer rights (at least on
initial release) as an adult member of contemporary U.S. society than someone
who is a formerly institutionalized mental health patient. As Simon (1995)
notes, "Rights, in short, are not inalienable essences, but specific prerogatives
granted by the commonwealth to groups and individuals who, at some point
in history, have fought to define and obtain them" (19). Therefore, a part of the
normalization of the ex-inmate in establishing herself in the community is the
degree to which she can negotiate the process of making claims for resources
and power. These include her rights according to the U.S. Constitution, her
right to other social and economic entitlements that are contingent on her age,
income, employment history, and familial status.

Access to the full exercise of social rights and responsibilities is frequently obstructed. A lack of education and literacy skills, as well as some
physical and mental limitations, may contribute to reduced opportunities to
derive social benefits. However, it is the condition of disempowerment and
marginality that accrues to the role and status of the ex-incarcerated woman
that may signal the greater need for redress in the environment. Rose (1994)
notes that when the "historical context [is] permeated by inequality, our
species character (that forms the basis for human dignity) is mediated, modi-
fied or distorted, perhaps even subverted by its inherent characteristics of
domination and exploitation" (32–33).

Women exiting prison experience stigma by virtue of their conviction for
a crime, regardless of having done the time associated with punishment for the
offense. The status of ex-offender is only one part of the person's identity, yet it
can become the most prominent defining characteristic for representing self.
With the label comes the baggage of distrust and lack of credibility that may
foster an attitude of hopelessness in the ex-inmate that she can be efficacious in
her life. Labeling also has the effect of making it convenient for others to view
the ex-inmate as like all other ex-inmates. Thus, the programming for people
on parole or under community supervision becomes generic: that is, everyone
so labeled needs about the same amount of the same thing.

Benard (1999) refers to external elements that contribute to individuals'
success as protective factors. These protective factors may include caring relationships with others, environmental reinforcement of high expectations, and
opportunities for participation in the life of the community. Other structural elements (economic stress, stigma related to ex-con status, prejudice) may atten-

uate these protective factors and the individual's ability to develop or regain an empowering or enabling niche (Taylor 1997).

Finding Initial Shelter

The women's narratives produced two overarching themes: the need for concrete resources and the inevitability of internal assessment and transformation. The women provide many examples of these two interwoven and overlapping themes of their recursive and ongoing processes for reasserting autonomy and well-being in their lives. All the women in the study described the initial necessity of finding shelter after exiting prison as crucial to the start of their transition into the free world.

A major component of the parole plan for women exiting prison is having an identified and verifiable residence. For most of the participants, having a place to be released to was the only element that they recognized as "pre-release planning." Women in the study either were released directly from the state facility where they had completed their incarceration or were released from a federal facility to a community placement facility (Dismas House[2]) for 90 to 120 days to complete their sentences before release to the community.

Women who had resided at Dismas House described a range of reaction to this halfway house experience where they remained under correctional control. Because they were not responsible for their total upkeep, the residents of Dismas House were enabled to move into their own residence more directly on their release in the community as compared with the state-released women who did not have the community placement opportunity. Participants who entered the community from Dismas House had made an average of 1.3 moves, while women released to the community from the institution where they were incarcerated made an average of 2.25 moves. Table 2.1 describes the trajectory of residences where participants lived after release from prison.

Participants such as Anita, Ashley, Bernie, Elizabeth, Mandi, Racque, Susan, and Suzy, who had not lived at Dismas House, tended to move from place to place, depending on more temporary supports until they had amassed enough money to move into their own place. Only Margi, Nicole, and Regina were all still living in the same location to which they had been paroled; in each case, the property in which they lived was owned by a family member. Sadie was unique in that she came out with financial savings: she was able to acquire a mortgage to purchase a house after only about six months of employment.

The women in the study described multiple steps they took to gain the financial (and legal) independence they needed to secure and maintain their own home. These steps included using institutional opportunities while they were incarcerated, drawing on the resources available to them through Dismas House, the support of family and friends, and sometimes the kindness of strangers.

Table 2.1
PARTICIPANTS' PLACE OF RESIDENCE
ON RELEASE FROM PRISON

Participants	Residence 1	Residence 2	Residence 3
Deeni	Dismas House	Rents apartment[1]	
Demi	Dismas House	Parents' home	Rents apartment (with boyfriend)[1]
Elena	Dismas House	Boyfriend	Rents apartment[1]
Jeanette	Dismas House	Rents apartment[1]	
Nan	Dismas House	Rents apartment[1]	
Rene	Dismas House	Rents home (with fiancé)[1]	
Ashley	Parents home	Boyfriend	Rents home[1]
Anita	Treatment center	Father's home	Rents home[1]
Bernie	Former inmate	Subsidized apartment	Buying home[1]
Elizabeth	Mother's home	Rents house	Buying home[1]
Mandi	Brother's home	Friend's home	Rents home[1]
Margi	Rents deceased grandmother's home (with fiancé)[1]		
Nicole	Shares father's trailer (with spouse)[1]		
Racque	Motels	Shared apartment with ex-inmate	Rents apartment with spouse[1]
Regina	Parents home[1]		
Sadie	Friend's home	Buying own home[1]	
Susan	Parents' home	Rents apartment (with spouse)[1]	
Suzy	Parents' home	Rents home (with spouse)[1]	

[1]Residence at time of interview.

Institutional Opportunities and Experiences

Women described their participation in a wide variety of programs while they were incarcerated. However, it was their participation in specific educational or skill-building classes or particular employment opportunities that enabled them to address their future economic needs.

For a number of the women in the study, getting a General Education Diploma (GED) or taking classes while they were in prison helped them identify new opportunities for employment when they were released. Three of the women obtained a GED while in prison (Nicole, Demi, and Nan). Specific job skill development mentioned by women in the sample included horticulture, word processing, tutoring in the literacy program, building maintenance, nursing assistance, real estate, and office technology. This list includes those programs that were offered to women in the state system as well as some offered only to federal inmates.

Those women who, as Suzy puts it, "took advantage of all that was offered," not only came out with more identified skills than when they became incarcerated, but also were able to use the classes as a way to cope with the boredom of prison life. Using whatever was offered also promoted a sense of motivation that may have been suppressed in the women's lives before their incarceration.

Nicole discussed in detail the classes that allowed her to get her GED even though she served time in several state prison facilities and a county jail. In each location she worked toward completion of the test by working with volunteers who came into the facility to tutor inmates, and she took the pretests until she completed the whole exam and participated in the graduation.

> When my scores came back, I passed it. . . . They make a deal out of it, just like you were graduatin' out here. They give you like a gown thing and your cap with the [tassel]. . . . I had been out of school about thirteen years . . . I had my GED, which I didn't have before, and I felt like at least on an application I can write down that I got this instead of "I made it to the tenth grade." So, I knew that I had something that I could look to go towards.

Nan used her time while in prison to build her repertoire of marketable skills.

> When I went there, motivation was strong. I went to prison pregnant and was in school the whole time I was pregnant and got my GED. I got Certified Nurses Aide in the community there. I got my license in real estate. You got nothing else to do but go to school and some women just play around and sit there day by day and let it rot with nothing to do. I felt the need to get active, to get involved in something to help my time.

Demi used the everyday structure of the boot camp as a motivating force.

> I got my GED right off the bat when I got down there. And, I also en-
> rolled to go to school. So, as soon as I got back here, I was enrolled for fall
> classes at Penn Valley. I mean, just things you never took—that's exactly
> why I didn't ever go to college before. I just procrastinated, "Oh, I'll do it
> next semester."

Deeni decided during her long term of incarceration that she was going to take
advantage of everything that was offered to maximize her chances for future
employment, including help from prison staff.

> I took college courses and I always took computer courses. And I plunged
> myself into health and fitness. I taught aerobics while I was there, and that's
> what I decided I really wanted to do. I knew there wasn't a lot of African-
> American instructors. And there was people in prison that helped me. I
> had some really good supervisors in there that really paved the way for me
> and taught me a lot about what I should be doin' to get myself prepared.

The length of sentence limits the type of work assignment that is available
to the inmate. Since Elizabeth had a relatively short time to serve, she was not
eligible to enroll in classes. However, after an incident with a guard whom she
believed was "after something that I'm not willing to give," a staff member in-
terceded so that she was able to enroll in courses that, when she was released,
helped her in one of her first jobs.

> The next thing I knew, I was in school. I took a Word Star word process-
> ing course. Word Star is like the most primitive thing, but it was new then.
> So, I took that and a little Applied Math class or something. I almost fin-
> ished both classes. I didn't make it for the finals, but I'd done everything
> and passed all the tests up to there with A's and stuff. Then it was time for
> me to leave. So, when I went to the job, and I was doing the inventory
> control using one of the computer programs they trained me on.

Although Mandi had previously received a scholarship to a community
college based on her high score on the GED exam prior to incarceration, she
had dropped out of college due to both her drinking and an abusive relationship with her former husband. While she was in prison, she took office skills
courses and computer classes. She described her delight in discovering that she
could figure out the passwords to get into software applications:

> Well I seen a pattern in those two passwords, so I'd go back to my dorm
> room, and I'd really think about it. I ended up going through all these dif-
> ferent ideas, and I'd go back to school, and I'd try 'em, and those were the
> passwords.

Mandi's problem-solving aptitude as well as the computer skills she developed in these classes helped her obtain one of her first jobs at a business doing data entry after her release where her speed and accuracy resulted in regular promotions.

Many of the women's jobs in prison provided them with only enough compensation to meet some of their personal needs. However, some of Jeanette's assigned jobs, for example, pipefitting and heating and refrigeration, provided her with marketable skills. She also developed talents that enabled her to barter within the prison economy.

> You know, I don't mind working, because it helped pass the time. But I made like a level II wage, which was, oh, $17 a month or somethin'. I didn't feel like I could ask my mother to send me money and take care of my children. So, I learned to crochet. I made things for people, and that's how I got stamps. Some girls can't read or write, so I'd help 'em read letters, and they'd give me stamps for that, or I'd write letters for 'em.

In addition to specific classes or work assignments that enlarged post-prison vocational possibilities, prison employment provided some women with savings that enabled them to have some start-up money when they exited prison. Sadie and Susan in the state system and Nan in the federal system made a minimum wage salary in their prison industry employment. Sadie and Susan both worked in a privately owned electronics assembly plant. Nan worked for a sign production company within Unicor, the trade name for Federal Prison Industries, Inc. Sadie, who exited the institution with almost eight thousand dollars in savings from her four years of employment, recalls the benefit of having savings when she came out for initial expenses such as a car.

> Well, the money certainly was a major thing. I wouldn't have had any money at all when I came out. They [the prison] made you save like 10 percent or something like that. . . . they put it in a bank in Lansing. . . . You never got any interest even though you had your money in a savings account . . . but then you could send as much as you wanted someplace else. You just couldn't have an account with your name on it so if you escaped you didn't have a bank account you could access. . . . I sent it to my mom. She opened a savings account for me in her name. I didn't have a car . . . I got one within the first week I was out.

Likewise, Susan immediately was able to get a car from the savings she had from being employed while she was incarcerated.

> My mom and dad picked me up. I had been working at [the electronics assembly plant]; they gave me a whole lot of money when I left. So I gave mom and dad some of it, and I got a car so I could have transportation.

Private industry jobs that some inmates acquired not only can provide the inmate with savings, and currently support the inmate and/or her children during incarceration, but they can also offer valuable job experience. As Nan recalled:

> I worked in Unicor, which means I made $300 to $600 with overtime a month. That's good money inside the system, because I didn't pay no bills. I saved $3,500 and some change while I was in prison. I got excellent experience. I worked at a printing shop. I printed up nine-color jobs. I printed flags for Washington, D.C. I got a beautiful portfolio of the jobs that I done.

Employment in a private industry also can promote a woman's sense of self-worth by enabling her to go outside the prison environment. Sadie described the benefits of working at the assembly plant in this way:

> It was a hard job, pretty hard physical job in a factory. So you weren't on the hill all day, you weren't in the facility so you didn't get caught up in all this stuff that went on. Most of the people that worked [outside the institution] didn't get involved in near as much just the everyday life in the prison.

Table 2.2

PARTICIPANTS' INVOLVEMENT WITH PROGRAMS DURING INCARCERATION (N = 14)

Participant	Vocational Skill Development/Employment
Ashley	Head chef, unidentified classes
Deeni	Computer classes
Demi	GED, forest preservation
Jeanette	Drug treatment
Nan	GED, Unicor (Federal Services Industries), CNA
Rene	Parenting
Elizabeth	Word processing computer class
Mandi	Computer classes
Margi	Parenting (PATCH-MO)
Nicole	GED
Racque	Pre-release life skills development
Sadie	GED tutoring, private prison industry
Susan	Life skills, private prison industry
Suzy	Parenting, dorm maintenance

Women coming out of prison with both skills and savings were better able to marshal their resources for finding a place to live. Table 2.2 describes the types of programs that fourteen of the eighteen participants reported they engaged in while incarcerated.

At the time I interviewed them, of the four women who did not report receiving any particular training while they were incarcerated, Anita and Bernie were employed while Elena was working to complete her GED and Regina was dependent on public aid and her family for support for her and her infant.

Participation in pre-release classes is another means for women to secure experience in employment that would enable them to address concrete needs. Only Susan and Racque, two of the state incarcerated women, had any pre-release classes. During the last several months of her incarceration in the Kansas system, Susan participated in an educational program that focused on developing an assortment of life skills for managing her transition. Racque had twice attended pre-release classes in another state's system in the last ninety days of her prior incarcerations. She found them useful because they taught job-search and interview skills and focused on building self-esteem. However, she also observed that the same exact program the second time around was not helpful.

COMMUNITY PLACEMENT

The federal system provides an option for some inmates to complete the last six to nine months of the sentence in a community placement in the city where the inmate will return after release. In the Kansas City area, Dismas House is the only federally contracted community placement. Not everyone who applies for community placement is accepted. Eligibility is determined by criminal history and risk to the community as well as good behavior while incarcerated. Residents at Dismas House work through various levels of increasing privilege and free time by adherence to the rules of the facility and participation in therapeutic groups.

Six of the seven federal ex-inmates in the sample had resided at the Dismas House. For those six (Deeni, Demi, Elena, Jeanette, Nan, Rene), the halfway house environment both promoted and hindered their process of establishing their foundation for release. Some resented the continued control and monitoring of their day-to-day lives and the consequent difficulty they had in seeing family members and their children until they had earned enough free time away from the facility. Rene recounted her great disappointment at not getting to see her children when she was recommitted to the Dismas House after a drug violation:

> I ended up there on Friday, which is their last workday. I been there before, so I basically knowed the program. And, the thing about it that was hard for me was that on Monday I found out that I was in the red book, which is restricted and can't do nothin' 'cept work. No pass time. I was really upset because the kids was expectin' to be able to see me. I had to work out with

the caseworker and people to bring 'em to me. It was hard because the things that go through my mind is, "You know, these kids are expectin' to see me, and now they're tellin' me I can't go anywhere." But, they finally would let me out. You have to go through a lot of things. I got out Friday— on Monday, I called my old employer. I told him that I had another eight days before I could get out to work. Okay, by the 20th, I was workin'. I hadn't been out two weeks, and I was already workin'. Then, you're workin' and you're on this restriction. You know, there's a lot of rules.

Women in the study often had negative reactions about residency at Dismas House. They felt frustrated by the lack of privacy, the intrusiveness of the staff in their daily lives, the restrictions that made it difficult for them to reconnect with their family members or children, the requirement that women pay a subsistence fee, and what they perceived as unsupportive staff attitudes. Elena "hated that place," for example, because she often had conflicts with one of the "reverends . . . because he told me I was like one of their statistics, that I would end up goin' back." She concluded that she would have "rather stayed in prison than deal with him."

Most of the women who had lived at Dismas House mentioned the difficulty of paying the subsistence fee of 25 percent of their gross income that made it difficult to save money for other expenses. However, Nan was so happy "with bein' that part of free," that even though she complained about the subsistence requirement, she asserted,

> Honey, they could have said, "Work and give us your whole check" and I would have gave it to 'em. I just wanted to be able to come and be here on the weekends with my kids and just be free.

Nan believed that she had been fortunate in making her transition from prison because she had savings from her private industry job she held while incarcerated, and a sister who had essentially managed the concrete part of finding a place for her and her children to live. As she observed, many women staying at the Dismas House are not as lucky:

> If you're payin' subsistence and tryin' to save money and pay for a place to stay and start all over, that can be hard. So, that's where the subsistence part I didn't like came in. Some women there were strugglin' to try to get set up. Some of 'em, their kids was in foster care and in order to even go back before the judge to reconsider getting' 'em back, they had to have a place to stay, stable home, stable job and all of that good stuff, and if they couldn't get that, then they're through. And, they go back to doin' the same thing, either usin' or sellin'. They need help when they get out. You can't come out of prison without money. It makes you go back to doin' wrong, even though you free, you might as well go back to prison.

Demi talked about what it was like to try to follow the rules while living in an environment in which almost everyone is struggling against the temptation to relapse.

> There's a lot of temptation. The most, especially, especially at the halfway house. I think the halfway house is very hard. If you can make it through the halfway house, you can make it through the rest of it.

The women recognized several positive aspects of their stays at Dismas House, including the presence of a dynamic drug counselor. Elena, for example, found that "Mr. G." was "down-to-earth" and encouraged her to "prove 'em all wrong." She attributes working with Mr. G. to her decision to abstain from using drugs.

> When I came out of prison, I had the same attitude that I was gonna do everything like before. I wasn't gonna change. I just thought, "They made me wiser, you know." I got caught one time. I was just gonna be slicker, and that was my attitude when I first came out. I had a terrible attitude. I think my drug counselor was the one that really helped me decide on what I really want out of life . . . he was like my inspiration, somebody that I really looked up to. If he could do it. I could do it . . . I learned a lot off of him.

Jeanette and Demi both also identified Mr. G. as a role model since he had not only served time and but had also come out on the other side of a drug addiction, as well as coped with many other troubles in his life. Jeanette observed:

> He is excellent. He's just one man spread so thin. Sometimes people need that extra attention. He does an excellent job for what he's tryin' to do. I think Dismas House has one of the best, highest rates of people not goin' back, and you can attribute that directly to (Mr. G.)— he did time himself, a lot of time, drug addict. Okay, he's really made some changes . . . he's from the streets. He knows how to talk to ya. He knows what you're goin' through.

Demi was so inspired by what she learned in Mr. G.'s groups that she periodically returns to Dismas House so she can hear his stories:

> . . . they are more personal stories and temptation stories. You can tell that these things have happened to him, and they are not out of a book. I have nothing but praise for that guy. I even bring friends who have never had a drug problem, you know, to group sometimes with me, just so they can hear him. I still have a lot of friends who go, "Why do you go?" Because I need that inspiration. When I start feeling stressed during the week, I feel at home there.

Deeni was the only member of this subgroup of participants who specifically discussed the importance of the Dismas House in providing her a place to live while she worked and saved money so she would not have to depend on others to support her when she was released. Dismas House also served to test her skills and determination for meeting her goals of self-reliance.

> The halfway house was very helpful for me . . . because I really didn't have any place to go. I'm always welcome with my family, don't get me wrong, but I didn't want to be there. I'd rather just do that and be there and know what I had to deal with there, and go ahead and do what I had to do, because I'm a warrior. So that thing was a challenge for me. I had to be there for 6 months. One of my goals was to save my money and make sure I had my apartment and everything ready to go when I got out. I set my goals and reached my goals.

Although the benefit of having time to meet financial goals was not widely discussed by those who stayed at Dismas House before being released to the community, the reality of dealing with the responsibilities of the real world certainly demonstrates a benefit of the halfway house. Nan summed up some of the real-world issues that women face when they leave the temporary and constructed security of Dismas House:

> When you leave the halfway house, everything comes to an end. You kinda like have to get up and get started fresh, because at the halfway house, they furnish a place for you to stay and you know all of the bringings that go with it. But, when you get out of there, you're responsible. You have to have a place to go live. You need a car, a job, you know, your own money and you just need other things.

The methods women chose to assume responsibilities in the world outside of Dismas House and the institution where they had been incarcerated are represented in the next section. These include all the themes expressed by the women that relate to what they had to do to maintain their home, once they had found it. These themes included the vagaries of getting and keeping employment and the types of concrete supports available from friends, family, and intimate partners.

OBTAINING AND MAINTAINING EMPLOYMENT

Once women had located a place to live after they had been released into the community, the challenge of supporting themselves became more demanding. In various ways, the women discussed how their incarceration was a barrier not only to their obtaining employment but also to having a realistic notion about how they would assume the responsibilities that quite possibly they had not assumed previous to their incarceration. Goffman (1961) discusses this type of separation from the outside world as part of the phenomenon of "institutional-ization" within the closed inmate world. Elena expressed the difficulty she had resuming responsibilities for her and her children when she came out of prison:

> In there [prison], it's like vacation time. I mean, you really don't have no re-sponsibilities in prison. Here, if you got children, you gotta take on the re-sponsibilities of your children or goin' to work and gettin' back on your feet, tryin' to get on the right track, you know, if that's what you really want.

Although other women's statements contradicted Elena's perception that there were *no* responsibilities in prison, all of them discussed the issues related to getting and keeping a job after not being held accountable to any great degree within the prison environment. Suzy compared the new responsibilities she faced to the everyday unchanging routine of prison life with some nostalgia.

> I knew what to expect. I knew where I was and what my responsibility was. You had a routine and knew what you had to do and how you had to do it, and it didn't change. And, here in a normal life, it changes every day. All these different responsibilities and stress factors. I didn't have 'em then there.

Anita discussed how the prison culture reinforced the lack of planning for the future responsibilities that women face when they exit the institution.

> . . . they know when they was in there, they can eat for free. They don't gotta pay no bills. They don't worry about no kids. They don't do nothin' but be there and do what they want ya to do, and that's the same daily routine, clean up for a few hours and then you got the rest of the evenin' to watch TV.

Nan discussed the relative ease with which she could manage her ex-penses while in prison as compared to the worries she had to assume in man-aging the day-to-day life of caring for a family.

> . . . if you've been locked up so long, you ain't paid no rent . . . no bills there. You went to the commissary, and you purchased your little personals that you needed. You never had to purchase anything from that store that cost you more than fifty bucks. Well, my God, you didn't have nothin' to worry about.

In contrast, the women who resided at Dismas House were expected to seek employment as soon as they completed an eight-day orientation to the program. A staff member assisted the residents to assess their skills and prepare them for job interviews. Women were referred to other agencies that also spe-cialized in assisting people to find jobs. In addition, the house culture supported women who were going through this process. For example, Jeanette recalled that she received the most help from other women at Dismas House.

> . . . the ones that have already been there for awhile and have already worked the ropes, they already know what's goin' on. They tell ya how to get clothes . . . get around . . . where you can get a job. . . . I feel like at least with the feds, which they should as long as they keep ya, they at least gave us bus passes and they had somebody workin' there when I was there . . . they did help to drive you around and help you get a job.

Since the women from Dismas House were already identified as ex-inmates by virtue of their residence, they did not sense as much stigma related to finding a job as did those women who came out to the community directly from a prison facility. Jeanette described her relief when a computer skills class sponsored by a local community-based agency provided her an opportunity for employment; in that setting, the fact that she was a felon provided her with some additional currency:

> I'm female. I'm white. I'm a felon. So, I covered a lot of slots for them in one big hiring, you know. I appreciate really the opportunity. That's a big fear. I've got to have a job.

However, Jeanette expressed her concerns about both maintaining her current job and her future employability. She indicated that since her record was known by her present employer, she felt insecure about her future:

> I feel the biggest drawback in the future is the felony. That will follow me for the rest of my life. There are several jobs that I'm very capable of do-ing that I'm not going to have the opportunity to [acquire]. I worry about providing for my kids, because, for example, I have a pretty good job now in a community-based organization. The felony doesn't matter. But, the lady I work for—the place I work, they hired me when I was still in the halfway house, and I feel like she holds it. Like a trump card. You know, to keep me in place or thinkin', "Well, she's gonna take this abuse because she needs this job." And, I do need this job. Jobs are not easy to get these days. Whereas before I had a good work history and I just eliminated myself from that kind of a job market.

Thirteen of the eighteen women in the study said that they had been subjected to discrimination on the basis of their criminal record that prevented them from getting the job they wanted. Study participants discussed the strate-gies they used in deciding when and how to disclose their ex-inmate history while obtaining and maintaining employment. Failing to disclose previous criminal records can be problematic even if to avoid perceptions of stigma or discrimination. When Elizabeth came out of prison in 1984 a friend who owned a car repair business offered her her first job. After the friend was killed in a car accident, and she could no longer work at the business, she obtained other office jobs. She avoided the potential stigma associated with her status by not disclosing it on job applications. In two different situations, Elizabeth believed that she was subject to discrimination when she was terminated from jobs in which she had proven herself a good employee because she did not initially disclose her record.

> After I'd worked there two and a half years, I went to dinner one night with one of the behind-the-scenes partners. Normally, I wouldn't do that, but he just like says, "Oh, come on. You're gonna go have a drink with me and have dinner." So, I did. And, a couple of drinks, and I talked a little bit. So, I don't know whether—I'd like to think that he would not have repeated that, but it is very possible. I suddenly lost the job about a month later, and there was no reason. There was no problem with my work. There was no conflict in the office.

She found another job working at a hotel chain where she again did not reveal her background.

> Two and a half years later, and I had a couple of friends that I had confided in, I'd had three promotions and many opportunities and a boss that was just fantastic. Everything was goin' along cool, and somehow somebody got wind of it. . . . my boss tried to get them not to terminate me, but they were adamant that because I had lied on the application, "that was the only choice they had."

After that experience and a short term of parole supervision, Elizabeth requested that the state expunge her record so that the public would not have access to it. The judge who originally heard her case granted her request and she is no longer under a legal obligation to reveal her ex-inmate status. Currently Elizabeth works as a bookkeeper in a setting in which other formerly incarcerated women seek assistance. She believes that her experiences should enable her to assist some of the agency clients. Yet the memory of her past terminations prevents her from disclosing her former status in this work setting.

Many of the women had friends, family members, or community resources that facilitated their securing initial employment and managing their concrete needs. Ashley used the employment preparation and placement services of the Women's Employment Network (WEN), an agency that focuses specifically on the needs of women in transition.

> I really went through [WEN] to get a résumé made. And, it was a good experience. I liked it. There was a lot of networking there. I got a great résumé. And, that's actually how I got the job at that social work place,

because they tap into the state agencies. They do a lot of good things. They show you self-respect. They show you how to interact with people. They teach you how to do interviews. They do a lot of career searching, so you can find out what it is you want to do.

Although Ashley was able to get a job at a residential group home for which she was referred, she later quit it because the salary was so low. She feels that her biggest obstacle in the transition continues to be employment since she has yet to find a good job, which she defines as one paying at least $10 an hour. Although Ashley attributes her getting the residential job to luck, it is evident that she also was able to present herself in a manner that attenuated the stigma of having been incarcerated. She recalled:

I had to go in there and tell this lady, you know, "I was in jail for this but I want to do social work." And, I basically sold myself. "I know I can do this. I love kids." And, she hired me as a social worker aide, and it was under the assumption that she would help me to go to school to finish my degree. Well, after being there like three months, we started talking about funds that were available, and there were none. So, I just got up and go. I'm not goin' sit here and work for $6 an hour like this. But, that was a good step in the door, if it would have went somewhere.

At the time of the interview, Ashley worked two jobs, one at a childcare center where her mother also works and where she can see her daughter during the day, and another at night doing telemarketing. She indicated that she is still not making enough money to adequately support her daughter and herself. She drew on other resources, such as her workplace and sometimes her family, so that she can pay her bills and regularly see her daughter. She relates that she has also learned how to better mange her finances:

Sometimes I don't know how I can afford to pay all my bills, but I do. I can do without a lot of things. I can do without going shopping. I can go without buying food to pay my bills to keep everything on, to make my car payment, to pay my insurance. And, the average person could not live without buying food. Well, I work at a day care center, so I can eat all day long if I want to and not pay for it. I can even bring food home if I want to from the day care. I mean, I can go to my mom's and eat. But I refuse to have anything turned off. I have to live comfortably.

Mandi was certain that acknowledging that she was an ex-felon would prevent her from getting a job. She drew on personal contacts to find her initial jobs.

My parole officer, when I first met with her, she gave me this sheet of paper and said, "When you find a job, your employer has to sign this. That way they know you're on parole." I thought, "I'm never gonna get a job."

> I ended up getting a job at Taco Bell because my brother's wife's sister was the manager there. That was the only option that I had. Then she told me she used to work at this other place, an office building. The office was the direction of the Taco Bell when I walked. She told me she used to work there and that they were always hiring.

Some of the women indicated that a serendipitous encounter propelled them into unexpected job opportunities. However, the women had to take advantage of the opportunity that presented itself. Mandi, for example, did not have a car when first released in the Kansas City area and so she would walk to her two part-time low-wage jobs located close to her apartment. She recalls that she would stop in periodically at McDonald's on her way to or from work.

> The manager there would tell me when I went in, "You're very friendly, I'd really like for you to work here." That's kind of funny, when you're in prison, you're setting goals for yourself . . . "I don't care if I go work at McDonald's, I'm gonna get a job." So, here I had the opportunity to work at McDonald's. I've already got two jobs. I don't need McDonald's, but I'm thinkin'. One time when I walked in there, she said, "How about I make you a manager?" I told her, "I don't know what a McDonald's manager does." "I don't like nights." "I have meetings to go to." There are more meetings offered at nights than during the day. So she said, "That can be worked out." The next time I went in, she said, "How 'bout it?" I was only makin' like $6 an hour at the office thing. I was only makin' like $5.25 at Taco Bell. It wasn't very much, but McDonald's offered me $6 an hour to start with a raise in sixty days to be a manager.

Sadie's involvement with an in-prison program became a support system when she left prison. She had become active with a battered women's shelter while she was incarcerated by participating in the training provided by staff members at the shelter and by co-leading a training on domestic violence for other inmates. Sadie used this support system "Seven and a half years experience in the criminal justice system" as a bridge in her transition.

> The support system needs to start before the person gets out of prison . . . it did for me. My major support system . . . was the people at Safehome who had been coming into the prison for all that time. I mean those women were a great support system for me. They were like friends, you know, and being in that group was real good. It was just for women and I learned a lot. I certainly learned a lot about domestic violence which benefited me in getting a job.

This outside connection also provided Sadie with her initial residence as one of the staff members from Safehome who had been co-facilitating the women's support group offered Sadie a temporary place to stay. Six months later she was able to acquire a mortgage loan that enabled her to buy the house where she resided. In her job at the shelter, the fact that she had been in prison worked to her benefit. She felt that she could draw from her experiences to assist other women who felt imprisoned in abusive situations. Sadie, who is part Arapaho, has never identified any discrimination against her in employment situations. She is quick to point out, however, that her "circumstances" of being both formally educated and having what she describes as "white skin privilege" provide her with advantages over other less educated women and women of color. In the nearly eight years since her release, she has worked at several battered women's shelters, as a contract employee for a landscaping company, and as a bike mechanic. Despite her background she reflects,

> I've always had work when I've wanted it. I don't have a lot of excess money but I've haven't ever been without. I have a cool home.

Both the Kansas Department of Corrections and the Federal Office of Probation and Parole require former inmates to disclose their status to prospective employers so that parole officers can confirm the individual's employment and monitor continued progress. Sadie and other participants often seek employment in settings in which a criminal background is not a detriment or might even be considered an asset—for example, in working with people who may have had involvement in the correctional system.

Suzy is another participant who has creatively managed potential obstacles that are related to the type of offense for which she was incarcerated. Suzy spoke bitterly of her initial parole officer who "forced me to work" as it meant that she would have to disclose her former incarceration and the nature of her conviction.

> I had tried to get a couple of jobs, but they kept wantin' to know where I was and why I hadn't had any work for the last thirty months. He was tryin' to tell me that I couldn't lie so I had to tell them I was incarcerated. They wanted to know why, and I refused to tell 'em, so it was bye-bye. That was like three or four jobs that I tried to get, so I had to settle for some stupid little temporary work. They had me workin' in warehouses and crap. I hated it.

When she and her husband moved to another county, she was assigned a new parole officer who agreed when she got pregnant that she could stay home to take care of her four-year-old son. When she later miscarried, she decided that she wanted to do something that enabled her to earn income and parent her son. The job she acquired also solved her disclosure problem.

> I started working right after I lost the baby with this guy. I just enjoy my work. I work nights with him. We go junkin'. I enjoyed the freedom it al-

lowed me. I knew that if I had another kid, I couldn't do it. You know, because bein' a mom is a full-time job.

Suzy takes great pride in her abilities to turn junk into salable items. She related
that in addition to having a sizable savings account, another benefit to the job
had been her ability to furnish her house with a number of the items she had
found on the streets.

UNEXPECTED SOURCES OF SUPPORT

Women identified other forms of discrimination that presented barriers for
them in obtaining resources during their transition. Racque was denied eligibility for subsidized housing due to a standard eligibility criterion that potential residents must not have a felonious record. Anita was denied admission to a
proprietary business school because the school could not guarantee job placement to someone with a felonious record who completed its program.

However, several women also identified times when strangers gave them
a second chance and anticipated discrimination never materialized. Mandi, for
example, related a story about an unexpected Christmas gift when she went to
rent a house. In much the same way that she had obtained a potentially better
job, Mandi used communication skills to offset the property owner's fears about
her suitability as a tenant, and identified a means so she would not have to pay
a deposit.

> I was supposed to have a house big enough for myself and my children for
> at least six months before they could come home. On Christmas Eve, I
> happened to be walking to work. There was this for rent sign in front of
> this . . . really nice home. I told my sister I called to see how much the rent
> was. It was $540. She said, "How are you gonna afford it?" I said, "I don't
> know, but I'm not gonna find anything cheaper." . . . I called this guy up
> and met with him. . . . he said something about, "Well, I'll run a credit
> check, and then I'll let you know." I said, "Well, I'll just tell you. You're not
> gonna find anything for me the last two years. It's like I disappeared on the
> earth, because I've been in prison." He just kind of stood there . . . I re-
> membered just talking to him. I remember the walls looked really bad. So,
> then I went on to, "I know how to paint and stuff. So, instead of deposit,
> I'll just paint the house for you." He really liked that idea. He ended up
> giving me the keys. I didn't give him a dime. I remember walking away
> from there crying. It was my Christmas present from God. So, I got this
> house, and I started paintin' it.

Bernie too received a gift when trying to obtain public housing. She related that when she got off the bus after she was released from her last incarceration she had no place to go. After seeking emergency shelter, and spending
several nights with an ex- inmate she had known while incarcerated, she applied

for subsidized housing. She expected that her criminal record would prevent her from eligibility and that "Donna" from Housing Authority would call to confirm her worse fears.

> Donna called me the next morning and said that everything was done and that I could look at an apartment. . . . I said, "Did my police report come back?" She said, "Yes it did, Bernie, I want to talk with you about that." I thought, "Oh, man, I'm not gonna get that apartment." She said, "Bernie, do you know anybody that works up at the Sheriff's office?" I said, "Yeah, I was up there, but I don't know any of 'em personally or anything." She said, "Well, you've got an angel on your shoulder." My APB come back: No warrants. No arrests. I know who did it now. So, that day I was in an apartment.

In addition, Bernie described the kindness of both strangers and acquaintances who provided her with furnishings when she was initially getting settled in her apartment. It is partially this memory that fueled her desire to assist other inmates returning to the community. All the women in the study related examples of friends, family members, professionals, intimate partners, and children who provided support to them in the transition. The following section describes some of those stories, as well as cracks in their walls of support that the women had to manage.

Family Contributions of Support

Only two participants (Bernie and Rene) had no family support either during incarceration or after release from prison. Many of the women believed that their families were also punished by the incarceration in that they provided financial support for the ex-inmate while she was inside as well as often caring for her children. As Nicole indicated:

> Basically, they say, "Well, you're doin' the time, and your family's doin the time, too." They go through more—probably just as much as you do bein' in there, because you bein' away and the visits—sendin' money, tryin' to take care of you.

All the study participants discussed the importance of having someone they could depend on when they were released from prison. Ashley recalled, for example, that her family provided a great Christmas when she was initially released:

> So, luckily, I had a lot of family and they've always cared, and we've always been really close, so you know, they gave me a lot of things. I got out around Christmas, I had a great Christmas, which helped a lot.

One of the major ways family members supported the participants was by caring for their children while the women were incarcerated, and for some of the women who were not yet financially stable, continuing to provide a home for the women's children after their release. Ashley's parents have adopted her nine-year-old daughter because Ashley recognizes that her parents' greater financial stability is more advantageous to her daughter than what she can currently provide.

> And there were, there were other reasons besides the fact that they raised her from a child. It's that there are a lot of financial gains for her. My dad is almost sixty-seven. He is getting ready to retire. . . . Um, he's gonna— she's gonna get a lot of money when he passes. There's no use in no one getting that money.

Jeanette depended on her mother to care for her two daughters while she was incarcerated or at Dismas House, and since her release her mother maintained physical custody of the girls while she works toward paying off old bills and saving enough money to rent a place with her daughters.

> My mom stays home with 'em. And, I have 'em all weekend long every weekend. But, you know, I make $8.75 an hour, and I owe from before I went to prison, I have outstanding utilities. Actually, I'm in better shape than a lot of people, and I know I am, but still it seems overwhelming some days. But, for me, in my situation, that is a lot of money, and to get a place to live that I can afford—I bring home $1,070 clear a month. With two kids, I don't have child support, you know. I'd have to pay those bills first and then—I want my kids to live with me.

One of Nan's younger sisters assisted her by moving, with Nan's four young children, to the town where Nan was incarcerated so that Nan could see them often. The sister also took care of Nan's newborn baby, who was born while she was incarcerated. Nan commented about the uniqueness of this form of support:

> My sister that you just seen left here today, her birthday was February 27. She just turned thirty, so she took on responsibility for them, and she was only twenty-five years old. How many twenty-five-year-old sisters would even take the responsibility of keeping your five kids while you gone? None. Because at twenty-five, she shoulda been out doin' her own thing. She took on that responsibility all by herself.

Some of the women who had family members with financial resources they could depend on stated that it was important to them to generate other resources for support during the transition. Sadie, for example, came out of a long-term incarceration with money in a savings account, a place to live, and a guaranteed job. She learned how to marshal the resources she needed to survive. Although Sadie's parents were supportive while she was in prison by visiting and giving her money until she obtained a private industry job that provided her wages, Sadie reported that she wanted to be independent and in a new environment for her own emotional well-being:

> The majority of people I knew went right back to whatever environment they came from which had at least something to do with, I mean that's true for me too. If I had gone to N——, I mean I wasn't living in N—— when I got arrested or anything but it's a teeny tiny town. I don't think I would have ended up back in prison, but it wouldn't been healthy for me emotionally.

However, it was important to her that she knew that she could rely on her parents for financial assistance if she needed it.

> I always knew that if I really had to and still do, if I really was in some kind of dire straits and needed some kind of assistance, especially financially, that I could count on them. They would do anything like that. All I would have to do is ask. I just never have and hope I never have to but it's certainly a benefit to know that's there.

Deeni also described her desire to "make it on my own" even if it meant that initially she had few furnishings for her home. Deeni used the example of one of the characters in the movie *Shawshank Redemption* to describe the difficulty in coming out after a long-term incarceration. She recalled that the assistance that family members and friends provided her in the initial days after her release from eight years of incarceration was instrumental to her transition.

> . . . if you don't have any money, you know, it's hard. That's why a lot of people go back to prison. You know, you have to look good if you wanna get you a good job. My mother gave me a charge card. She took me shoppin' and bought me clothes. My friends bought me clothes and put money in my pocket, and provided transportation for me. That's why sometimes you go right back to your old habits, because you don't have the help that you need.

Elizabeth said that she was the first person she had ever known who had been to prison. Her family visited her while she was in prison and offered her assistance when she came out. When Elizabeth first came out, she temporarily stayed with her mother until she had saved enough from employment to rent her own place. Several years later, she decided to buy a house. She did not have enough income to qualify for a loan so she went to one of her brothers to ask for assistance. She recalls her appreciation of her brother's willingness to help her:

> I went to him and ask him, "Would you co-sign?" He said, "No, I have children and a wife. I can't do that." This was really reachin' out there, because I'd never ask my brothers for a twenty-dollar bill before. I said, "Would you buy it for me, and let me buy it from you?" He said, "I can do that." So, it was very important to me to pay it off just as quickly as I could and to have that security. So, four years later, my house is paid for, and I got it back in my name. It was cool that I had my brother to help me and that he was willing to, and that it worked so smooth. So the fact that my house is run down and things like that, it's paid for. It's mine.

Financial problems that stemmed from the period prior to incarceration also created a need for family support by some of the women. Jeanette acquired a job while she was staying at Dismas House. However, as she explained, she had a lot of bills left over from when she had been using drugs that made it difficult for her to save money. Her mother kept Jeanette's two children for her during the week because she had not been able to rent a place large enough to accommodate them. Jeanette's father loaned her money to get a better car. Although she recognized that he had financial means, it was important that the assistance was a loan rather than a gift so she could maintain her autonomy.

> My dad helped me get another car. See, my dad and them are very financially well off, but it's a matter of doin' it on my own, and I did ask his help on getting' me another car. What he did was he got me a better car. It's reliable, and it's a nice car. But, I pay him for it. Dad gives me this. So, they are—my family has helped and they will help, as long as—especially my dad, who has money, and he seems to be really makin' an effort. I mean, I am trying.

Several of the women, similar to Jeanette, had to prove themselves to their family members in order to obtain assistance. Since Nicole moved into her father's trailer that is located some distance from employment opportunities in the metropolitan area, getting family assistance for buying a car became a major priority for her as well. She recalls that after she obtained employment, her mother agreed to help her get a car:

> The fact of getting [a car] was going to be the obstacle for me, because I didn't have any money saved. The only thing I had was what they gave me when I left there, and that's nothing. I didn't have a job yet. So, me and my mom had talked. She said, "You know, you start working and tryin' to save some money, and we'll go look for a car, and I'll try to help you out and see what I can do about co-signin'." So, that's what we did. It was kinda hard

startin' off at first, but I was lucky that I had the parents, you know, my mom, because what's important is if you have people to come out to that can help you.

Regina, the youngest member of the group, moved back home when she was released from prison; she lives with her parents and her younger brother and sister "as long as I show them I'm a responsible person." She depends on her parents as well as monthly payments from public assistance for the care of her and her infant son, whom she delivered shortly after her release from prison.

Not all families were responsive to the needs of a formerly incarcerated woman. Both Nan and Deeni were distressed with various family members who still expected them to provide some of the benefits that their criminal activities had offered. Deeni asserted:

> I've always been the backbone of my family. I guess bein' a hustler, bein' out there and always provided and did everything. So, when I came home, I knew that I could never live like that again. It was hard for me to adjust to not havin' anything.

Nan also felt that by no longer having the material goods that her lifestyle had provided, her relationship with her family had changed. She observed:

> I'm different for them. I was the one that even—because of my crime, you know—I lived in a big fancy house, and I did all the big Christmas dinners, and they came out to the fancy dinner, and they came over.

She also expressed some disappointment that she had not been able to rely on her family in general for help when she was in prison, and did not want to depend on them when she came out. Nan continued:

> But I won't, I don't want them to think that I'll ever need them for anything. My children couldn't rely on 'em, and I just don't want to be bothered with feelin' like, "Do you have some bread today?" If I have to bake a loaf from scratch for me and my kids, I'll make it.

After Margi's release from the Missouri prison facility in which she was held, she moved back to the small town in Kansas where she had grown up to be closer to family. When she first got there she worked in her parents' restaurant in town and rented her late grandmother's house. Still, she noted that she did not feel like her family was supportive:

> But, my family didn't want to step in neither. You know, after I got out, I didn't have no clothes or nothing. They gave me a couple of bags of clothes that didn't fit 'em or whatever. That's about all I've had since I got

out, except for what people gave me here and there. Then Christmas my
mom gave us some money this year, so I went and bought me about four
or five pair of slacks with the money.

Margi, of all the women in the group, seemed to be so financially overwhelmed
that it appeared that the lack of tangible support could become her rationale for
recommitting a new crime, much as it had done before when she said she had
stolen items in order to pay her rent. The difference in this current situation
may be the presence of a new intimate relationship, the father of her newborn
baby, as well as her ability to identify where she could go for assistance.

COMMUNITY SOURCES OF SUPPORT

Professionals from various private and public agencies provided some concrete
assistance to women in transition from prison. These types of concrete assistance
included everything from job preparation and referral to vouchers for clothing
or food. In one case, a parole officer provided referrals for housing and employment to Susan and her husband (also a parolee).

> Yeah, when I came back from Louisiana, they gave us lists of places that fit
> our price range for places to move. They gave Chris lists of places willing to
> hire people on parole. You know, they would say we could use them as per-
> sonal references or whatever. That's about all they could do. It helped a lot.

However, women expressed hesitation about using community resources
to acquire assistance because it put them in a position where they had to disclose their record as well as trust that others would help them. Nan was most
vocal in verbalizing what other women implied about depending on any system
for assistance once they were released from prison. She likened the intrusion to
an extension of control she already felt in her post-prison supervision. In response to a question about seeking assistance, she exploded:

> For what? For them to pry into my business—why I was in prison and
> what did I do and da-da-da-da. The federal government was all in my busi-
> ness and turned it upside down and told me what to do, when to do, not
> 365 days a year, [but] four times 365 days a year. I live with my probation
> officer that does the same thing. I don't want to go nowhere else and no-
> body ask me nothin' about my business. Can I have some privacy? Can I
> be a citizen? Can I have rights? Can I be human?

SUPPORT FROM FORMER INMATES

Although women did not draw on an extensive network of professional helping
services, if they were not connected with family members, another source of
support was former inmates. Bernie, for example, consistently used her network

of other ex-inmates by staying with a friend from prison when she was first re-leased. Bernie believes the principle of "we these people [helping] we these people" and has created a wide web of community connections, many of whom are former inmates, to assist other former inmates. Bernie reported that having someone to call when she arrived "on the streets" with little money and no place to go gave her enough of a starting point for exploring other options.

> I finally got up and called a girl— I'd helped her get her GED while she was up at Topeka. She'd been home a couple of months. So, I called Roberta. The minute I said "hello," she said, "Oh, Bernie, you're home. How're you doing?" I said, "Well. . . ." She didn't let me finish. She said, "You need some help?" I said, "I sure do." She said, "We'll be up to get you." So, her and her son came up and picked me up at that restaurant. She took me out to her house. So I stayed at their house that night . . . the next morning they got up and took me to get my records and all of the things I had to do.

Relationships with spouses/intimate partners, friends, and the women's children, although extremely important to the transition, proved to be a source of less tangible support and will be discussed in Chapter 4.

The findings in this chapter emphasize that women in transition from prison require an affordable place to start from where they can exercise autonomy and identify resources for meeting basic needs. Having a home—a place to go—is a taken for-granted part of structuring our daily lives. For women returning to the free world, identifying a place to live provides the starting point from which they can build the relational supports they need to facilitate the transition.

Securing and maintaining permanent shelter is a challenge for most women coming directly to the community from a prison facility because they usually have no financial resources to reestablish themselves, and they are faced with multiple and complex expectations for completing a sentence of parole and retrieving responsibilities, primarily that of assuming or resuming support for their children.

Dismas House provided a way station that, despite the sense of contin-ued control and intrusion, enabled the women to establish themselves to some degree before being faced with the pressures of making it without the obvious supports of room and board. Many of the women expressed a need for a tran-sitional and protected environment that would provide them with these initial supports for managing the transition. The halfway house model will be dis-cussed further in the final chapter on policy and practice recommendations. The themes in this section indicate that the critical period of community reentry is usually an extended process of trying on different situations to find the right mix of home and employment that best enables the formerly incarcerated woman to manage her everyday needs.

CHAPTER THREE

FROM THE INSIDE OUT

I had a lot of time to think, and I thought, Now look where I'm at and what am I gonna do to get out of here . . . I gotta do something positive or somethin' better.

—Nicole

Prison, for some people, is better than where they lived.

—Jeanette

Get up, brush yourself off, and just go on. You gotta walk for the rest of your life.

—Nan

Exiting prison is a crucial time for women in transition to the community, or "free world." Sykes (1958) notes various pains of imprisonment including deprivation of freedom, familial relationships, choice of associates, status, and material supports. But women also face an array of personal, social, cultural, and structural issues in reestablishing themselves within their communities. This chapter addresses some of the challenges formerly incarcerated women face as women; such as socialization to role functions and gender-specific identity as well as issues related to becoming an "ex" (Ebaugh 1984). There is some overlap with the next chapter on reconstructing relationships because the women's expression of their emerging selves was often intertwined with the development of relationships that promoted their sense of competence and well-being.

THEORIES OF FEMALE DEVELOPMENT
AND SOCIALIZATION

Much of the historical as well as contemporary literature that attempts to explain women's lawbreaking focuses on behavior that challenges female stereotypical roles. The dominant view of women is that they are nonviolent and passive, so criminal activities more easily attributed to men's nature are viewed as intrinsically not female. Historically, these deterministic beliefs contributed to the development of paternalistic treatment of lawbreaking women with an objective of moral reform (Rafter 1985). An undercurrent of these beliefs still ebbs and flows in the discussion of women's treatment in the criminal justice system (Robinson 1992). Theories on women's socialization and role development (Eagly 1987; Schaef 1992) provide additional understanding of the complexities of reshaping the sense of identity that women leaving prison have to address.

Feminists who emerged to address "the problem that has no name" (Friedan 1963) focused primarily on political and social liberation and equality. They strove to free women from the constraints of stereotypical sex role definitions, as well as economic and political oppression (Freeman 1995). Participants in the early feminist movement tried to minimize the differences between men and women, arguing that it was exclusively sexist discrimination that prevented women from full participation as community members. They also argued that changing social perceptions would rectify the situation (Alleman 1993; Weisstein 1970).

More recently, feminists writing about women's development have taken an alternative route, expressing a common theme that women are indeed different from men. They emphasize that these differences should be defined not as weaknesses, but as sources of strength (Aptheker 1989; Davis 1994; Gilligan 1982; Miller 1976). These strengths include women's orientation to relatedness, moral decision-making, and their ways of knowing.

THE PSYCHOLOGY OF WOMEN'S RELATEDNESS
AND TRANSFORMATION OF SELF

Psychiatrist Jean Baker Miller produced some of the early writings about women's capacity for relatedness and their different process of psychological development. She argues:

> Women stay with, build on, and develop in a context of attachment and affiliation with others. Indeed, women's sense of self becomes very much organized around being able to make and then to maintain affiliations and relationships (1976, 83).

Calling for a new approach to psychology that recognizes this different pattern in women's development, Miller asserts that the threat of disruption of a relationship is often perceived not just as object loss but as something closer to the loss of one's identity, thus requiring a transformation of self. She contrasts her findings with those based on observations of male development, which proceeds in the direction of separation, autonomy, and achievement of mastery in the world. Basic to Miller's perspective is the sense that human identity is inextricably bound up in one's relationships with others, and that complete autonomy is a fiction.

Much of Miller's (1976) writing, as well as that of her colleagues at the Stone Center for Developmental Services and Studies at Wellesley College (Jordan, Kaplan, Miller, Stiver, and Surrey 1991; Jordan 1997) is based on clinical case descriptions. While Miller places her theory of women's psychology within a critique of social inequality, her colleagues focus exclusively on psychological issues. Falling short of a complete feminist model that needs to account for class and race differences, Miller asserts that the forces she describes "affect all women, by virtue of the fact of being women" (x). Jordan (1997) notes in a second edition of writings from the Stone Center the importance of "engaging with difference in relationship" in their efforts to elaborate the centrality of connection in the diverse life experiences of women.

Members of the Stone Center group (Jordan et al. 1991; Jordan 1997) have formulated a theory of women's psychological development that also emphasizes relationship rather than separation as the vehicle of development. Based on clinical case studies, the group has found that mutually empowering relationships are the medium through which development occurs as well as the goal of development. Their work has involved a reconceptualization of women's development as a function of the capacity for relationships and competence within relationships. They believe that a growing capacity for empathy is the central organizing feature of women's development.

The relevance of this notion of self-in-relation is in the potential for women to develop and explore new forms of relationships, networks, and community. As women recognize their capacity for empathy and relatedness during the development of relationships with others, they begin to feel competence as relational beings. This recursive sense of competency is transferred to other relationships. Out of this mutual self-esteem building practice comes a revision of self. They define self-esteem as related to the degree of emotional sharing, openness, and shared sense of regard despite external stigmatizing or oppressive structures. This sense of self may be nearly impossible to completely achieve, especially in a culture that stresses separation as ideal and where validation of the need for relationship may become distorted and hidden.

Nancy Chodorow (1978) also sees the psychological development of women as embedded in relationships. She explains women's development from a psychoanalytic, object-relations framework, but rejects the view that biology is destiny. Chodorow argues that gender differences are influenced by societal norms, in accordance with which girls are nurtured by a parent of the same gender while boys begin their path toward adulthood in a primary relationship with a person of the opposite gender (the mother). Gender differences are not rooted in the child's experience of anatomical differences between the sexes, but rather in the different experiences and imperatives that grow out of nurturance by a person of the same or different gender. For women, social legitimacy comes not from self-assertion but from efforts to be like men, who represent power in the world; women may succumb to power envy rather than penis envy (Chodorow 1978).

MORAL DECISION-MAKING

Carol Gilligan (1982) further explored relational themes in the context of how people make decisions relating to moral dilemmas, including dilemmas that may lead to illegal behaviors. Gilligan reinterpreted and expanded Kohlberg's (1969) theory of moral development to include meaningful dimensions of possible gender differences. Moral behavior constitutes one significant aspect of personality, indicative of stable, underlying patterns associated with decision-making. Girls often score at lower developmental levels than boys, primarily because the developmental norms in Kohlberg's model were based exclusively on the experiences of males.

In three interview studies of identity and moral development, Gilligan (1982) discovered what she characterizes as "a different voice" among women participants, one that emphasizes relationship, commitment, and care. Women's experiences of morality organizes around issues of responsibility for other people within the context of investment in relationships and the development of an ethic of care.

Gilligan also found that moral and social integration went hand in hand, and that both were contingent on the women's sense of self-worth. As their self-worth increased, the study participants in her study (1982) began to make responsible rather than selfish decisions, and therefore moved developmentally toward social participation, or shared norms and expectations. Gilligan stated that the transition "requires a conception of self that includes the possibility for doing the right thing, the ability to see in oneself the potential for being good and therefore worthy of social inclusion" (78). Gilligan's model of relational development helps explain how lawbreaking may be an outgrowth of a complex interaction of relationships, feelings, and situations that might have led to a need for a sense of effectiveness in an inherently disempowering world.

THE PRODUCTION OF KNOWLEDGE

The most recent major additions to the growing body of literature on women's development seek to explore women's epistemology, or the construction of knowledge. Examining the nature of knowledge production provides important insights into understanding how some views operate in concert with socialization practices to maintain oppressive beliefs and practices.

While many versions of what we know as reality may be constructed (Berger and Luckmann 1967), only a few are legitimated. Minnich (1990) argues that it is privileged white men who have "generalized from themselves to all, establishing their sex/gender, their race, their class, as norms and ideals for all, while also maintaining their exclusivity" (68). This group, by virtue of its social power, establishes the normative standards against which everything and everyone is judged. Minnich argues that a transformation of knowledge would legitimize and empower women who develop versions of reality that more accurately reflect the worlds in which they live.

In *Women's Ways of Knowing*, Belenky, Clinchy, Goldberger, and Tarule (1986) present findings from interviews with 135 women of different ages and social classes. Their discoveries with regard to how women learn and how they find their truth parallel Chodorow's (1978) views of emotional and personal development, as well as Gilligan's (1982) findings concerning moral judgment. Belenky et al. found that several epistemological positions emerging in their study of women's ways of knowing related to age, self-concept, social class, and educational opportunity. They discovered that women as a group are more likely than men to use concrete knowledge in assessing knowledge claims. A substantial number of the women in the study, for example, identified themselves as "connected knowers," in that they were drawn to knowledge that emerges from firsthand observation. Such women felt that because knowledge comes from experience, the best way to understand another person's ideas was to develop empathy and share the experiences that led the person to form those ideas. Finally, these authors discovered that women's ways of knowing are socially constructed both through the roles they enact in family relationships and through their response to the socialization practices perpetuated by educational systems.

In an attempt to "have our ideas matter," Patricia Hill Collins, a self-defined black feminist, uses an "outsider within" angle on black feminist thought and experience to develop a black feminist epistemology, which relies on an understanding of the simultaneous effects of race, class, and gender oppression as well as sexual orientation (1991). Within that more complete standpoint, Collins describes black women's struggle as rooted in the legacy of enslavement and currently manifested through economic devaluation and ideologically controlling images, that is, "mammy, matriarch, welfare mom, and Jezebel" (67).

Collins (1991) argues that core themes in developing an Afrocentric claim to knowledge for black women include: drawing from concrete experience and the wisdom that comes from survival; the use of dialogue with others; the ethic of caring that values emotion and expressiveness; the adding in of the personality of each group member; and, finally, the ethic of personal accountability. This latter concept is one that Collins believes converges with Gilligan's (1982) model of moral development.

Each of these perspectives (self in relation, moral decision-making, and the construction of knowledge) is based on women's experience and provides a partial framework for how to assess individual development and the processes of change as formerly incarcerated women move toward developing empathy for self and others after release. The study is one attempt to shift the means by which knowledge is formulated about ex-incarcerated women by enabling these women to construct their own understanding from their lived experience.

THE SOCIAL CONTEXT

The reasons that women commit crime cannot be separated from their social and biographical context. In an early critique of male-derived theories about the psychology of women, Weisstein (1970) argued that any study of human behavior requires a study of "the social contexts within which people move, the expectations as to how they will behave, and the authority which tells them who they are and what they are supposed to do" (242). Weisstein supported the claim by drawing from other literature that examined how people behaved in groups.[1] Weisstein also discusses some of the social expectancy studies that have demonstrated an improvement among students when the students' teachers were told that some among the students "showed great promise."[2]

"Social expectancy" theory is important for understanding ex-offenders' behavior because stigmatizing beliefs about criminals contribute to the women's personal feelings of inadequacy and lack of self-efficacy. According to this theory, women who are striving to rebuild their lives and self-identity after release from prison are expected to fail due to assumptions about who they are and a lack of appreciation for their human potential.

Some socialization theories have focused more on adult behavior than on developmental origins. Eagly (1987), for example, has developed a theory termed the social-role theory, which implicates compliance to gender-role expectations as the major determinant of gendered behaviors. Social behaviors are, according to Eagly, "a result of prescribed social roles that stem from family life and occupational settings and produce the content of gender-role prescribed and limiting behaviors" (16). A related theoretical perspective assumes that while social roles are significant determinants of views toward the different personality traits of males and females, early socialization practices and experiences are of critical importance. Differential treatment by parents and other socializing agents, such as teachers and peers, shapes the personality characteristics of boys and girls from an early age (Ruble 1988).

Theories that promote the importance of socialization in shaping patterns of perception toward differences suggest the need for new models of the self. Theories that emphasize developmental areas such as relatedness and caring provide much more promise for the evolution of new models.

However, one outcome of the emphases placed on socializing females to maintain relationships has typically been negatively characterized as dependence, deference, or acquiescence. These labels of woman's desire for mutually fulfilling relationships have resulted in the development of the concept of co-dependency, yet another model for the negative description of women's relational behaviors. Collins (1993) found that this concept, initially used to describe wives of alcoholic men, has burgeoned as a disease model in which women's relational orientation is characterized as dysfunctional. Collins argues that such disease models are victim-blaming and they deny the strengths of women's relationships.

Gender patterns are also constrained by societal rules that maintain unequal power relations within the general society. Faith (1993), for example, provides a thorough analysis of the social construction of crimes, based on an analysis of the power relations that have historically established a double standard for persecution of women (i.e., the witchcraft trials, prostitution, and girl's status offenses) and the lack of prosecution of men (i.e., for solicitation of prostitutes, wife battering, and rape of women).

Another indication of unequal power relations in contemporary U. S. society is women's continued occupational gender segregation and associated gender-based wage discrimination. Women get paid less than men for doing the same job, and the jobs in which women tend to be overrepresented are low status and low paying, with few or no opportunities for advancement. The Bureau of Labor Statistics notes that women earned 76 percent of the median wage earned by men in 1998. On the average, women currently make seventy-four cents for every dollar a man earns (Bowler 1999). Dressel (1994) argues that a logical feature of capitalism is the phenomenon of unemployment and underemployment. She notes that when levels of social assistance are inadequate, some members of the population may be unable to conduct their lives within the usual legitimized opportunity structures.

ADDICTION AS A RESPONSE
TO POWERLESSNESS

Inciardi and his associates (1993) conducted an ethnographic study observing women's crack cocaine usage and associated lawbreaking activities and concluded that crack was such a physiologically consuming addiction that it overshadowed any other personal or socially protective, relational, or constructive behaviors. There are many critical factors in the drug-crime relationship among females that are unknown.

Claudia Bepko (1989) believes that "addiction makes special statements about issues of power and dependency" (406). She hypothesizes that addiction reflects a disordered power arrangement that is embedded in gender. Bepko examines the different subjective experiences of male and female addiction, as well as the gender-based factors influencing their differential access to treatment. Using a case study of a white, heterosexual couple with children, with both parents alcoholic, the woman additionally addicted to prescription drugs, she observes that the husband's drinking was socially accepted as an indicator of his maleness. Neither he nor those around him, with the exception of his wife, identified it as a problem because it did not interfere with his role as breadwinner. The wife's drinking and drug abuse were kept secret and went largely unnoticed until she no longer was available to her husband for caretaking duties; she subsequently sought help because he physically abused her. Bepko theorizes from this case study and other writings on patterns of addicted behavior that "the social oppression of women becomes internalized in female addiction as self-abuse and self-oppression . . . power over one's own self-destruction is the only power left to them" (417). These theoretical findings are important for explaining the importance of the process of recovery (as opposed to the attainment of sobriety within prison walls). Recovery can allow women to become the subjects of their own experience, able to negotiate their level of connectedness and build their ability to say "no" to others' needs and expectations, especially when they may involve them in lawbreaking activities.

These studies (Bepko 1989; Inciardi et al. 1993) imply that addiction is a health issue rather than a criminal activity. The response to women addicts, however, has typically been punitive, especially as related to recent responses to pregnant drug addicts. Young (1994) concludes from her essay on policy approaches to drug addiction among women that an ethic of care would mean greatly expanded public and private funding for drug treatment and social services. These services would take into account women's parenting concerns and the issues of victimization by sexual abuse, which constitute the life history of a high proportion of addicted women.

Oppression as a social force that diminishes women's possibilities is a common thread running through accounts of abuse and addiction. Women's personal lives and their choices are constrained by institutional structures, power relations, cultural assumptions, or economic forces. For women offenders, many of whom are also substance-dependent, an empowerment perspective that enables them to recognize social sources of individual problems would be a beginning step to community reintegration.

THE "EX-OFFENDER" LABEL

Goffman (1961) described the transition into the world of the inmate in mental institutions in which there is a deep initial break with past roles, dispossession of property and self-identity, an appropriation of privacy, and an enforcement of regimentation by bureaucratic surveillance. This disculturation in the total institution results in the loss of or failure to acquire some of the habits required to live in the wider society. When women are released from the institution, numerous challenges lie ahead for them in their efforts to return to or establish a conventional life, due in part to their necessary adaptation to the institution (Jose-Kampfner 1990; Larson and Nelson 1984).

THE "EX" ROLE

"Ex-offender" is an example of an emerging "ex" role, as the incarceration of women has become more widespread over the last several decades. Only a few studies (Chambliss 1984; Shover 1983; Snodgrass 1982) have focused on the lives of ex-offenders, and all sampled only males. These studies centered on the effects of prior attributes and activities on their subsequent lives. Only one study (Adler 1992) examined the factors affecting lawbreakers' reintegration into society. Other sociological studies (Ebaugh 1984; Herman 1993; Warren 1991) have examined the process involved in other types of role transition.

Becker's (1963) discussion of the internalization of deviant labels implies that transforming deviant identities is extremely complex. An ex-offender not only has to construct a new self based on the personal desire to create a noncriminal life, but also has to deal in some way with others' expectations. Such expectations are often derived from ignorance, outdated notions, or judgmental preconceptions. The person who is trying to harmonize self and role, therefore, has the added difficulty of remolding and reformulating others' expectations of him or her self. As Ebaugh (1984) and Herman (1993) observed in their studies on "role exit" and the reintegration of "ex's" into society, no formal rights of passage exist to mark the "ex's" passage out of formalized, and sometimes identified as deviant, identities and roles. Warren (1980) notes that this "empirical situation is paralleled by the theoretical situation; whereas there are innumerable studies of the transformation of normals [nondeviants] into deviants, there are fewer studies of the transformation of deviants into nondeviants" (59).

Warren (1980) conceptualized a theory of destigmatization whereby the individual is reborn nondeviant by virtue of a moral cleansing, and, thus, transcends the deviant label by development of an alternative better self, or allies with others in order to collectively overturn the stigmatized label. Warren's theory highlighted the importance of exploring the possible positive impact of providing public attention (and therefore reinforcement) for the ex-offender who establishes a exemplary life after prison. Brown (1991) likewise focused on the reintegration of deviants who became professional "ex's," individuals who capitalized on their deviant identity and status by moving into therapeutic counseling careers.

Ebaugh (1984), in her study of Catholic nuns leaving a religious community, examines the process of becoming an "ex" related to role exit and self-transformation. Ebaugh asserts that ex roles represent a unique phenomenon because a previous identity often shapes the definitions of self and societal expectations. This determining process produces what Ebaugh (1988) calls a "vacuum experience," whereby an ex in transition is caught between two worlds and must resolve feelings of anxiety tied to the efforts of creating and adapting to a new role in society (45). Of the six stages that Ebaugh identified that nuns went through in the process of role exit, the third stage of "trying out options" may be especially important for incarcerated women, as they prepare to exit the institution, because it involves "role rehearsal . . . the process of anticipatory learning and acquisition of social roles before one actually assumes them" (166).[3]

Adler (1992) conducted a follow-up study to an ethnographic study of mostly male upper-level drug dealers and their reintegration into society and found that individuals returned to the mainstream more often when trafficking became more anxiety-provoking than enjoyable. Moreover, Adler documented the problems that ex-traffickers faced in attempting to secure or return to mainstream and legitimate occupations and the career-based factors that aided or inhibited reintegration, such as age at onset in illicit activities, the lack of (or intermittent development of) prior interests and skills, and the social class in which they were born and raised. In the case of the last factor, the sample members were all middle-class people who aspired to an elevated lifestyle and were reluctant to engage in the downward social mobility they felt a middle-class job entailed. Adler (1992) found that expressive aspects of these dealers' lives were also significant for reintegration. The strength of associations outside of the drug trafficking trade, for example, kept traffickers from totally removing themselves from society and provided a bridge back to society when these individuals felt an internal push to reenter it.

MANAGING STIGMA

Herman (1993), using a stratified random sample of 285 ex-psychiatric patients, identified all the ways in which they learned the "social meaning of their failing" (300). Herman found that the former patients were able to transform their deviant aspects of self by actively negotiating how they managed disclosure of their ex identity and how they avoided behaviors that projected a mentally disordered image. An additional study finding is that ex-psychiatric patients learn they can't be cured of their "stigmatizable attribute," that is, the mental disorder that resulted in their hospitalization or treatment (302). The stigmatizable attribute may be analogous to the perception of ex-offenders who are generally mistrusted despite having paid their debt to society.

Stigma contributes to the further devaluation of women when they carry an additional label of ex, irrespective of attempts to engage in personal change or treatment. Warren's (1991) reinterpretive analysis of interviews with couples in which the women had a history of psychiatric hospital admissions, for example, found that uncertainty in the discharge process of diagnosed schizophrenic women in the 1950s contributed to the selective interpretation of the ex-patient's mental wellness according to rigid gender-role expectations.[4] Warren also notes "the provisions of conditional discharge allowed a return to the mental hospital to be used as a threat by husbands against wifely misbehavior" (154).

Women's release from prison is similarly conditioned. Parole officer monitoring operates on assumptions about the appropriate roles and responsibilities of women after they exit the institution. In fact, some of the previously hospitalized women in Warren's study described the conditional discharge provisions as being like a form of probation or parole where follow-up services provided by social workers had the effect of reminding the women of their identity as a mental patient, rather than as an *ex*-mental patient.

In his theory of crime, shame, and reintegration, Braithwaite (1989) argues that individuals are steered away from their former deviant activities by individuals who can accept them as essentially good and reject their bad behavior. Rather than labeling and isolating them as deviant, these friends, associates, and acquaintances aid reintegration of former offenders. Braithwaite suggests that a process that he conceptualizes as "reintegrative shaming" (1989, 55) is effective only prior to individuals becoming ensconced in the criminal subcultures, which support criminal behavior through their criminal norms, values, and opportunities. At a macro level, Braithwaite's theory suggests that communitarian cultures, which he characterizes as an "aggregation of individual interdependency" (85), provide the most reintegrative form of shaming by nurturing offenders within a network of attachments to conventional society. Braithwaite hypothesizes that women offenders are more often the objects of reintegrative shaming, due to the social expectation that women "swap one form of dependency (on the family of orientation) for another (on the family of procreation)" (92), making them more susceptible to shaming by those on whom they are dependent.

Braithwaite states that shaming should be followed by efforts to reintegrate the offender back into the community of law-abiding or respectable citizens through words or gestures of forgiveness or ceremonies to decertify the offender as deviant (101). He claims that shaming is more effective than stigmatizing the offender, because it offers gestures of acceptance that enable the ex-offender to develop the self-confidence and social support to recognize that they are once again a part of the noncriminal community.

To what degree ex-incarcerated women experience stigma in the process of rebuilding their lives after prison is an important question to address. It is possible that post-prison stigmatization may be reduced by the extent to which the ex-offender maintains outside associations with others, although the notion that women's less stigmatized identity evolves from their putative dependence on others, principally males, is problematic for testing this theory.

When women are empowered, they are able to experience themselves as efficacious, or capable of making an impact on other people and situations. Women who are not empowered become vulnerable to persons and situations where they may achieve a false and transitory sense of power. In some cases, this ephemeral sense of power is achieved through antisocial and/or lawbreaking acts.

Bettina Aptheker (1989), drawing on the science fiction of Ursula LeGuin, the poetry of Adrienne Rich, and other contemporary women writers from very diverse cultures, traditions, and histories, describes a "web of life" that includes an "invocation of tribal values, a visioning of ancestral communities, and a centering in values associated with women's everyday lives" (240). A tribal person could not exist apart from the tribe: The stories that reinforced the individual human dignity also placed her within cultures that were characterized by egalitarian and peace-loving principles.

Just as the spider's web connotes the individual spokes that create the strength of the whole, so too does this vision of community life reflect the connecting points that reinforce its viability. The connecting points may vary in weight, thickness, and durability as they change over time to meet different needs. Despite the myth of American self-sufficiency, we all rely substantially on our social web.

Creating a web of social relations is intrinsic to developing an enabling environmental niche for women in transition from prison and may be similar to Braithwaite's idea of the "reintegrative community." In addition to the family members and/or intimate partners who may constitute spokes of the web, other potential connections for support and reinforcement of noncriminal activities might include neighbors, work associates, spiritual companions, and bowling team members. In an earlier in-depth interview study of a woman who had served ten years in prison, for example, I found that Sherri[5] identified multiple relationships of support that she could count on within the first several months of her release from prison (O'Brien 1994). Each person in her web had a specific function that facilitated her successful transition during the first few months. Since she was released to an unfamiliar community, they provided her with concrete support, as well as with affirmation of her reentry to the free world. Although all these relationships promoted Sherri's competence, as she became more confident, she also reciprocated in a number of ways, which in turn helped her feel more a part of the community where she had chosen to live.

EMPOWERMENT AS AN INTERNALIZED PROCESS OF CHANGE

Although writers have overlooked the social context for women's lawbreaking behaviors, Sommers (1995) asserts that "women are psychological as well as social beings" (23). An analysis that is limited to women's position as passive victims in the social structure is just as skewed as those early studies that examined their cranial characteristics for criminal tendencies. Kondrat (1995) states "When individuals or groups become empowered, they become active agents, more effectively directing their lives in keeping with their own needs and purposes" (414). The notion of agency, the ability to act in one's own behalf, has a variety of concepts ascribed to it that include self-esteem, self-worth, self-identity, self-efficacy, and confidence. The individual's movement toward agency is not linear, nor is it likely to have a temporal reality for steps of completion. Rather, the movement toward agency is the result of a dynamic interaction between the person and the environment. The following section describes some of the necessary elements in this internally derived part of the process.

An overarching theme for the individual manifestation of empowerment is one in which the woman sees herself as motivated toward and capable of engaging in change. Any woman exiting from prison, regardless of time served or type of conviction, will have to develop a different way of existing outside the institution. This, in and of itself, reflects a process of change, as it relates to making choices about where she will live, how she will support herself, and with whom she will construct and maintain relationships, including relationships with her children.

Gutiérrez and Lewis (1999) describes the psychological changes necessary for moving women of color from apathy and despair to action. These include increasing self-efficacy, developing a group consciousness, reducing self-blame, and assuming personal responsibility. Although Gutiérrez and Lewis conceptualized the model based on their observations of the social marginalization that women of color experience in the face of the dual oppressions of sexism and racism, the model is applicable to women coming out of prison, due to the disproportionately high representation of women of color in the prison population and the added stigma of having been incarcerated.

Self-efficacy stems from beliefs about one's ability "to produce and to regulate events in one's life" (Bandura 1982, 122). Developing self-efficacy involves developing a sense of personal power or agency by rising to the challenges of everyday life, developing initiative in identifying needs and wants, and increasing

the ability to act (Solomon 1976). Bandura (1989) suggests that a model of efficacy that combines self-belief, affective perceptions, and environmental events
contributes to a reinforcing cycle of high accomplishment of tasks, persistence in
the face of adversity, and an optimistic view of one's personal ability to influence
life events. A woman is most likely to develop and/or extend her self-efficacy in
the immediate post-incarceration period when she has experiences that test her
fears and enable her to master new skills to manage threatening activities. Self-
efficacy is also reinforced by supportive interpersonal relations. Bandura (1992)
argues that people can exert some influence over their well-being "by the environments they select and the environments they create" (30). He cites research
demonstrating that people with a high sense of social efficacy create systems of
social supports or webs for themselves (Holohans in Bandura 1992). People
within the social web serve as a model of useful attitudes and strategies, provide
incentives for beneficial behavioral choices, and promote success by modeling
that difficulties are surmountable. Although Bandura recognizes that "simply saying that one is capable" does not make one so, especially when it contradicts pre-
existing beliefs, he concludes that converging lines of evidence indicate that
perceptions of efficacy play a central role in the exercise of personal agency
(1992, 32).

One manifestation of the overemphasis on ex-incarcerated women's individual and family characteristics and pathologies in attempting to explain their
lawbreaking behaviors has been an indifference to resiliencies and strengths.
Wolin and Wolin (1993) describe a "damage model" based on their work with
survivors of troubled families. In this model, survivors are regarded as victims of
their parents' poisonous secretions and forever after are doomed to repeat their
parents' mistakes and further spread that toxicity. The best survivors can do is
to adapt at considerable cost to themselves. It is possible to replace "troubled
families" with "criminal history" and see that the same dynamic currently dom-
inates the expectations of people who have been convicted and served a sentence for illegal behavior.

Wolin and Wolin identified seven resiliencies culled from clinical interviews with twenty-five adults who had bounced back from adversity: insight,
independence, relationships, initiative, creativity, humor, and morality. In addition to these resiliencies, O'Brien (1995b) found, in her sample of twelve low-
income African-American long-term residents of a public housing complex,
that they identified spiritual beliefs as a support for their survival and that the
challenge of living in a challenging neighborhood sharpened their will to do so.
Higgins (1994) interviewed forty mostly upper-class white participants who
had been hospitalized for psychiatric disorders relating to their previous experiences of abuse and/or family troubles and found that their adaptive and resilient
strategies focused on loving well and working well.

Benard (1999), from his studies of resilient children, recognizes the self-righting nature of individual's mental health and functioning but also identifies the necessity of environmental resources for well-being. He concludes that

> if we hope to create socially competent people who have a sense of their own identity and autonomy, who are able to make decisions, set goals, and believe in their own future, then meeting their basic human needs for caring and connectedness; for respect, challenge, and structure; and for meaningful involvement, belonging, and power should be the primary focus (6–7).

It seems probable that for women exiting prison, a balance between the "doing and achieving part of life" and "the quality of one's relationship with (self) and others" as described by Baruch, Barnett, and Rivers (1983, 18), is the foundation for the internal transformation from the criminal identity through the process of empowerment.

The women's stories in this study demonstrated that in addition to establishing a physical shelter and meeting basic needs, they had to address a multitude of internal issues related to how they chose to present themselves in the world. Implicit in many of the women's narratives were their reflections about the impact of incarceration on their relationships, their everyday behavioral choices, and how they thought and felt about themselves as a consequence. Many times women expressed insights about their experiences that they had not been aware of up to the point of their articulation in the interview.

Women discussed both the anticipated and unanticipated ways in which the changes manifested in the transition were established by them prior to their release from prison. This section includes elements related to how women dealt with challenging aspects of their incarceration as well as recognizing elements within the experience that promoted some sense of efficacy that they could later draw from after release from prison. Central to almost all these women's accounts is a sense of their ability to experience prison as if it were a growth-fostering environment. Making the best of an untenable situation by taking advantage of all opportunities within the environment so that they could develop a sense of themselves as efficacious in the day-to-day life of prison is another way of describing the facilitative effects on the transition that began while they were incarcerated.

MANAGING INCARCERATION

Some women identified new roles for themselves while in prison. Bernie recognized through her many years of incarceration experience, for example, that she had become a "leader" and expressed a sense of satisfaction from knowing how to negotiate the system to "keep somebody out of trouble":

. . . every time I was in prison, I was always put in a leadership position. I always had the respect of the women [and] the officers. I was always the one saying, "Hey, guys, don't do it this way. You're just playin' into their game." I'd see some of 'em go off, and "Oh, we're gonna riot." I'd say, "What's that gonna do? All it's gonna do is get you locked up." But, they're [the prison administration] the driver and no matter how wrong they might be, you can't just say, "No, I ain't gonna do this." You can figure ways to get around 'em, you can manipulate 'em . . . but you can't just stand up, because they'll tell you in a minute that you're forgettin' what you are and where you are.

Nan identified her role as that of a counselor while she was in prison. In her statement to others about how to deal with their incarceration, she also reflected a belief in herself for how she could manage it. She relates that she told another inmate:

Look, girl, get up out that bed and stop all that cryin', because you can be cryin' 'til 1997, that's when they say you goin' home, you be cryin' 'til then. Get up, get yourself together, go and do somethin' that's beneficial, not only to you, but to your children, because of the mistake you have made. The mistake has already been made. Get up, brush yourself off, and just go on.

Deeni reflected about a turning point of growing self-awareness while she was incarcerated that reflects doing just as Nan suggested. She recognized that she wanted to be alive to the possibilities in the environment instead of "dead." As she stated:

I did not want to live the rest of my life in a prison. I had too much to do. Then, you know, as conscious as I am, I could see it if I was dead, like so many people are in there . . . they are mentally asleep. They don't know what's happening . . . you send yourself to prison, but what are you doin' while you're there? I started learnin' how to use my time instead of doin' my time. That's what made me grow up. I read all the time. That's somethin' I had never done before. I studied and worked out, and I did all those things that my religion taught me to do.

The recognition that she was mentally alive, unlike some of the women she saw around her, also led Deeni to taking care of herself physically, as a means of resisting a system that she felt could sap her spirit.

What happened—one day I was sittin' in the TV room, and there was all these big fat women, sittin' around, eatin' and playin' cards, and cussin' each other and watchin' TV. It was just so disgusting, the way they was talkin' to each other. They lived to see the soap operas, to sit around and play cards, to waste they life away and just be a part of the system. I just refused to be a part of that. I had already been workin out, but that right there, it was just somethin' . . . they watched me all the time, as if I was gonna escape, because I was a black woman that ran and did a lot of things that most blacks didn't do.

For Elizabeth, a major benefit to incarceration was that she developed a friendship with another inmate who is still a good friend to her in the outside world. She described the "shield of power" that she was able to draw on in this context of mutual empathy and support that helped her better cope with incarceration. She recalls:

> It was a good friendship. She went about [the compound] with a lot of quiet, and nobody bothered her. When we became friends, it was really strange. It kind of rubbed off. Nobody bothered me after that, and it wasn't an intimidation thing at all. It was like she had this shield to protect her somehow. And, anyone that was a friend fell under that shield too. It was really a spiritual thing. I was grateful for the friendship. That was more valuable than anything.

This relationship enabled Elizabeth to reduce her sense of powerlessness in an environment in which she often felt traumatized by what she experienced or witnessed. It even provided her with a sense of mediated normality in an abnormal situation. Elizabeth related a story, for example, describing how she and her friend found the freedom to laugh despite the control that made their laughter suspect and intolerable:

> There was one incredible cold winter day. It was way below zero, and the snow was deep and sparkling . . . it was just, my phrase I stole from an old movie of June Allyson, "a day of diamonds." And the snow crunches, and S. says, "Come on, let's go for a walk." So, we got permission to go for a walk, because a certain amount of exercise is supposed to be healthy. So we were goin' our certain path, and midway we decided to stop, lay down and make angels in the snow, and we're laughing and having a good time, and that was our mistake. We started laughing, and the guards could see us from the guard room, and they motioned, "Your walk's done." We were in the allotted space and the allotted time but we laughed and we were havin' a good time, so it was stopped.

Another way women manage their incarceration is by their choice of programming. Jeanette went to prison on a drug conviction. She decided to take advantage of the drug program, initially only because it provided her with a major benefit in prison, a "two-man" room rather than a dorm bed. She did not expect that the program would actually motivate her to face her addiction. She recalls thinking:

> "Well, you know, two-man room, and I do got a problem. Okay, let's go see what they got to say." I had had enough with these people with their

bullshit, though. I got in there with a group that they were new, and they
were good. You get pretty bonded with the people in your group, because
you're together a whole bunch. And, some of those girls sat there through
that whole program and said, "I am going to get high, and nothing you say
or do is going to stop me. And, as soon as I get out of your reach, I'm
gonna get high." They were like, "Okay, well, I'm glad you're being honest. That's what we need here." It was just the right thing for me. I needed
a place where I could be honest.

Jeanette was forthright in indicating that she had not planned to stop her drug
use once she got out of prison. When she got involved in the program, a nine-
month milieu type of treatment, she found that she looked at her drug use in a
new way because she recognized that she had chosen her drug use and she
could choose not to use drugs. She concluded:

> It works, because they give you the facts, and it's up to you what you do
> with 'em. . . . you have some education on the drugs themselves and what
> they do to you. You know, then you're given some programs on choices
> and behaviors. They cover the whole spectrum. Of course . . . this is in a
> time in your life that you're really goin' through major things. And it is
> probably the best time for you to do something like this. You're away from
> the outside influences, and you don't really have drugs to tempt you like
> you do on the street.

Perceiving Efficacy from the Experience

Examining why she used drugs in a surprisingly supportive environment where
she could be honest without threat of reprisal provided Jeanette an opportunity to see new possibilities for herself.

> What I do now is I have goals. Part of it was in that drug program. It's not
> that they said that, it's just somethin' I figured out on my own when I was
> in there. When I got out, that if you set a goal, then you know what
> you're workin' for, instead of just doin' it everyday. So, if you reach a
> milestone, then it's like, "Oh, I've done this. This is the next thing I need
> to do." I want to achieve more, because this is the first time I've ever not
> done drugs, and I have a little streak of ambition runnin' through me that
> I never knew.

One-half of the participants had been incarcerated more than one time in
their adult lives. For the women who had been reincarcerated, their efficacy
may be episodic or developmental. Susan, who had been incarcerated twice, recalled how she used the second time to break out of her previous criminal behaviors and decide she could make different choices for herself.

The first time I did everything that I thought would get me released. I didn't do anything for me. I just did what I thought was expected. The second time, I knew I had to do my time. I knew there was no early release. You don't get furloughs, nothing. So I worked all of my time but since I had the time, I decided I was going to try to use it. I guess I cared more the second time. The first time what I did wrong, I did to get out of an abusive relationship. I didn't know what I was doing could actually put me in prison. It wasn't a conscious thing. The second time, I knew what I was doing. And that I could get caught. I used it to get away, break out. I sort of felt better about the second time.

Similarly, other women described multiple periods of incarceration as time when they could review some of their former choices and make a determination about how they wanted to shape their life after prison. As Bernie stated, "I never come home, and I don't think anyone does, without the desire to do better." The desire to do better is often born while women have time to look more closely at the experiences that resulted in their incarceration. Ashley, Deeni, and Rene all recognized that if they were not in prison, they might have ended up dead. In retrospect, Ashley believed, her experiences made her a stronger person.

I've seen a hell of a lot. An awful lot. To be real honest and not meaning to sound silly, I wouldn't change what's happened. I think that it's made me a hell of a stronger person. I don't think that there will ever be anything on this earth that I cannot deal with. I think I have a lot of potential to help others, and I see things in ways that other people may not.

Deeni believes the years that she spent in prison helped her to "grow up" and change her life so that in a sense, she could die to her old life by leaving old thought patterns, attitudes, and behaviors behind, something she recognizes that not all women in prison can do. Again, she relates her changes to a developmental process.

I guess if I hadn't have done time, I may not be here right now. Some say, "How can she say that?" But, let me tell you, until you walk the mile in a person's shoes . . . people say, "How can they smoke crack?" You know, it's easy for you to say unless you been there, unless it has hit close to home. Uh, I don't know where I'd be if I hadn't gone to prison, because I carried guns. I lived a dangerous life. I wasn't afraid. And, I had this really gangster mentally. So, me goin' to prison, it was probably the best thing in the long run. It changed my life. But, I see so many people go to prison and it never changed their life. I mean, they keep the prison doors open, because they constantly stay in that revolving circle. They come out and then go back.

Rene observed that not only might she have ended up dead, but that the incarceration promoted her well-being in such a way that she can clearly see the connection between her previous behaviors and the way that she has parented her children, both of whom have been in residential treatment centers during the time Rene was incarcerated. She believed that the incarceration gave her another chance to deal with things differently.

> You know, some people would say, hey it was a blessing. I could have been dead today. I tell you what, I wouldn't be where I am now. No, because the person I am now is not the person I was before. I'm still stubborn, but I was too headstrong . . . you got to let go of this takin' the whole world on by yourself, because it don't work. Anybody says it works—I don't know anybody that can take the whole world on and things will work by themselves. There's no way. Keepin' yourself sane is basically what it is. I never abused my kids physically, mentally possibly, but when you abuse yourself, you abuse your kids indirectly. I realized the physical things you're doin' to yourself, like drinking, what it does to kids—because my kids and I have always been able to talk—they tell me, "I'm glad you're not drinking. I'm glad you don't take pills anymore."

For Demi and Regina, the choices that took them into prison had been unconsciously made in the context of their relationships with other people. Neither one of them had thought too much about the consequences of their choices prior to their incarceration. Each of them discussed the incarceration as a turning point that helped them understand the seriousness of consequences for criminal behaviors and allowed them the time to make a new start.

Demi observed how the discipline of the boot camp where she was incarcerated taught her to take responsibility for her choices even in the day-to-day expectations of the camp.

> A lot of it was discipline. I had never had anything bad happen to me in my entire life. I didn't have my priorities straight. I was party, party, party all the time. I didn't neglect my kids or nothing, but my outlook on life just wasn't like it is now. I learned a lot of discipline.

Several participants mentioned that it was respect for the law that generated new thinking during their incarceration. Sadie, although initially reluctant to see that there had been any gain to her in the experience that affected her ability to make it on release from prison, obliquely noted that certainly the sentence had been long enough to get her attention.

> I don't know that this is something I'd want too many people to know but probably because I was there so long, I certainly took it a little more seriously than I would have eight months, twelve months, you know. And more determined to not do that again.

Suzy was more direct in noting how she had developed respect for the law from understanding the consequences of behavior:

> I have more respect now for the law. . . . Before, you know, I didn't care if I got into trouble or if I beat up on someone or if I was violent. Consequences didn't mean nothin' to me before. Now they do. I don't go over fifty-five in my car. I'm very adamant about havin' my insurance. Um, if I see somethin' wrong bein' done around me, I report it. I take an active interest. I didn't do that before. Some of my changes are real evident to me.

Elena tearfully recalled the pain she felt on the day of her delivery of her son while incarcerated and the consequent loss of him during the next year of her incarceration.

> He was my only son. They snatched him from my arms within twenty-four hours. That hurt me really bad. I think that was the worst part of my sentence. I only seen him the first day he was born, and that was it, you know, I never seen him after that. He was about thirteen or fourteen months when I got out.

Despite and perhaps because of Elena's horrible experience, she recognized her efficacy in her role as a parent and likened her commitment to meeting the needs of her children to a life sentence that would motivate her to stay clean.

> I got my kids, you know. Like I told my mom, "After I get off of parole," I said, "it ain't gonna change anything, because I got eighteen years of it with my children. I got a life sentence with them. They don't need no mother that's a junkie or who sells drugs or anything like that. They need me, and now they got me, and so I don't plan on jeopardizin' that for nobody."

Finally, all the women expressed a determination to succeed that came from an unwillingness to suffer the pains of imprisonment any further. Anita captures the idea of transformation when she represents her new identity with "new clothes."

> . . . I done put on new clothes, and I'm a new person, and I'm not gonna let nothin' get in the way, because I don't ever want to go back to the penitentiary again, not ever. So, I know what I need to do to stay out.

Seeds planted in the period of incarceration were sometimes incubated so deeply in the soil of everyday coping and maintenance within the institution that the women did not recognize their potential for growth at the time. However, all the study participants in retrospect were able to identify their efficacy in how they handled the incarceration that nourished their belief that they could make it in the free world.

Managing the Intrusion

Similar to Goffman's (1961) description of life in a total institution, many of the women described peers who had grown dependent on the prison for making their everyday decisions and meeting their survival needs and therefore were sometimes unable to make their own decisions after leaving prison. Anita, who did not make it the first time she was released, expressed it this way:

> They pay the bills. You don't have to worry about your lights. I think that's why a lot of people get institutionalized, and they come out here, and you go to try to fill out for an apartment, and they turn you down, and then they get frustrated, and then they say, "Forget it. I'm goin' to smoke" or whatever they're doin', and they just say "To H-E-L-L with it."

Elizabeth, who says that she was quickly "institutionalized," recalled a time soon after her release when she was at a discount store and had the awful feeling of being out of place. Her feelings of being institutionalized extended to the community after her release so that she had difficulty in regaining autonomy.

> I'm not where I'm supposed to be, and it's all over now. A policeman on the road, if I'm driving, even if I wasn't speeding or wasn't sliding through a stop sign, there was that, "Where am I supposed to be? Is everything right? Do I have my pass?" It [that feeling] stayed for a long time.

The extension of the institutional control is maintained through the system of supervision. All inmates on release to the community are assigned a supervision status for a designated length of time based on their offense history and sentence. The terminology depends on whether the ex-offender is supervised through the Federal Office of Probation and Parole or a state office of parole. Ex-inmates in the state system, for example, are referred to as parolees and are supervised by parole officers. Ex-inmates on the federal level may be referred to as parolees or probationers, or as "cases in custody under supervision," depending on whether the individual is completing a term under old or new sentencing guidelines. Federal and state sentencing guidelines passed on the federal level in 1987 and implemented in Kansas in 1993 also have an effect on the length of parole or supervision. However this period of monitoring is specified for the individual, all the study participants had some time after their release in which they had to meet certain conditions in order to become eligible for discharge from the system in which they had been convicted (also called "getting off paper" by the participants).

Table 3.1 identifies the participants' supervision status at the time of the interviews. For some participants, the interview was conducted some time after the completion of parole or supervision, while, for others, they were continuing to negotiate the systems' monitoring of their day-to-day activities. Of the ten participants who continued under supervision, six are federal ex-inmates who were convicted of drug-related crimes (possession, trafficking, conspiracy, sales).

The ways by which women negotiated meeting their conditions of supervision and their relationship with their parole or probation officer were instrumental to the women's transition. Since seven of the participants had been incarcerated previously, they were even more cognizant of the difficulties of getting through this initial part of the transition.

Racque, who essentially married out of her life on the streets by moving from Oakland, California, to a small town in Kansas, recalls that in her long history of repeated incarceration for property and disorder offenses, there were several times when she was only able to stay out for a night before she was arrested on a new charge or for violation of her parole. At the time that she met the man she eventually married, she had only been out a month and realized her chances of staying out were slim. Racque reported that she was "watching [her] back and more or less bein' sneaky, and tryin' not to get caught doin' whatever [she] was doin'." Racque attributed her problems to the fact that she hung around with the wrong crowd and did not have a support system in the area that could assist her in getting a new start. However, she recognized that she needed a change if she was going to make it out of the cycle of one incarceration after another.

Table 3.1
PARTICIPANTS' SUPERVISION STATUS[1]

Released from Federal Incarceration	Released from State Incarceration
Ashley—on federal supervision	Anita—on parole
Demi—on federal supervision	Margi—on parole
Elena—on federal supervision	Susan—on parole
Jeanette—on federal supervision	
Nan—on federal supervision	Bernie—discharged from parole
Rene—on federal supervision	Elizabeth—discharged from parole
	Mandi—discharged from parole
Deeni—discharged from federal supervision	Racque—discharged from parole
	Regina—discharged from parole
	Sadie—discharged from parole
	Suzy—discharged from parole

[1]At time of interview.

> I was tired of living that life. I stood a chance of goin' back to prison for a long time and never getting' out or I might ended up dead somewhere. If you're gonna change your life, you ought to be able to do it around the environment you was dealin' with then. But, then, it didn't work for me. It took me to where I had to leave California in order to change my whole life around, but it worked out for the better and we're happy.

However, moving to Kansas placed Racque in jeopardy with the California criminal justice system because she was adjudicated to have absconded from their custody while on parole. She was able to solve that problem with her "understanding" parole officer.

> I just took the chance and came over here, and then called 'em when I got over here, and then had to go back to California to straighten that mess out. The parole officer I had in California. He was pretty cool. He was understanding.

No other participant had such a geographical opportunity for a new start. Most of the women returned to the area where they had previously lived or were near to the towns in which they had grown up. The rules or parole conditions under which the women were placed are meant to provide ex-inmates with the motivation to steer clear of former criminal associates in their previous settings. However, participants often found that the expectations were overwhelming and, sometimes, impossible to meet.

Nan described her frustration in a typical day in her life that she describes as being "under the roof" of her supervision after her release from Dismas House.

> I work 11 P.M. to 7 A.M., I have a Code-A-Phone number I need to call Monday through Saturday to see if I need to come in and leave a UA [urinalysis]. So, I'm responsible for makin' sure I remember to call every day, workin' a job. I have five children. Then on Thursday, I go for a counselin' session up at Research. Right now I'm not free, even though I left the halfway house and I felt I was free, because I was away from their jurisdiction. They had their own rules and regulations. I had to abide by them. I felt like, "Okay, I'm goin' to the house, and I'm on my own." I'm not. You know, I have three years paper. So, until that three years of paper is up, I'm not actually free. I'm always up under the roof.

Other women also expressed the frustration of being free as a consequence of being outside of prison, but still feeling confined or controlled because they were still accountable to the correctional system.

Participants who were currently on parole or supervision at the time of the interview often described a feeling of being overwhelmed by the conditions imposed on them. Mandi not only had to meet conditions placed on her for her parole period, but also had to meet court-imposed conditions to demonstrate her ability to parent her children in order to regain physical and legal custody that she had lost previous to her incarceration. Many of Mandi's initial obstacles in meeting her conditions of parole related to her precarious financial condition.

> Well, getting a job and getting there. I had to walk from home. When I was in my own house, I didn't have a car. I found a house within walking distance from Taco Bell. It was probably about a mile. Obstacles were no vehicle. Trying to meet the parole requirements. Like, I had to report once a month by phone; however, I couldn't have a phone in my name because of an outstanding bill, so I couldn't get a phone in my house, but I had to report once a month by phone and you get charged for that. So, finances were a real big struggle, getting to work without a vehicle, trying to go see the parole officer without a vehicle.

As summarized by the following quote, Mandi described some of the conditions that she had to meet to address both the parole conditions and the court to regain custody of her children. She described a strategy she used of taking it one step at a time in order to mediate her feeling of being regularly overwhelmed. She exhibited some of the same dogged persistence she had shown in cracking the computer codes while incarcerated to manage her process of reintegration, although she did not immediately perceive the advantages of doing so.

> I went to court . . . like a week after I got out of prison. So, I went, the judge was like, "You can't have 'em back, because you don't even know where you're gonna live tomorrow." The judge gave me a list of things I had to do to get the kids back. So, I remember during that week, and I remember especially since I was reminded a few months ago, when I went back to court, how when I went home and I got the list in the mail. It was just so overwhelming, because here I am thinkin' how there was this whole list to do to get my kids back and I got this whole list to do for my parole officer, and I thought, "How am I gonna do all this thing?" I was like court ordered to AA meetings three times a week. I was court ordered for parenting class once a week. I was court ordered for intensive psychotherapy at least once a week, plus I was court ordered to have a full-time job, and I was court ordered to maintain my own home. I was court ordered to do everything. I thought, "If I'm gonna maintain a full-time home, I'm gonna have to work two jobs. If I work the two jobs, when am I gonna go to the meetings, and when am I gonna go to [see her children]. . . .

Mandi met all her conditions, but not without some cost to her personally, and at great risk to her parole. She tearfully recounted how she relapsed by smoking crack on two different occasions during the first year of her release, after she had started employment and was attempting to do it all. With the assistance of an understanding employer, she was able to acquire the substance abuse treatment she needed, successfully regained legal and physical custody of her children, and received a discharge from parole supervision.

NEGOTIATING DEMANDS OF SUPERVISION

Many of the women in the sample, attributed their success and/or difficulties in part to the type of parole officer or supervisor they had. Table 3.2 summarizes the women's perceptions of negative or positive responses of the parole officers toward them.

Study participants had positive relationships with parole officers who treated them as a person rather than a number; left them alone, without daily

Table 3.2
CONTINUUM OF PAROLE OFFICER'S
RESPONSE TO PARTICIPANTS

Inhibits Progress	Neutral	Promotes Progress
Invades privacy	Does her job	Treats me with respect
Arbitrary in making decisions	Tells me what I need to do	Can be flexible based on my individual situation
Goes by the book		
Doesn't believe me	Manages the paperwork	Believes in me
Forced me to work outside the home	Left me alone	Proud of me
		Wants me to succeed
		Knows that I am different
		Provides information about resources in the community
		Modified my conditions based on my changing needs
		Requests early discharge from parole

intrusions into their lives; willingly responded to changing circumstances by modifying conditions when appropriate; provided specific information about the parole process when requested; and in several cases, requested early discharge from parole. Among the participants, four of the Kansas parolees shared the same parole officer and two of the federal parolees had the same officer. In each of these cases, the participants made positive observations about the ways in which their parole officer had promoted their transition.

Mandi, who as described earlier, faced many obstacles in dealing with all the conditions placed on her, negotiated with her parole officer a modification of her condition for attending AA/NA meetings.

> I told my parole officer that I wasn't making it to three meetings a week because I was going to parenting group, I was goin' to therapy besides working two jobs. My parole officer agreed that if I didn't work and make my income, that I would lose my house and, therefore, I'd be back on the streets. So, she ended up changing my conditions to go to meetings basically as desired.

In addition, when Mandi did not have the transportation to report to the parole office to report in to her parole officer, the parole officer met Mandi at her house and gave her a ride to one of her jobs. Mandi recounts how she made the request:

> I was reportin' to her. I wasn't just reporting by phone. It was by phone and reporting to her once a month. Like, one day she came to my house. I called her up, and I was like "I just don't know how I'm gonna get over there." She said, "Well, you have to report." I said, "Well, I have an idea. How about you meet me in the morning?" because it was kind of cold that week, I remember. I had to walk, so I asked if she could come over to my house and see where I was livin', and give me a ride to work. I think she kind of chuckled and said, "Okay, I'll do that." So, she did. She came in, and I took her through the house. I said, "I work right down this way." We visited in the car in the parking lot for a little bit. She told me she thought I was doin' good. Definitely, she knew I did have a home, she definitely knew that I had a job.

Nicole recalled that the same parole officer treated her with respect and praised her progress on parole:

> I think she looked at me for the person that I was instead of where I'd been. I mean, you can pretty much talk to a person and tell what their situation might be, and I think she just knew that it was something I had to go through. But, I think she seen that I was determined, and I was not gonna go back, and so she knew right off the bat that I was gonna be easy to work with.

When Sadie got into a personality dispute with co-workers who put her at risk of revocation because they made a complaint to her parole officer, the same parole officer checked it out, and when she found that the accusations were false, immediately requested an early discharge for Sadie.

> . . . this deal happened with these two people trying to making all these phone calls to her telling her that I was crazy and that I was violent and that I was doing drugs. She thought they were the ones that were crazy, fortunately for me. It could have been the opposite, it could have been to-tally the opposite but I think she felt confident about me. Then she did it immediately, about a month later I got my [discharge] and I got a nice let-ter from her with it.

Sadie felt as though she had developed a good relationship with her pa-role officer, which helped her when she had problems. That relationship prob-ably evolved in part due to Sadie's perception that she was willing to take responsibility for her behavior.

> I think I was probably a little different than a lot of people she had dealt with. Maybe it was kinda like a breath of air, to not have to be dealing with a lot of problems, a lot of stuff, excuses for not showing up, excuses for not send-ing in this or excuses for why you moved and never said anything, whatever.

Elena was primed by other ex-inmates to have difficulties with her parole of-ficer but became aware that it would be her own behaviors that would "send her back:"

> Yeah, I thought she was out to send me back. I didn't trust her. I didn't like her. My mom fell in love with her when she first met her. And, I just heard stories about her from other girls at the halfway house, but later on I found out that they ended up usin' and they send their ownselves back. She didn't send 'em back. They sent their ownselves back. That's one thing she don't tolerate is drug usin'. She's even told me that if I ever had a dirty UA or anything that she was sendin' me back. But, like, if I have any problems or any questions, I can call her up and talk to her and she's very understanding.

Study participants reported that they sometimes had difficulties in dealing with their parole officers, and in two cases the women felt that the parole offi-cer hindered their successful progress on parole. Negative characteristics men-tioned by the women included arbitrary interpretation of the rules, excessive intrusion in their lives, and a lack of understanding of the obstacles they had to address coming out of prison. When Suzy was first discharged from prison, she was assigned to a parole officer whom she described as having no backbone when a mental health provider reported her resistance to a course of recommended treatment.

> One of the conditions of my release was mental health. I didn't have no problem with that. I knew that, so I had to contact Mental Health. I started goin' there, and the therapist that I had, was, you know, I was havin' problems adjustin' to bein' a wife again and bein' a mother again. So, she was tryin' to tell me that I needed to go to counseling for my family and for my son, and parenting classes and all this stuff. She wanted me to do this, and I didn't have any money. I had just gotten home. My husband was on a low paying job. I told her I couldn't afford it, so she called my PO. She called my PO twice tellin' him that I couldn't do it, and I was refusin' to do it. So, he was ready to send me back.

At the same time that Suzy was struggling with these expectations from "mental health," she and her husband moved across county lines where she was assigned another parole officer who was more responsive to her situation. She recalls that he also treated her respectfully by validating her work as a mother:

> Yeah, and I met up with Don S. He was great to me. He treated me like a person, and he treated me right. He allowed me to stay home. He asked what I wanted out of life. I told him I wanted to stay home and I wanted to be a mom. He let me stay home and be a mom. I went to mental health, and I had no problem. Anytime I needed to talk to him—he gave me his pager number, and I just picked it up and called him. He was always there for me anytime I had a problem or just wanted to talk. Most people bitch about their POs, because they treat 'em like they're just a damned convict or disrespectful. Don never treated me like that. I was his only female parolee, and he was proud of me.

Although most participants found some way to manage their conditions and develop a mutually respectful relationship with their parole officer, Ashley in particular expressed frustration about what she considered arbitrary intrusion into the choices she made in her daily life. She felt, for example, that her officer projected his moral standards on her relating to her sexual behavior. She related several conversations she had with her officer about his expectation that he be able to know her whereabouts at all times. She recalls asking him several years ago, "I understand you're married, but I like sex. I can't go to a hotel and have sex?" To which the parole officer answered, "No, you have to be at your house." Another conflict erupted again when she attempted to assert her rights to privacy:

> About three months ago, he called me and said, "Meet me at your house. We need to talk." Okay, he comes over here. Now, there were several

reasons why he wanted to talk. One was that he came by my [house] at 6:30 in the morning and did not see my car and wanted to know where the hell I was. Well, sometimes I leave to go to work early. "Well, you don't have to be to work until 7:00." "Well, I get there at 6:20 or 6:30 or 6:40 or 6:55 or 6:59. It just depends on how I feel that morning. I might have left early." "But, you weren't here." "Well, I was at work." So, he really believed that I was sleeping somewhere else. And, I think that's hard to ask an adult. I brought that to his attention. I said, "What if I liked somebody and wanted to spend the night at their house." "You have to call me and get permission." This past Thanksgiving and this past Christmas, two days before the holiday, I had to call and get permission to go spend the night at my mom's house out of fear he would violate me if he happened to pass by and didn't see my car.

Ashley protested what she considered was an unfair extension of control over her individual choices and discovered that she was accountable for her location, and that the parole officer could decide how to enforce that accountability.

I called his supervisor a couple of days after Christmas to discuss this issue with him, and he said that it's more of the parole officer's initiative as to how far they can take it. He didn't have any guidelines, but he said, "It's up to your parole officer." I didn't think that was fair at all, because that's not in my manual, but I'm not gonna test y'all and fuck with y'all. So, I'm gonna go with what he's sayin'. So, I don't spend the night anywhere. If I have to have sex, it has to be here. I do not go into your house, and I'm not goin' to a hotel. I mean, I think that's just takin' it to the extreme, to the utmost extreme. . . . And, I think that a lot of times he oversteps his boundary. But, I'm not in a position to push it.

Rene observes that it is difficult sometimes to follow the rules even when you know what the rules are, want to be responsive to the rules, and are behaving in a way that is consistent with the rules. As federal ex-inmates move through the levels of supervision, eventually they are assigned a number they are required to call on a daily basis that randomly identifies anyone who has a drug abuse history to report for a urine analysis. Failure to make the daily call can result in a revocation, even if, as in Rene's case, it was an inadvertent mistake. She recalled that she was working and doing her best and still felt scared that she could be reincarcerated due to what she characterized as a human error.

I worked, and that's why you work, and you save so much of your own money, and you get a place. You know, I was already doin' my part for the home. Just, basically, stayin' clean, goin' by the rules, and just knowin' that I wasn't gonna go back the life I was. When you're clean and you want to do right, it's a lot easier than to have a guilty conscience when things aren't—like, I missed a UA and I got into panic. It could cost me my freedom, and I'm not even doing drugs or anything. Now, that's what scares you to death, you know. It's just, you might not be doin' anything, and you can lose your freedom. There are things that you have to do. That call. What happened that day was I had to go to the unemployment office, and my schedule got off track. I usually call at 7:30, and I forgot—totally forgot. But see, they don't care. You're not allowed to be human. You're not allowed to make an error, and that error could cost me my freedom. That's my main stressor there is that number I got to call on Monday through Saturday.

Many of the participants described the parole or supervision process as "doing what I have to do." The process was facilitated by parole officers, most of whom the women described as promoting their transition, despite the context of supervision and control they represented in their daily lives.

Women wanted to know about the expectations of their parole of supervision. Some women expressed deep frustration related to their perceptions that parole officers sometimes transgressed their privacy in the name of supervision or the overwhelming nature of the conditions they were assigned. Mandi represented the extreme example of these challenges: in order to complete parole and meet the demands for regaining custody of her children, she had to manage a number of treatment conditions, report to her parole officer, and work two jobs to generate enough income to rent a house large enough for her four children and herself.

Harris (1993) suggests the imposition of "needs-based" conditions, which she defines as those that derive from perceptions of women's complex life situations, results in an unfair and unequal extension of surveillance of women during parole. Erez's (1992) study of parole officers' decision-making found that the more objectively determined areas of needs did not differ between male and female parolees, but that there were significant differences in the factors used by parole officers to arrive at their classification and treatment decisions. Erez reported that, for male parolees, the risk level was the more important determinant of parole conditions while women's conditions were more often linked to relational indicators such as marital status. Further Erez (1992) found that with respect to attitudes, criminal orientations are not seen as appropriate for the female role; women, unlike men, are not expected to be hostile or belligerent. Thus, a change in negative attitudes is perceived as important for female parolees but not for males.

Some women in this study displayed what they characterized as "bad" attitudes about parole supervision expectations of them. The effects of the conditions that women may have felt were unfair or inexplicable were attenuated in part by the positive relationships that many expressed that they had been able to develop with their parole/supervision officer. Women did not just happen to have good relationships with these officers; they were empowered by a sense of their own competence and desire to "make it" after prison. They were assertive in claiming the right to information and support. The next section describes the variety of beliefs that helped them withstand some of the indignities of prison life. These beliefs also provided them with comfort in dealing with some of the uncertainties of the transition period.

DRAWING ON SPIRITUAL SUPPORT

The participants expressed a wide variety of beliefs that had helped them withstand some of the indignities of prison life, and provide them comfort or security in dealing with the challenges of the transition. Nicole emphasized that spiritual guidance is an important factor in helping her to get through periodic bouts of depression about how things are working out. Mandi's involvement in religion began as a way to support her children's continued participation in a church. She discovered that the church she chose, however, was a source for some of the positive people she needed to bring into her life.

> I go to a Lutheran church. I think that's real important for my kids. They were really active in the Lutheran church when they lived with my mom. So following through with that. It helps myself. I've been goin' since before the kids got home, since I've been out. Ever since I quit Taco Bell. Now I go to church every Sunday morning and Wednesday evening. I have a sponsor at church, too. She's really nice. I talk to her a lot.

Sadie's spirituality evolved from a blend of Native-American traditional beliefs and a metaphysical understanding of the connection between mind and body. She observed that these practices "helped me with day-to-day-living while I was there and now too":

> I do a lot of meditation. I used to be running—running to me is part of a spiritual thing—running is a meditation. I don't run anymore but I bike and that's similar. You can't separate spirit and body. It's real important I think and part of my spiritual life. I do a lot of ritual, probably not traditional organized religion but spiritual certainly.

Nan provided a powerful testimonial to the faith that took her through her almost five years of incarceration. She emphasizes, however, that she did not expect the Lord to take responsibility for her getting to prison or getting out of prison:

> I know that there is a God, and I believe in Him. The Lord didn't send me to prison. The Lord allowed man to sentence me, because durin' my sentence, I was originally up for ten years. Now, I do believe the Lord stepped in and intervened in that and seen to it I only got five. If you need to have

brain surgery, you can pray until you turn another color. The Lord is not comin' to give you surgery. He gives the doctor the power to give you the surgery. He sends the angels to watch over you in during the surgery. He already gave us our blessin' when we were sentenced. We didn't have to go to prison. We could have went to death. We went to prison, and we're still livin'. I look at the Lord knowin' that He's here with you and I today. Without Him, I could have been dumped in the road.

Nan's faith in the Lord was strong but she was very certain that it was up to her to do what it takes to make her own choices in everyday life.

Sort of like a lot of people today, they use Him, just like they use drugs. They lean on Him and use Him. He made a way when you was given life this morning to wake up, when you was given knowledge and sense to go look for a job and pay your own bills. My spiritual growth for the Lord has become stronger when I was away, because I had the time to sit down and read the Bible. I had the time to practice and make sure I was sayin' my prayers. But, sometimes in a busy day when you lay down, you so tired you just call him and say, "Oh, Lord Jesus, thank you" and go on.

Susan grew up attending a "Bible thumpers" church that did not provide her a meaningful spiritual base. After her release from prison, she found a church where she felt welcomed.

I mean the church we went to when we were kids is what we call Bible thumpers. I never would go back, until mom told me about Unity. It was somethin' we liked—and the kids love it. It's someplace where you feel accepted. You don't have to put on a face. We're pretty much into the old church thing here. But, it's not a church of sermons. If you make a mistake—it's forgiven. You just deal with it and correct whatever you've done. I don't think we'd stick with it if it was a—you'll go to hell for doing that and doin' this. It's a feel-good church. You walk out of there with a smile on your face.

Although not all the women belonged to a church or claimed a particular spiritual practice, it was clear that for those who did have a means for expressing their spiritual beliefs, this was an important aspect of maintaining themselves when they felt challenged by life's daily struggles. The themes of this chapter related to the women's spurts of internalized confidence that derived from managing the rules imposed by their post-prison supervision and identifying sources of support and solace. The next chapter examines the ways in which relationships provided a foundation for the women's continued progress in the transition after release from prison.

CHAPTER FOUR

RECONSTRUCTING RELATIONSHIPS

It's like when you go to prison, they act like you're dead.
—Jeanette, 1996

Who knows better the needs of these people than we these people?
—Bernie, 1996

Common to the stories about women's moral, social, and psychological development is the ethic of care. Women's focus on relationships with others is a major source of self-worth and empowerment that defines their perceptions of the world and their role or place within it. In this chapter, I discuss the importance of relationships in assisting women to find their place in the free world after release from prison.

There is no indication that lawbreaking women are any less likely to develop a web of connection with others than women who have not been convicted of an offense. What may be different, however, is that the primary relationships that lawbreaking women create is often characterized by a high degree of abuse, violence, and exploitation. The character of these relationships echoes the challenge that lawbreaking women face in trying to maintain relationships while also asserting their own needs and desires.

Because women's central relational orientation is often devalued, their lack of shared empathy with others is sometimes expressed in lawbreaking behaviors. Although women currently have more access to social power and identity in the world than in the past, they do not perpetrate crime like men. However, it is almost predictable that many women, as a social worker in the Kansas correctional system stated, commit crimes "with a man, for a man, because of a man, or to a man" (Blaine Saunders, personal communication, July 1991).

In interviews with sixteen first-time incarcerated women offenders, Sears (1989) found that a majority of the women identified "being used and/or conned by a man" as the number one reason for their conviction. Women in the Sears study also identified a fear of loss of their primary relationship with a man or abuse by a man; to a lesser degree, the women reported economic or drug-pressured motivation. The Sears study is limited by its nonrepresentative sample as all interview participants were white. Black women or other women of color might describe a different perspective on the impact of their relationships with a primary partner.

Thomas (1995) reported that an incarcerated woman, convicted of selling crack cocaine and sentenced to more than ten years in prison in Kansas, was granted a new trial on the basis that she was forced to sell drugs by an abusive husband. Although this is a new application of the battered women's defense,[1] which has generally been used to explain mitigating circumstances in cases when women are charged in the homicide of their abusive partners, the association between women's drug-dealing activities within her intimate relationship has been supported by other studies of women's criminal activities.

For example, Wilson (1993) examined the differing and gender-related patterns of male and female criminal work by an analysis of *Uniform Crime Reports* data from 1970 to 1989 for ten income-productive crimes. Wilson identified that the economic crimes that women commit tend to fall in the "amateur" category because they engage in these offenses on a part-time basis. On the other hand, men were engaged more often in what Wilson defined as "subcultural" crime that relied on greater discretionary time, geographic mobility, and freedom from other domestic responsibilities such as childcare.

Of interest, however, is the role that women play in relationship to men's criminal activities. In the realm of drug dealing as an income-producing activity, Wilson found that the two aspects of amateur and subcultural crime merged in the sexual alliance of a heterosexual partnership. Men rely on women's work in the home in several ways for its provision of a stable base: It enables them to steal or, alternatively, deal drugs. Wilson notes that men and women together create drug distribution networks, in which men do the outside sales and contact work and women provide the base of operations. Wilson's conclusions are exploratory; more research is needed to describe the ways in which this type of partner crime is developed and the roles that each partner play within it. The implications for women's increasing conviction and incarceration for drug trafficking crimes that evolve out of their business and sexualized relationships with men are significant.

Another risk factor related to women's intimate relationships is their possible exposure to violence or abuse. Although all methods for studying incidence rates of violence are flawed to some extent, by confounding environmental influences, diverse methods in data collection, and unreliable instrumentation (Gelles 1987), conclusions drawn across multiple studies suggest that men victimize women more often than women victimize men. The most conservative estimates suggest that a minimum of 12 percent of women are victims of spousal abuse every year (Straus and Gelles 1986) and that at least 30 percent of all women are battered at least once during their adult lives (Straus, Gelles, and Steinmetz 1980). Estimates based on the Straus, Gelles, and Steinmetz study suggest that over 1.5 million women are the victims of major assaults by a partner each year.[2] A recent survey confirmed these estimates (Tjaden and Thoennes, 2000).

Why abuse against women is, to some degree, socially tolerated is an unanswered question. Feminist scholars have argued that male domination within the family, social institutions, and society itself provide the structural and ideological foundation for violence against women. Yllo (1984) conducted a series of studies examining how women's status correlates to violence in the family, using quantitative analysis of secondary data on wife abuse. Yllo constructed a "Status of Women" index and used it to rank thirty American states regarding the economic, political, educational, and legal status of women. She compared this index to the state rates of wife beating drawn from a representative survey on family violence (Straus et al. 1980) and found that there is a curvilinear relationship between the status of women and wife abuse. Violence against wives was highest in states where women had low status and was lower as women's status improved. Rates of abuse increased, however, in those states in which women's status was highest relative to men's. One implication of this study's findings is that if patriarchal attitudes, as reflected in women's social status, reinforce abuse of women, it will be much more difficult to eradicate the problem.

Among incarcerated women, the rate of abuse by their male intimate partners (the correctional national survey data does not discern battering or assault between women), as well as prior experiences of abuse by partners and/or family members, is quite high. In fact, as indicated by self-report studies, it is much higher than the incidence of violence toward women in the general population (Bachman 1994; Comack 1993; Gilfus 1992; Robinson 1994). The BJS (Snell 1994) survey of women in prison in 1991 indicated that 43 percent (as compared to 12 percent of the men) reported prior physical or sexual abuse; about 32 percent said that the abuse had occurred before age eighteen, and 24 percent said they had been abused since age eighteen. Women in prison reported prior abuse three times more often than incarcerated men, and sexual abuse or abuse since age eighteen at least six times more often than men. Seventy-nine percent of the women incarcerated for a violent offense of homicide or assault had experienced prior abuse at the hands of an intimate partner. The reported statistics, however, do not identify whether the victim of their violent crime was an intimate partner (or male, for that matter).

In addition to the multiple physical problems women experience as a result of battering, the psychological effects of violence have been identified as low self-esteem, clinical levels of depression, overcompliance or lack of assertiveness, feelings of powerlessness, strong fear reactions to threatening situations, vulnerability to medical illness, and a sense of needing to hold one's aggressiveness in check because of a fear of being overwhelmed. McHugh, Frieze, and Browne (1993) caution against reading these characteristics as only passive responses; many battered women develop strong coping mechanisms to manage the stress related to the abuse, others fight back, and some end up in prison as a consequence.

Once in prison, women's need for affective relationships with each other may be an obstacle to long-term well-being. Larson and Nelson (1984) attempted to develop a theoretical model to explain the short- and long-term consequences of incarceration related to different forms of adaptation to prison. These authors found that a strategy of adaptation to prison that relied on solidarity with other women inmates was "the central socializing agent(s) shaping a criminal identity" (613). Larson and Nelson used "criminal identity" to represent a woman's "willingness to think of herself as a criminal" (606) and consequent long-term involvement in a criminal career. Criminal identity was also related to opposition to the legal system and conflict with the correctional staff. Furthermore, Larson and Nelson hypothesized that individual affiliations among women prisoners may mediate the loss of control and powerlessness that women experienced while incarcerated. These authors found that some women develop solidarity relations as expressed in friendships, while others remain more autonomous through isolation from other inmates.

The effects of these adaptive strategies are attenuated by relationships women maintain outside prison and/or expectations about post-release life. Larson and Nelson's (1984) analysis of women at three state prison facilities produced several interesting findings. First, women who have negative post-release expectations, low trust in other inmates, and feel they have little control over events develop hostile attitudes toward the legal system. This effect was exacerbated for those who maintain few or no free world contacts. Second, women having extensive and intensive friendships with other women while in prison ("solidarity" adaptation) and negative post-release expectations have a more salient criminal identity. Other types of adaptation (isolation and efficacy) were generally accompanied by a favorable disposition toward others. Larson and Nelson suggest that women who feel positively toward friends and relatives outside prison, and those who maintain these bonds, perceive themselves as being more in control of their life while in prison. They also found that, "as the release date approaches, prison friendships become less important and the orientation to post-release society gains behavior influencing significance" (607). A critical omission in this study is a fuller understanding of how the inmates themselves describe their prison friendships and the purposes the relationships serve during the women's incarceration. The authors imply that the sole function of friendships is to reinforce criminal behaviors and/or provide an adaptive response to incarceration.

Larson and Nelson's findings related to women's friendships are contradicted by Schulke's (1993) cross-sectional study of formerly incarcerated women. Schulke found that the informal social supports women developed with each other while in prison were helpful in creating and maintaining a noncriminal identity because they reinforced positive attempts to reestablish themselves after release from prison.

Neither of these studies (Larson and Nelson 1984; Schulke 1993) examined the influence of substance addiction on criminal or noncriminal identity. Since the bulk of current criminal offenses and convictions among incarcerated women derives from drugs (Beck and Mumola 1999), it is important to examine the connection between substance abuse, perceptions of self-identity, and lawbreaking behaviors to better understand the additional weight of addiction on the ex-offender in transition. In addition, given that women often had to depend on family members for support during the initial period after release, how they dealt with some of the unresolved issues from abuse they experienced in their families of origin reflected the internal change processes that they initiated while incarcerated.

CREATING AND RECREATING
RELATIONSHIPS TO NURTURE GROWTH

Relationships can nurture or inhibit personal growth. Generally, the initial relationships study participants described as facilitative during their transition were with family members as the women proved themselves to be clean or straight, as well as when they were able to resolve previous disappointments or cutoffs with family members. The women's relationships with their children, whether or not they had custody of them, were a pivotal source of nurturance and efficacy. The women also discussed new relationships with partners or spouses. Finally, relationships with social workers and counselors and other helping people, as well as former and new friends, provided emotional support at challenging points in the transition.

RECONSTRUCTING FRACTURED RELATIONSHIPS WITH FAMILY MEMBERS

For a variety of reasons, ten of the eighteen participants in the study described their relationships with their mothers as problematic and sometimes abusive. Working out the difficulties in their relationships with their mothers contributed to the women's sense of well-being and growth following incarceration, even if mothers were no longer living. For some women, regaining the ability to parent their children also depended on their being able to reconstruct their fractured relationship with their mother. Participants' fathers were mentioned very rarely, if at all, signifying perhaps a less volatile or an absent relationship.

Study participants described how the mother's anger became an obstacle in the women's process of reestablishing their relationships with their children either during their incarceration or afterward. Mandi, for example, recounted the story of a day prior to her incarceration when she realized that due to her drug use she was unable to adequately care for her children. Not knowing who else she could depend on to take care of her children, she called her mother to pick them up. Mandi's mother at first reacted with disbelief and denial, and then anger. While Mandi was incarcerated, her mother started proceedings to adopt Mandi's children without her knowledge or consent. Mandi tearfully recalled her panic after a visit during which her oldest son asked her; "How come Grandma's gonna adopt us?"

> Then I called her, and she didn't accept my call. I was really emotionally upset about that. They put me in the Psych Ward because they said I was considered for suicide because I was so emotionally distressed. My counselor and I called to see about the proceedings, and they told her that they couldn't start adoption proceedings . . . that the court was going to give it the chance that I was going to be rehabilitated.

Mandi's mother also used control over the children's visits with Mandi as a way to further punish her.

> My mom was really negative. When I was in jail, I'd say, "How come I don't get to see them more often?" "If you wanted to see the kids, you shouldn't have went to jail." You know when you're in jail, you don't have much money. I saw my mom and said, "Can you give me some bucks?" "If you wanted money, you shouldn't have been jailed. You should have stayed out and had a job." My mom wouldn't give me nothin'. She was not about to help me.

As Mandi demonstrated her commitment to remaining free of her crack addiction and to parenting her children again, her mother became more supportive by providing assistance and facilitating the children's visits to Mandi, before she regained custody.

> Well, after I think I was doin' good—now she seems more supportive of me. She says she hopes things works out. She brought a carload of stuff. She helped work with me to have visitation every weekend.

Ashley, Jeanette, Rene, and Susan described much more complicated relationships with their mothers. Their mothers either abused them or did not protect them from others who abused them. For Ashley, finally being able to assert her needs to her mother opened the door to their creating a more bounded relationship, in the sense of maintaining both separation and connection.

> My mom and I were never close, and that was the main thing, because she did abuse me. I would never open up to her and talk to her. So, about a year ago, I just sat her down one day, and I said, "Look, Mom, this is me and this is the way I am. You either deal with it or you don't, because you don't have another daughter. But, I'm not gonna let you downgrade me and talk bad about me. You have to accept me the way I am, because, if not, I can just walk out of your life like I've come back in, because I don't need this shit. I'm old enough to take care of myself." You have to make those steps forward sometimes.

Ashley believes that the experience of surviving the incarceration gave her insights that have enabled her to feel more secure so that she can make better choices about what she will tolerate in her relationship with her mother. Apparently this new behavior had a different effect on her mother as well.

> Because, there is no way I would have said anything like that before [the incarceration]. Just knowin' I would have got back-handed.

Having an improved relationship with her parents has helped Ashley feel better about her decision to allow them to adopt her daughter because she believes they can provide a more financially secure life for her daughter than she can. However, she still has to negotiate with her parents about her participation in her daughter's life.

> She has full health benefits as long as he's her father, so it had to be on paper. I thought that I was taking responsibility in allowing that to happen. I thought that that was a wise decision. About eight months ago, my mom and dad and I would get in big fights because they wouldn't let me see her when I wanted to. They wouldn't let me take her here and there. You know, I just had to say, "Hey, look, she's my daughter. You guys have custody, but she's still mine." They have problems with me takin' her just to hang out. They want to know exactly where we go all the time. So, I just have to say sometimes, "I don't know. If I have to tell you, she can just stay. I don't know where we're goin'." They get pissed, but I just don't have an answer. Sometimes, I am an adult and just let me take the initiative, and it will be okay.

When Jeanette went to prison, she threatened the family system by confronting the "family secret" because of her fear that her stepfather, who had molested her as a child, would also molest her daughters if they stayed in her mother's home while she was incarcerated. At first her sisters, who also had been molested by the stepfather, agreed that they would care for her children, but then they later "ganged up" on her and accused her of making trouble. After a long history of secrecy and denial about the abuse, she did not feel as though her mother would protect her daughters.

> Well, my stepdad when we was growin' up molested us. I have two older sisters, and now I have a little sister, too, but there's three of us. Well, we never told nobody. My mom knew, but she didn't want us to tell nobody, because she was afraid my dad would kill him [stepfather], and we wouldn't get to see her no more. So, when I went to prison, these are the people that have my kids, two little girls. You're not only goin' through all the changes when you first go to prison—get locked up, but then I had that to worry about, and I couldn't tell nobody because I was afraid that the state would get my kids. I didn't know if he was molesting them or not because they were such little babies, and he didn't molest us until we got a little bigger. You tell yourself this shit. But, then you lay awake at night and you worry about it. My kids don't have dads. Their dads aren't in their life. There was nobody there, and if I depended on my mother to protect my children, she didn't protect us. She made us available for him, so she could see us. I figure, if it came to that, she would allow him to molest my children before she would do somethin'.

When Jeanette was unable get anyone in her family to provide shelter to her daughters other than at her mother's home, she made a legal complaint that resulted in his removal from her mother's home where her daughters continued to reside.

In addition to the cover-up of sexual molestation within the family, Jeanette, similar to Mandi, had a difficult relationship with her mother due to her mother's response to her crime. Jeanette described the power that her mother used to punish her by not bringing her children to see her at the federal prison "basically clear across the damn country."

> You know, my mother was very mad at me and wouldn't talk to me for several months and wouldn't let me see my kids. See, you have to take that kind of abuse because when you go to prison, you're at other people's mercy. It's like when you go to prison, they act like you're dead. It's like, I say that, and it sounds mean, but it's so true. It's like you're never gonna get out. . . . maybe I would have acted the same way . . . I just know it was me that was in there. This was the first time she was in a position with power with me and my children, and she ran with it. I tried to be understanding, you know. She was goin' through a lot, too. You know, I am her daughter. She wasn't just angry at me. She was angry at the feds. But, the feds were doin' their job, bottom line. I try to talk to her about that still.

Jeanette indicated that her mother finally got beyond her anger enough to recognize that she could be supportive to Jeanette by bringing the children to visit her, despite the difficulties involved in bringing young children to a prison facility.

> I guess she just got over bein' so angry, and then she started worryin' about what was gonna happen to me. And my kids needed me too. My baby wasn't quite so bad, but the two year old was with me always. This was like I was there one day, and I was gone, because what they did was they revoked my bond. You can't explain to someone that young what's happened. She brought 'em to see me in Lexington, and that's an ordeal for your family. They have to go through so much shit . . . it's humiliating. I can do that, but I don't like my family doin' it. They didn't break no laws. Do you understand what I say when I say they punish your family? It's little things. You know, all through the whole thing, they know how to get your attention. To get your attention to get you in line, they mess with your family or your visits.

Jeanette currently works a full time job. Her two daughters, now five and seven years old, live with her mother during the week and spend the weekends with her in a small rented apartment. Still, she has a backlog of debt and is not certain she can support them. Although Jeanette recognizes that her children are her mother's "whole life," she is making plans for the time when she can adequately support them. She also feels that she has to prove to her family that she is free of the drug addiction that led to her incarceration.

> Then when I got out, they all waited. It didn't bother me a bit, because I had a goal and a plan. I just thought, "You know, all these years, through all of this stuff, they need to have a chance. They have never seen me not use drugs, okay? Just because I know I'm not usin' drugs, let's give them a little while to get used to it." And, so, it's not like, I could say, "I'm perfect now, and you know, I'm gonna do everything right." So, all I do is get up and go to work every day, and I do everything I'm supposed to do.

Susan also took responsibility for the behaviors that resulted in her imprisonment, but she has examined the abuse in her family that she feels led to her criminal behaviors.

> From the time I was three, my mom was real abusive to me and I grew up with it so all my boyfriends were guys who were abusive and everything's always my fault so I was very big people-pleaser and I did whatever I had to make them happy and a lot of times it had to do with money so I would

steal money whenever I had to give it to them so I wouldn't get beat or so they wouldn't just fly off and leave me.

This examination began during Susan's last incarceration and continued when she was referred for mental health sessions during the initial part of her parole. Meanwhile, her mother also got into therapy and began to understand and own some of what she had perpetrated on her daughter as a child.

> My mom and dad—the first time I went in is for a crime against them. I used them . . . and when I did that, it was more of a get back in touch with what I felt like my mom had done to me as a kid instead of, there wasn't nothing I needed, I used it to help a friend, it wasn't like for spending money. But that's another problem that I get into what other people need instead of what's right for me. The first time I came home, it was like no contact, particularly with my mom. The second time, my mom had started counseling a year before I went in and I did a lot of counseling while I was in and so we both worked through a whole bunch of stuff and they came up and talked to me a lot; they were really there for me. I mean, there was no, "I blame you, what you did was wrong, what I do is right," there was none of that stuff; they were there to support me and stood behind me, and they helped me when I came out. And they're still there, I mean I'm closer to my mom and dad than I've ever been in my life. . . . part of her therapy is acknowledging the things that she's done to me. Me and her talk about it a lot.

This opportunity for healing between her and her mother became especially important when Susan became pregnant because she worried she might become abusive herself.

> She asked me to go to her [counselor], she knew I needed to go back. When I got pregnant, I was scared to death it was a girl. I didn't want a girl, because I was afraid I would be like my mom and I'm the only one of the kids she abused, so I was very scared that if it was a girl, I would hurt her. I didn't find out until I was six months that it was a girl but I went to counseling the whole time I was pregnant. And so far it's worked. I get really really mad but I don't touch my kids.

Rene traces much of her criminal history to the sexual abuse she experienced from the time she was five years old. Again, the fact that her mother protected the perpetrator (Rene's uncle) made it difficult for her to rebuild a relationship with her mother once she started dealing with the consequences of the abuse.

> For me, it was a lifelong lot of things, but I made a change in my life. There was a point I came to I couldn't deal with anymore, and I took it all in my own hands, just like I did on everything gettin' me there. I've drank since I was five years old, 'cause mom and them drank beer. The

beer was there in the 'frigerator. So, when these things went on, I drank to try not to remember what was goin' on. I still remembered. The mere fact, that 'til I was up to ten or eleven years old, I went through over five years of this. I just told 'em, right out. My grandma couldn't believe it and still don't believe it to this day. My mom finally accepted it. I remember one time, my mom says, "Well, how could you do that to my mother?" I said, "Well how could you let that happen to us kids?" For a long time, the door was closed on us. We were rejected for the mere fact that we made the statement that we was sexually molested by the baby brother that everybody thought was so good.

Rene believes that most of her self-destructive drinking and drug-taking behavior came from her attempts to cover up the pain from the abuse. Only when she confronted the abuse was she able to make the necessary changes in her life.

There was a heavy burden in my whole life that I had to let go of. And, I done everythin' from drinkin', just on and on, and basically just tried to cover up the pain. And all the things that's gone on, and then I come to a point when they locked me up this last time, I kept sayin, "I'm not a bad person. I beat myself to death all the time already. I'm not a bad person."

For both Elizabeth and Bernie, the older women in this study, resolving issues with their mother depended in part on resolving some of their guilt about their behaviors that had led them to prison. Elizabeth moved in with her mother for the first several years after her release from prison. She recalls that she felt grateful to have a stable place where she could recover from the fears that had emerged from her prison experiences. She did not feel very connected to her mother at the time: "I withdrew from my mother. As soon as I'd come home from work, I'd go to my room." She also recalled that her experience made her a source of shame to her mother:

My mother, that was awful when I told my mother, "Mom, I might go to prison." Then, when I was in prison, my mother was mortified and did not say anything to anyone. Still that's an area I never discuss in front of any of her friends. She kind of hobnobs with all these old fuddy-duddy little old women. So that's real important—all that image stuff. It was really hard for me.

Elizabeth's brother helped soothe some of her feelings of shame and re-solve her sense of her mother's disappointment in her when he told her that he believed that everyone does something wrong but that only some people are held accountable.

Bernie struggled for years with feelings of being unwanted by her mother. She recalls that she spent years trying to "be somebody I wasn't." She relates her criminal behaviors to her alcoholism, which she referred to as an emotional problem that stemmed from her rocky relationship with her mother. Confronting her mother about the unfair expectations that her mother levied on her allowed Bernie to finally resolve some of the difficulties in their relationship.

> Every time I went home, I would go straight to my family. Straight to Mama. And Mama was going to change, but Old Anna never changed. Maybe the last few years before she died, and I was forty-some years old then, when I told her, "You gotta let me grow up, I gotta live my own life, and I've got to do what I think's best for my kids." She didn't speak to me for a year. I went back on one parole violation. She wrote me, "Well, at least you could send me a card and let me know if you are still alive." Finally after that my mother and I had the best relationship we had ever had right before she died, and it was very shortly after that, I got my life straightened out. I guess I grew up a little bit. I think mostly it was that I didn't feel I had to be somebody I wasn't anymore after Mom died.

Suzy acknowledges that she feels "a lot of anger at my mother," whom she believes is still trying to control Suzy's relationship with her son. A major part of Suzy's struggle in the transition has been to reassert her role as mother to her son. She observes that her mother undermines that role by not respecting Suzy's wishes.

> The whole time I was gone, David, my husband, was stayin' with my parents, and my mom had taken over the role of mother, and she did not and to this day does not want to relinquish the role. That infuriates the hell out of me. So, that was a lot of adjustments. My mom was tryin' to control every aspect of my life, like when I could shower and when I could feed my husband and when I could do my laundry. It was worse than bein' in prison. So, I told David, "You got to quit this job and get us a good job, so we can get the heck out of here," so he did. We saved every penny we had. We moved into a run-down little dump, but it was out of my mom's house.

Suzy also learned from counseling that some of the ways that her mother acted around her as a child, and currently exhibits around her son, reflect "inadequate boundaries." She has since worked to establish more healthy boundaries and rules that appropriately distinguish her parenting role both with her mother and her son.

> . . . it was kind of rough, you know, the first couple of months, but after we got away from Grandma, and I started workin' with [the counselor], he made me see things and taught me how to protect myself from possible risks so I won't offend again. He made me aware of some of my red flags

around my son, so that helped. 'Cause when I first got home, and I'd go in to take a bath, J. would want to crawl in the bath with me. I didn't think nothin' of it, because my mom did it when I was a kid, but I don't do that now. Just little things that Randy taught me about bein' a parent. Some boundaries—my mom didn't teach [J.] boundaries. I mean, she goes in to go to the bathroom and J. follows her. She goes in to take a shower, and J. follows her. She walks around in front of him like that, and I just think it's totally wrong. I never thought nothin' of it before, but it's totally wrong now. When he goes and spends the night at her house, I mean, we get into some arguments because I do not want her behavin' like that in front of my child. So, there's been a couple of times, I told her, "If you don't start doin' it right, he's not comin'." She doesn't like that.

Suzy accepts responsibility for her offense (aggravated incest). She has been in treatment during and after her incarceration. However, her mother is still in denial about Suzy's behaviors and Suzy feels she cannot depend on her mother to support an improved relationship with her son.

She's in denial, because I was in denial for so long about what I did, and she still believes what I used to tell her that I was innocent, because for years I believed it. She still believes that I didn't do it. I told her the truth but she still believes that I'm just sayin' what I have to say. That's where she's at, Fantasy Land.

Jeanette recognizes that her foundation of support from which she can draw is not entirely secure. Yet she described her own efforts to create an adult relationship with both her parents by taking responsibility for her problems.

You know, with doin' drugs and all of that, you destroy a lot of relationships. I'm lucky in that my family, you know, I did damage. They did damage, too, like my sister is an example, but she does drugs, too, so that's part of it still. But I have made a conscious effort to have a relationship with my parents as an adult, and that goes two ways. It's not just because they are my mom and dad. It's because, you know, a lot of the problems I had before, I blamed other people. I never took responsibility for my own faults or problems. It was always somebody else's fault. When you start takin' responsibility for your own problems, and you look at other people and you quit judging them so much and you try to understand.

Finally, some study participants found they were able to draw on their mother's support when they came out of prison despite other family problems. Jeanette observes:

My mom, you know, she drinks. I've got over things with her with our childhood, but she's still my mom. So, and plus, she's helped me with my children regardless of everything else that's happened. She's always been there, and, you know, I have more support than a lot of girls do comin' out of prison.

As Elena has proven to herself and her family that she can meet the challenges of supporting her children without resuming her drug use and other activities that resulted in her incarceration, she has been able to develop a different relationship with her mother that is based on her success.

> My mom is so proud of me . . . and I don't want to ever disappoint her like I have before. She knows I've changed. I don't run the streets all the time. I'm not doin' [or] sellin' drugs. I'm not getting' involved in no abusive relationships. I take care of my kids good now, and she can rest in peace. I know she used to worry about me. She used to say she was prayin' and prayin' that I would change. Then when I got incarcerated, I came out and I changed, she said God answered her prayers. I got somethin' to live for now. My mom and my father, they praise me all the time with how good I do, and that makes me feel really good.

These examples indicate a recognition among the study participants that anger does not have to eliminate the possibility for restructured relationship. Anger is a part of relationship, an expression of caring, and can ultimately contribute to building better connections. The women also expressed their capacity for "mutual empathy" (Jordan 1997) by their willingness to engage in reconstructing and nurturing the relationship with their mothers despite past hurt and disappointment.

Reassuming Relationships with Children

Sixteen of the eighteen participants had a total of forty-four children, including children who had been born to Elena, Margi, Regina, and Susan since their release. Table 4.1 provides a summary description of the ages and sex of the participants' children, as well as the current status of child custody.

At the time of the interview, eight of the participants had alternative physical or legal custody arrangements for their children. Those children were not residing with their mothers and/or their mothers had relinquished permanent custody of the child(ren). Ashley had voluntarily relinquished both legal and physical custody of her daughter to her parents because she felt they could better financially support her daughter. Her parents lived near her and she had arranged to work at the after school childcare center that her daughter attended, so she had almost daily contact with her. Mandi, Margi, and Rene were regaining full physical and legal custody of their children, a process that depended on demonstrating their ability to financially and emotionally care for their children. Both Margi and Rene had children in residential foster care, due to the children's behavioral difficulties or disabilities.

Table 4.1

PARTICIPANTS' CHILDREN AND
CURRENT CUSTODY STATUS

Participant	Number/Sex/ Ages of Children	Custody Status
Anita	14-year-old son	Son lives with his father.
Ashley	9-year-old daughter	Daughter lives with and adopted by Ashley's parents.
Bernie	Five adult children (30–50 years old). Also has eleven grandchildren.	All living outside of metropolitan area where Bernie resides.
Deeni	23-year-old son 25-year-old daughter Also has two grandchildren	Deenie provides primary care for one grandchild and a 9-year-old niece.
Demi	4-year-old daughter, 8-year-old son	Demi has physical custody of daughter; son lives with her mother and stepdad.
Elena	1-, 6-, 8-, 10-year-old daughters, 3-year-old son	Had son while incarcerated; all except oldest daughter who lives with her father, live with her.
Elizabeth	24-, 26-year-old daughters, 22-year-old son	Son currently living with her.
Jeanette	5-, 7-year-old daughters	Daughters live with Jeanette's mother.
Mandi	5-year-old twin daughters, 9-, 11-year-old sons	Mandi regained legal as well as physical custody of all children.
Margi	2 months, 4-, 9-year-old sons, 8-year-old daughter	Daughter (diagnosed as mentally retarded) remains in state custody in foster care. Sons live with her.
Nan	4-, 10-, 12-, 15-year-old daughters, 18-year-old son	Had youngest daughter while incarcerated; all children in Nan's custody.
Racque	15-year-old daughter	Lives with her.
Regina	4-month-old son	Lives with her.
Rene	13-year-old daughter, 15-year-old son	Son is in residential setting in state custody; daughter lives with her.
Susan	4 month-old daughter, 4-year-old son	Daughter and son live with her.
Suzy	4-year-old son	Son lives with her.

Anita, Demi, Elena, and Jeanette had chosen for one or more of their children to reside with another caretaker (either the father of the child or the participant's mother) or had decided not to pursue regaining physical custody of the child at this time.

Nan was the only participant who had made a Herculean effort to maintain a strong parenting role with her children during her incarceration. Her sister's willingness to move to the town in another state where Nan was incarcerated facilitated this ongoing contact. Other women had to depend on their children's caretaker to bring them, usually a long distance, for brief visits.

When Elizabeth was incarcerated, her three children stayed in the care of their father. When she was released, she separated from her husband, and from her children too. In the intervening years, she has developed a close relationship with her now adult children, all of whom I met in the course of two interviews at her house. Although she described needing some way to make up her absence to her children, she had never, prior to this study, talked to any of them about the time of her incarceration. She indicates that when she was released, she knew her children were safe, and her main focus became dealing with the effects of incarceration and reestablishing her life. She wonders now how her absence during that period has affected her relationship with her children. Of the eldest daughter, she mused:

> I've never asked her if she felt like she missed something. I'm always concerned with what can I give her now. Sometimes I wonder if I'm trying to buy back some of that guilt.

All the parents discussed the pain they had experienced in the separation from their children while they were incarcerated. And for those who had not yet resumed their residential parenting role, enduring relationships with their children gave them an opportunity to address some of the trauma that the children had experienced prior to and during their incarceration. But they felt discomfort because they were not able to materially care for their children. Both Ashley and Jeanette, for example, discussed their difficulty in talking to a potential partner about the fact that they did not have custody of their children. Jeanette relates:

> Because, when I meet somebody, it's never mind that I've been in prison. The hardest thing for me to say is my kids don't live with me. You can give 'em all the explanations you want.

Although children are not often recognized as promoting an adult's experience of efficacy, that was the consequence, particularly for Mandi, Nan, and Suzy. Reclaiming their parenting role gave these women an indicator of having proven something to themselves related to their ability to resume an important component of their identity as mothers.

Nan explained how she was able to overcome the need she previously had for good living that resulted in criminal behavior by creating a home for her children made up of love, rather than only material things.

> Havin' to go to prison, livin' in a matchbox room and only havin' X-amount of dollars and havin' nowhere to go and nobody to turn to. I don't ever want that again, honey. All them fine fancy clothes and good livin', I don't want that because I had all of that, I wasn't even happy. Now, I'm so happy bein' right here with my kids. With little money because it's real, true love right here in the home with me and my kids. Then, it wasn't. I didn't love my kids then. I loved to supply them with materialistic living. So, why I thought I had to live in a house I was payin' over a thousand dollars a month. I'm fine livin' right here payin' $325.

Mandi, at the time of her interview, had physical custody of her children only a few months since her release over a year before, and only recently regained legal custody. She recalled the process she followed to prove her competence to care for her children. Acquiring and maintaining a home she could afford became a symbolic as well as a material accomplishment and a reflection of her ability to surmount the crack addiction that led to her incarceration. After describing the conditions placed on her by both the correctional system and the family court, she concluded, "I remember feeling real overwhelmed, but I did it."

Suzy found that resuming her job of running the house and parenting was a major source for reestablishing her identity with her spouse after release from prison.

> It was hard for David too, because before I went in, I always took care of everything. While I was gone, he had to do it, so it was kind of hard to get my reins back from him, because I run the house now. I did then, and I do now. It was hard for him to relinquish all that. That's my job. You know, gettin' J. [her son] to adjust to me bein' mom and me bein' home was the hardest.

In reestablishing their relationship with their children, the mothers in this study had to avoid the notion of children as "objects of sentiment" (Dougherty 1998, 144) to motivate them to go straight. They had to actively pursue the economic resources that could enable them to regain all aspects of care of their children. Some of the women also recognized the implicit dangers in their efforts to move too hastily in resuming the role when to do so could trigger illegitimate behaviors or parole violations that would return them to prison and result in further separation from their children.

CREATING NEW RELATIONSHIPS WITH SPOUSES/INTIMATE PARTNERS

Six of the women were in current relationships with male partners. These partners provided support during the transition, but in less tangible ways than family members.

Racque's husband was a man she met on the streets of Oakland who lit-
erally offered to marry her and bring her to visit "Toto and Dorothy," as
Racque characterized her move to Kansas. The move enabled her to make a
new life for herself and her daughter, whom she had not had in her physical
custody for years due to her frequent incarcerations and lifestyle.

Five of the women had developed new relationships with partners since
their release that contributed to a greater sense of security, in some cases because
the partner actually contributed to the costs of maintaining the house, and in several others because the new relationship reinforced the woman's competencies.

Rene, who at the time of the interview had only been released from Dismas House for a few months, described the process of building the walls of support for her and her children brick by brick, with the help that her new fiancé
provided.

> I started while I was there in prison . . . it's just like doin' a diagram of a
> house, and you're gonna have this what's gonna hold it up, and you're
> gonna do all these things to keep it standin'. And, it's like keeping all the
> bricks in place. You don't do this, then you got this, and so, the basic thing
> is keepin' straight. Keep straight and maintain, and then workin' every-
> thing around. That's what I did, because my boyfriend was there. We was
> friends before I got locked up. He came to see me. He stuck in there with
> the kids.

Nicole met her husband, whom she described as her "knight in shining
armor," at the first job she had in a bakery after she was released from prison.
Together they are working to save enough money to move out of her father's
trailer so that they can have their own place and have children. Nicole described
the full-time job she has held for more than a year in the period since her release from prison and the difficulty of saving enough to meet their goal:

> Overnight stocking at a department store. It is a pretty good place to work
> for. But the money's not good . . . they have other good benefits, that and
> the fact that you get paid every week. . . . My husband, he makes more
> than I do, but it's still not enough after taxes. And, when you've got other
> bills to pay on top of tryin' to pay rent, food, utilities, you need a phone.

Susan met her future husband while incarcerated. They resided in the
same facility for several months, and they became reacquainted after having initially met in high school. When Susan was released, they got together after her

relationship with a former boyfriend did not work out. Susan describes the almost magical transformation that has infused her transition from prison:

> I mean, five years ago I would have never looked at my life and saw myself down the road livin' in a nice place with nice stuff with great kids and a nice husband. I always thought I'd have kids but other than that I didn't think of it. Now, you look back, and you can't even imagine any of that was you. I know I've done the things I've done. It's just doesn't seem like I could ever do that again. There has been opportunity. There have been times, especially within the last five months that we've been really hurtin' for money to make our house rent. It just comes to that. I just can't imagine that we won't make it.

When Susan was initially released, she worked in a family-owned business. Later she began working in a nursing home when she acquired her Certified Nursing Assistant (CNA) license and from there decided to return to school to become a Licensed Practical Nurse (LPN). Her husband agreed to support her financially through this process for the future good of their family, even though it means more of a struggle for them in the short term. In addition, as Susan notes, her mother's support also contributed to the family's security:

> That's one thing that boy knows how to do is work. My mom got him the job he's workin' now. It took her a while to realize he wasn't going to do anything wrong. I'm not so worried about where's the groceries going to come from, and how I am going to live without working while I go to school. It's probably given me a lot more confidence to have a husband who thoroughly supports us financially. He doesn't say nothing about me going to school, or how much money we have. It gives me the confidence I need to go to school and not doubt myself . . . I know I can go to school and graduate in May. When I do I'll probably be bringing in as much as he does, we'll be able to make it, which is very nice.

Of the women in the group who are in intimate relationships, Suzy's is most tenuous. She's not certain that she and her husband are going to stay together, now that she no longer has parole conditions that could effect the physical custody of their son. Although her husband's income has been important, especially in allowing them to have their own house rather than to continue to reside with her parents, it is the fact she has savings that enables her to feel secure.

> He's an upholsterer. He makes nine bucks an hour. As long as I'm workin' and he's workin', we can do it. And, even if I wasn't workin', because like I said, I'm good with money. I got $3,000 stashed that I've managed to save from my job.

As these women discussed newly formed and evolving relationships with intimate others in their lives, they reflected authentic connections that were mutual, empathic, creative, and empowering to them.

CONTINUING RELATIONSHIPS WITH FORMER INMATES

One of the more controversial resources that some of women drew on was former inmates. This resource is controversial because it is tied to the prohibition by the state parole office and the federal office of probation and parole against the association of former inmates for any reason. With the exception of Bernie, most of the assistance that former inmates gave the women was limited to emotional support.

As many of the women discussed, seeing other women they had known while incarcerated could be construed as a violation of their parole or supervision after their release from prison. Yet they also recognized that peers could be a valuable resource by already knowing the ropes and potential obstacles after release. Jeanette acknowledges that association is one of the rules of her supervision that she violates because of the greater value she perceives in having support from former inmates she knew in prison. She rationalizes her choice by distinguishing the difference between a "rule" and a "law."

> The only thing I do wrong in their eyes and see, there's a difference in their eyes and my eyes, to them I can go back to prison for association, okay? To me that's breakin' a rule and not a law. There's no law against it. It's some rule they got. I'm sure they have very good reasons for those rules, and in some cases, I believe they need 'em. But, I break that rule because I have friends who are also in recovery that are convicted felons, and some of 'em are goin' through the same things I go through, and that's my best support group, and I can't tell them about that, because that's against the rules.

The ability to give back in some way was also an indicator to many of the women that they have been successful in their transition from prison. Many of the participants who felt stabilized in their residential situation and had an internal sense of having met the challenge of incarceration and the transition from prison identified ways that they recognized that their experience could be useful to others. In fact, as is reflected in some of the recommendations that the women generated, many of the women believed that it was *only* those people who had experienced the pains of incarceration who could be really helpful to others coming out. Nan, for example, sits down with her fifteen-year-old daughter to write letters to her friends that she left behind.

> I have her do that, and she's enjoyed it, because they write back talkin' to her. And, she's really been getting' a kick out of that. She'll always say,

"Mamma, let's go to the public. Let's volunteer. Let's go help somebody. Help somebody's daughter whose mamma's locked up, those kids." She's startin' to get feelin's from helpin' the girls up there.

When I asked why it was important for Nan to write other women inmates, and to inspire her daughter to do the same, she recounted the frustration she felt when other former inmates wrote back only about the good times after their release. She recalls that she had wanted to know about their "real time" experiences of transition:

> It's very important to me. When I was locked up and I got close to people there and they went home, they used to piss me off when they used to write back and say, "Girl, I got laid last night. I had me a beer. I went to the club." I don't want to hear that shit. I wanted them to write me back and tell me that how they felt when they first hit the street. Were they nervous? Did they make a mistake and put a dime in the pay phone and it cost a quarter? I wanted them to tell me the problems they had with getting' a job. Did the people say, "Well, what were you in prison for?" I wanted them to tell me their first visit with their children and families. Did the kids break down at the airport or bus station? Did you cross the street at the red light instead of the green light?

Nan believes that she can now provide some of what she needed to some of the women that she left in prison.

> When I got out, I wrote back to those girls about how my kids came to get me. I wrote back and told them about how stupid I was when I went to Hardee's. I wrote 'em and told 'em about how when I had 500 cash dollars in my hand, how I responded to that. I wanted them to know the importance of when I first went to apply for a job and when I first rode the public bus. I wanted them to know the experience of getting' up in the middle of the night, goin' to your refrigerator, openin' it up and just lookin' in there. They wrote me back and . . .they just cried over my letters because it was what we wasn't used to. I always told 'em, "When I go home, I'm gonna write back and tell y'all stuff we was dyin' to hear."

Nan is also able to share with the women she writes some advice about what she has learned about managing her supervision while out on the streets.

> If you're a federal offense, and the next person, your best friend is an excon, you're not even supposed to be affiliated. That's a violation. So, I tell women now, "If you know you had trouble when you lived on 95th Street, all your friends are still druggies or whatever—whatever, break away from that."

The issue of association with current or former inmates was a topic of mixed opinions among the study participants both in terms of the purpose and the extent of the contact and its duration. Bernie and Ashley were at the extreme points of the discussion, although there was a lot of variability among the individual women.

Bernie, for example, in spite of her age (sixty-seven) and deteriorating health, saw it as her mission to aid people coming out of prison so that they had a place to go, clothes with which they could make themselves presentable, and help with finding employment so they could support themselves and have a sense of pride. Although Bernie, an AA (Alcoholics Anonymous) adherent, used many community and city-wide resources for assisting former inmates, she strongly believes in a self-help model among former inmates. It was a former inmate who provided her a place to stay when she first came out of prison when she had no other options. She remains cynical about the correctional system's ability to respond to the needs of ex-inmates or the public's willingness to give women a second chance. Bernie believes that the inmate herself should be able to discern who she can risk associating with and calls the prohibition of association "a bunch of crap." She observes:

> . . . there are people up there that if they told me I could associate with 'em, I'd run, you know, because you just know who's right and who's wrong. If you're tryin' to make it, you're not gonna get involved with some fool that's not gonna make it, that's not tryin' to make it, and you know pretty quick who they are. But, who knows better the needs of these people than we these people? When these people can turn to one another for support and help, then that is half the battle.

Bernie tells many stories of women who have made it because of their contact with her as well as other people in the community who care about assisting former inmates. Other participants in the study had contact with former inmates because they were members of their own family (Ashley, Deeni). Several women (Nicole, Margi) mentioned friendships they described as supportive while they were incarcerated, but those friendships faded away once they were released.

For some of the participants, making the transition from prison meant that they had to turn away from the friendships that they might have made while they were inside, in order to reorient themselves to the outside world. For example, Elizabeth expressed it this way when describing what happened when she returned to the facility to visit the friend that she had made during her time of incarceration:

> I made application to be able to go back in to visit her (laughs) and it was a while. And, the first time I went back in and passed through that gate,

I just knew they would never let me out again. There's no logic to it, but inside me, I was supposed to be there, and I didn't think they'd let me go back out when it was time. I was really glad to see my friend but it was very painful at the time I went there. I found that each time I would wait longer before the next visit, because it was so painful. I had no idea what was going on, but there was this real strange conflictive emotion. I stopped going completely. I even stopped writing to my friend. It had nothing to do with her. It was all this weird thing that was goin' on in my head. When she was released, then she did contact me, and our friendship was renewed tenfold. I haven't really said these things to her, but I know that she has friends there, I don't think she communicates with them at this point. I wonder if she's feeling there was something pulling her back, and she knew if she didn't break that, maybe she wouldn't be able to reach out here.

The friend that Elizabeth refers to is Sadie, also a study participant. As Elizabeth mentions, their friendship continued when Sadie was released after her much longer incarceration. They have continued to be a strong source of both practical and emotional support to each other. Sadie also perceived the conflict, however, between staying in touch with inmates or former inmates and the need to take care of herself. Sadie, who had been employed at several battered women's shelters in the first few years after her release from prison while continuing to be a role model and support for women on the inside, recalls:

I'll never forget that I was in prison, you know, I mean seven years of your life. That doesn't just go away. I kind of grew up there, too. I was like almost twenty-two when I went in, and I was thirty when I came out. But, there came a time when I needed to remove myself, and take one step farther away from when I was there and no longer working in battered women shelter was a part of that . . . I also quit goin' up to the prison. That was a positive thing for me. I had done what I could up to that point and realized that I didn't have anything else to give right then and that I really needed to take care of myself. I don't think that's a bad thing. I think it was a real good thing for me to recognize that. I think we all have somethin' to give.

Anita indicated that there is perhaps a difference between staying in touch with another ex-inmate and attempting to stay connected with other inmates. She said that she still corresponded with another ex-inmate whom she met while in prison, a woman who is "doin' real good." She also observed that the first time she was released, she used to write people in prison:

. . . and send 'em money and stuff, and I ended back in there. But, this time I didn't look back. I didn't write nobody. I didn't tell nobody I was gonna write 'em. I just kept on movin'.

Jeanette also expressed her need to use the support that she received from other inmates in recovery, and her willingness to risk violation of her supervision in order to maintain the contact she thinks vital to her sobriety. Ashley, of all the participants, was the most concerned about being violated for association, going so far as to express her concern about the possibility of being violated when she attended the participants' group meeting with other ex-inmates. Ashley stated:

> I mean, you just don't know people. You don't know what they've gone through. Like I was saying, if you meet somebody, you don't know if they've gone to jail for a bad check twenty years ago. That's an association, and it could probably get your parole taken away. That's the hardest thing for me, I think, And having gone through what I've gone through and not wanting to go through any more of it, I think I'm overcautious, but that's a good thing.

In the group meeting after the completion of the interviews, the issue of association was hotly debated among the participants. Although it was generally noted that ex-inmates could provide information and support to each other that promoted the woman's individual transition, some women felt that being able to associate with other inmates or former inmates depended on the individuals' having already managed some of her own transition so that they are not susceptible to criminal activities. Yet as one woman,[3] who had been incarcerated ten years prior to her release, expressed at the group meeting, that it was having these friends that had been so instrumental to her success:

> My close friends remain [the] people that I was locked up with. You know, we're doin' well. I couldn't have done without their support because I had been in for so long. When I came out and there were things that I had to deal with and my family didn't know what kind of advice to give, I would call them up and say, "Help, I've got such-and-so obstacle." They'd be like, "Okay, I went through this, and this is what you do." You know, if you want to get into trouble, you're gonna get into trouble. If you want to do well, you really need support, and I think that you have to network with the success stories, because seeing that they did okay and that they were succeeding gave me some hope, "Okay, well, they're doin' all right, so I think that I can do this."

There was no agreement among the women for when and how they believed ex-inmates should be allowed or perhaps encouraged to draw on each other's experience for managing the transition, but it is clearly an important issue for further exploration.

OTHER RELATIONSHIPS

As previously mentioned, Demi, Jeanette, and Elena noted that their counseling relationship with Mr. G. while residents at the Dismas House was crucial for them in recognizing that they could make different choices. Suzy discussed the importance of her counselor from the mental health center, who provided her the information and skills to better parent her son.

To maintain and grow the fragile seed of her sobriety, Mandi has surrounded herself with what she describes as "positive people," including her AA group, her church sponsor, and the boss from McDonald's who first noticed her potential as a manager. Mandi recalled something that a correctional officer told her while she was incarcerated that she believes is a good guideline for her life:

> "The company you keep will determine the trouble you're in." . . . I think that how I got in, that was the company I was keeping. They say in the program that if you hang out in a barber shop long enough, you're gonna get your hair cut. If you hang out in a dope house, you're gonna smoke dope. If you hang out in a bar, you're gonna drink. So, where you hang out and who you hang out with.

Common to these reflections about creating new relationships with professional helping people or other mentors is a sense of the women reaching for more real and honest approaches to engaging in relationships that contrasted markedly from the ways they related to others prior to their incarceration. Since studies confirm that women's criminal involvement often came through relationships with family members, significant others, or friends (Chesney-Lind 1997; Owen 1998), much as the participants in this study described, it is important to focus on how physical, sexual, and emotional exploitation and/or abuse and the lack of legitimate opportunities converge to provide a pathway to involvement with the criminal justice system.

BOUNDED RELATIONSHIPS

Not all relationships that women chose promoted their transition from prison.[4] Several of the women moved directly from prison or the Dismas House into live-in relationships with male partners (see Table 2.1). For both Ashley and Elena, this was a mistake. Ashley recalled that she was not ready for a relationship and had to move into her own place so she could better deal with the demands of her supervision and the need to become financially self-sufficient. Elena discussed an abusive relationship that she had with her now ex-boyfriend. She recalls that she initially moved in with him so she would not have to live at her mom's house:

> I was pregnant again, and—my boyfriend—my ex-boyfriend, we was livin' with each other. And, I think I jumped into that relationship too quick . . . he treated me just like (snaps fingers) worser than if I was in jail. It was really terrible with him. That was the worst year and a half that I spent after I got out of prison was when I was with him.

Elena continues:

> I quit workin' because I was about to have her, so after I had her, I stayed home and kept the house cleaned up. . . . If I would go somewhere, he would check the gas mileage. I went to my mom's house, and he was callin' every five minutes until I got home. It was really terrible with him. I never had no friends come over or nothin'. I think I got with him because I didn't want to go to my mom's house. I mean, I love my mother, don't get me wrong, but we're just two different people.

Elena related that when the abuse became physical, she sent him to jail. Since she was further along in her transition by this time, she was already in an apartment and connected to the resources she needed to support herself and her children, so she was better able to see other options.

> I just got tired of it. He hit me one time, that was back in September. I told him, "If you ever hit me, that would break up our relationship." And, I did. I sent him to jail, and we broke up.

However, managing the responsibilities of caring for four children alone, including an infant, has been a major challenge for Elena.

> Taking on the responsibilities with my children. I've never done that. I always let somebody else take care of 'em, and my mom always had 'em. I never really took the time out with 'em . . . and to pay bills and everything . . . when I was with him, I never thought I'd be a single mother, and now it's really hard—just me and the kids. It's really hard tryin' to get 'em everything they want, birthday parties and if it ain't Christmas, it's birthday parties, Easter and all these holidays in between and makin' sure they got everything they need and want.

Nan had a unique way of reframing what she had considered rejecting behavior of many of her family members and friends in the sense that they "kept (her) growin'." She recalls that it was perhaps the fact that she did not have support from expected sources that forced her to look to herself for support:

> My best friends and my family members, they kept me growin', because half of 'em turned on me. When I got home for Christmas this year, you know what I sent out? Thank you cards. Everybody got a thank you card from me from Alabama, to Tennessee, to Atlanta, Georgia, Indiana, all my relatives, families and friends. I was thankin' them for allowin' me to fall, not bein' there for me like I used to be there for them, so that I could get up and be the person that I am, because sometimes you can allow yourself to use people to be the crutch, and lean on 'em forever. But, when I went

to prison, they felt that I shamed them. They was embarrassed and, honey, I growed. I never had the chance to know that I could get up and didn't need you or didn't need him, or didn't have to accept this abuse or didn't have to be bothered with this. I never knew I couldn't do that. When I went there and was by myself, nobody but me, I realized, "Hey, I can do this." I did it for almost five years. Now, I can do it for the rest of my life. It finally hit 'em. As a matter of fact, when I came out, it was a big shocker to everybody. It was a new me. They thought that I was goin' to be bitter, but I wasn't. I made my mind up. I'm not gonna be bitter or angry.

Healing the pain of past abuse and betrayal as well as identifying family members who can promote participants' growth in the transition, although elusive for some of the women, is an ongoing process for most. A theme for those women who discussed how their relationships had changed since their release from prison was that they established boundaries about how people behaved toward them. For several women, asserting themselves sometimes meant that other friends perceived them as cold or unreachable.

Yet most study participants recognized that in order to maintain the growth they had experienced since their incarceration, they had to behave in a certain way to reflect a difference in the way they thought or felt about themselves. Nan, for example, felt that what some might describe as being "mean," she knew as being protective of what she has reestablished for herself and her family. In addition, the increased need for explicit boundaries with friends may also be a reflection of the extended surveillance Nan has felt by a system over which she has no control. She can control the intrusiveness of her friends and family into her privacy. She observes:

. . . they say "You so mean." But, I'm not—once you get to know me, you know that is just me. I'm not mean, I'm just straight. I don't go around the curve to get out what I got to say. So, once they get to know that, they understand, but even on the phone, I don't allow them to say, "Girl, where you goin'?" "What! Excuse me? I done had to tell where I was goin' for so many years, don't ask me where. I'm goin' out here to kill myself. Don't ask me where I'm goin'." I want to go without somebody knowin' where I'm goin'. It's not your business.

In a similar way Ashley identified her ability to assert herself, even if she has to sometimes temper her bluntness, as a strength that she never knew she could draw on when she was dependent on others to provide her material well-being.

Now I really say what I feel to people. Sometimes I have to say, 'Look, I'm not meaning to offend you, but this is how I feel or this is what we should do." It's made me more of a blunt person, but the people around me in my circle know exactly how I am, and they know that I will just say how I feel. But, if I'm around people that I may not know, I may have to phrase it differently, but it will still be more forward than the average person.

Nicole observed that some people who knew her before her incarceration believe her to be hard. She describes the hardness as emanating both from surviving incarceration and other difficult times, as well as a proactive need to protect herself from exploitive or abusive relationships as she has experienced them in the past.

I'm pretty much the same person I was before—a little bit older and a little bit wiser—I guess it's just part of growin' up and goin' through hard times and realizin' that things can get better, which they have for me in a lot of ways. I think I still relate to people the way I was before I was in—some people say I'm a little hard—I've been called an evil woman by an old friend. He said it was something about my eyes or somethin'. But, I said, "Well, when you've been where I have and gone through the things that I have, I learned to build a wall and it takes a lot to get through it." If I feel that somethin's not right, then I'm goin' the other direction. I woke up and realized had I not went there and went through the things I had, I don't think I'd be where I am today. I've just learned especially I wasn't goin' to get into relationships that I had been in before [incarceration] . . . if it meant bein' cold or building a wall around myself . . . that's what I would do, I wasn't goin' let anybody get in and hurt me or get me in the place I was before.

All of the women sought a balance between asserting their own rights and identifying how they can appropriately relate with others. Susan believed that she has learned how to communicate with friends about conflicts and this has made a major difference in how she manages her life since her incarceration. She reflects:

I believe if I wouldn't have found the things that are truly important to me and found ways to learn how to talk to people, instead of acting out all my anger, that I would have went back. There are things that people do now that I'm just "I'd like to hurt you." But I just tell 'em exactly what I think and how I feel about it. I feel better. They still come back around. You got to find new ways of dealing with things that really get you. I think a lot of people are in [prison] because they act out of reflexes and reactions instead of thinkin' about things.

Despite her sometimes blunt stance toward others, Susan feels that her relationships are better now because they are "honest." She believes that this authenticity in her relationships has also provided her with a dependable and mutual network of support that she has been able to draw on in challenging times.

I know I have stronger relationships now with friends than I ever had. I've always been a one or two person friend but I was too scared to get too close. And now I have more than that, and it's a bigger bond. Chris was in a real bad accident, he was in the hospital. All of our friends coming over, watching B., cooking dinners so I could stay in the hospital with him, they helped us through those four months. I can say honestly that none of my friends before would have done that. They'd have their own agenda and not anything that would include helping somebody else. It's just where I want honesty with people instead of trying to hide things.

A sense of dormancy and growth runs through these narratives. The women project a wisdom born of experience about how they must function in order to free themselves from correctional involvement and how they can address some of the embedded strains in their relationships. In addition, they discuss how they can use their power with others, not in a negative or exploitive way, but as a means of setting firm and respectful limits of what they will tolerate in their relationships. The willingness to choose new friends also reflects a deeper understanding of the potential of mutual relationships to nourish their growing sense of confidence and competence.

Finally, a recognition of women's psychological capacity to "build on and develop in a context of attachment and affiliation with others" (Miller 1976, 83) provides a template for developing tools for correctional programs and policies that strive to enhance this capacity for building mutual, caring, and empowering relationships. Healthy relationships become a crucial ingredient for a woman reconstructing her life after release from prison. The study participants reconstructed and used their relationships as the ground for emotional growth and healing and the blossoming of their ability to divest themselves of old disappointments and anger.

CHAPTER FIVE

IT COULD BE OTHERWISE

It has to be a combination. It's just like bakin' a cake. You can't leave
out the flour. You need all the ingredients to make it come out right.
—Denni, 1996

Two overarching, intertwined themes dominate the narratives of women's transition from prison.[1] First, women marshal external resources to meet concrete
needs. Second, the women's internal strengths and capabilities empower them to
transcend their former identity by nourishing their sense of survival and hope.
These themes are neither sequential nor hierarchical. They can be likened to the
life of the garden in which there is a continuous process of plowing, seeding,
fertilizing, weeding, and enjoying the blooms. The beauty of the garden is in the
anticipation, the variation, and the surprise, as well as the tending of the garden
through the various seasons of change and growth.

ADDRESSING THE STUDY QUESTIONS

The research questions guiding this study provided the structure for the interviews as well as a framework for the conceptualization of the findings.

1. *How did women exiting from prison initially establish a residence and address con-*
crete needs?

Women described multiple sources of concrete support and direct and indirect
paths to establishing their housing. Twelve of the eighteen participants were employed at the time of the interviews. The other women received Aid to Families
with Dependent Children[2] (Elena, Regina), Supplemental Security Insurance
(Margi), or unemployment compensation (Nan, Rene). Susan was attending

117

nursing school. Of the six, Rene and Susan had other income support from intimate partners, and Regina was partially supported by her parents. As the women discussed, it is difficult, if not impossible, to stay out of prison if an ex-inmate is not able to quickly establish a legal means of income to support her and often her children.

Of the studies that examine formerly incarcerated women, Jurik (1983) found that a consistent means of income support reduced repeated property type crimes, and Lambert and Madden (1976) found that women ex-offenders who demonstrated stable employment patterns were less likely to reoffend. In my study, having a means of legal income became a springboard for everything else that the women had to do in reestablishing themselves after prison. This finding converges with other literature that suggests much of women's criminal behavior is economically motivated (Carlen 1988; Chapman 1980). In addition to producing income, many of the women described other intangible benefits to their work such as a sense of personal reward and autonomy that accrues to demonstrating competence and confidence through work. Ashley's employment at the childcare center, Bernie's thrift store, and Suzy's junking, for example, also provided a means for the women to feel as though they were making a difference by contributing to making life easier for others.

Of the six women who were not employed at the time of the study, two had other family demands they had to address, two had newborn infants, and two were taking classes (GED and nursing) to further develop their employability. The two women with the newborn infants seemed the most detached from a consistent means of financial support: one has never had any job experience and is vague about her vocational goals; the other has been diagnosed with a mental disability.

Participants in the study generally followed two divergent paths for establishing a home for themselves. One path was followed by the women who first resided at Dismas House, a federal "community placement" where they served the remainder of their sentence prior to release. Although they were responsible for paying a percentage of their income for room and board, it was much less than they would have paid on the open market for both rent and food expenses. The period of residence at Dismas House, usually six months, provided these women the time to obtain employment and save money for acquiring a house after their release to the community.

The second path of reentry was that traveled by the women under state parole supervision who were released to the community directly from prison. These women depended on family members, friends, and, occasionally, the kindness of strangers to assist them in obtaining a residence. For these women, the initial residences they chose were often temporary and problematic. They were more likely to bounce from place to place before they found an affordable and safe residence.

2. *How did women's relationships support or inhibit their process of reentry?*

Although the participants described their need to have autonomy for making choices guiding their everyday lives, they also identified the need to feel connected to and affirmed by others. Keeping in mind women's developmental needs (Chodorow 1989; Gilligan 1982; Jordan et al. 1991; Katz et al. 1993; Miller 1976) and their position in the social structure (Faith 1993; Rosaldo 1974; Schaef 1992), I studied the network of people that the women described and uncovered two common threads that appeared in almost every woman's story: the centrality of relationships to the women's lives and the struggle for instrumentality or empowerment within those relationships.

One element of frustration for the eighteen women in the study lay in their struggle to remake their relationships, particularly with their mothers, or to connect with significant others in the hope of moving toward empowering development and ongoing support. Some of the women had suffered severe losses of relationships, and some had experienced prolonged pain and disconnection in relationships, some had very long histories of abuse endured in either family or intimate relationships. Twelve women committed the crime for which they were incarcerated with, or for, a family member, an intimate partner, or someone else with whom they had an unspecified relationship.

The women's struggles to maintain and repair relationships were individualistic and complex. Because women had previously attempted to sustain relationships by meeting the unrealistic and sometimes harmful expectations of family members and significant, though often abusive or exploitive, partners, a major part of new relational strategies tended to focus on two aspects of relationships. The first was having a focus on self in relationship to others rather than a self defined only by relationships with others. In examining of the ways women developed in the context of relationships, researchers at the Stone Center at Wellesley College (Jordan et al 1991) found that mutual empathy is the mechanism by which contacts become affirming and growth-enhancing connections. Miller (1982) offered a working definition of power that has great relevance to this particular group of women's experiences as "the capacity to produce change" (2). According to this conceptualization, a woman gains a sense of her own power as she develops her ability to produce change or movement in another in the context of mutually empathetic relationships. The participants demonstrated "mutual empathy" by talking about the focus on their own needs and aspirations, determining limits on what they would tolerate in their relationships, continuing to bring "new" and affirming relationships into their lives, and describing ways in which they were able to reciprocate in relationship with others.

The second aspect of relationship building had to do with the willingness of the women to elicit assistance through their relationships with professionals, recovering people, ex-inmates, and peers for the information, support, and skills they needed to normalize some of the initial feelings of alienation. These mentors reflected a rootedness in reality and exemplified survival and growth as a possibility to the women. The women also looked for such support to decrease their sometimes overwhelming sense of powerlessness in handling the challenges during various points of the transition. The participants commonly felt that relationships with ex-inmates could be a source of support and affirmation. This was qualified, however, by both an understanding of the parole condition prohibiting such contacts and the woman's own sense of self-preservation.

An additional source of complexity in the women's relationships lay in how they retained contact with their children while incarcerated, and decisions they made about custody of their children after release. Most writers about women's incarceration recognize that separation from children is the source of much of the pain that women experience while incarcerated. Zalba (1964) noted that the woman's separation from her children and the concomitant major change in her role as mother strikes at her personal identity and her self-image as a woman. Participants in the study who were mothers of minor children discussed this particular aspect of the incarceration and how they dealt with it in detail.

Schulke (1993) found in her study of recidivism among women that the threat that women would lose custody of their children after their release from prison constrained the women from further criminal behaviors. I found, however, that reunification with children is not a major indicator of success in the transition.

Five of the participants in the study chose to not regain either legal or physical custody of their children after release from prison, preferring to leave their children with family members because it was more financially advantageous for the child or children. The decisions to relinquish physical custody of their children or, in one case, to allow the woman's parents to adopt her child, reflected a pragmatic reality that they did not have the financial resources that would enable them to support their children. In addition, they did not usually have the personal emotional support at the time of their release to resume the role of primary caretaker.

Most important to the women, consistent with other studies of the effects of the mother's incarceration on children (Beckerman 1989; Bloom and Steinhart 1993; Johnston 1995; McCarthy 1980), is having the means to reestablish and/or nourish their relationships with children while they are incarcerated and then have access to regular visitation with their children after they are released. In only two cases in this study were women not yet able to regain regular visitation, one because her fourteen-year-old son was in the custody of an ex-husband and in the other because the child, diagnosed with mental retardation, remained in another state's custody.

Two of the women in the study delivered infants during their incarceration. Wooldredge and Masters (1993) note the difficulties that incarcerated mothers of newborn children often face. In my study, one of the women had to release her baby to her mother after birth and did not see the baby again for thirteen months when she was released. The other woman's sister moved to the town where she was incarcerated, so that the woman was able to maintain contact with the infant, as well as with her four other children.

The relationships that women develop with their children are often an integral aspect of their progress in the transition. The actual outcome of reunification with children, however, is shaped by how the woman has resolved issues related to how she parented prior to incarceration, as well as financial and emotional factors that affect her ability to support them after her release.

3. *What are the internal or individual elements that facilitate or inhibit women's processes of reestablishing themselves after release from prison?*

Women in the study used institutional treatment programs that were available to them, but they also found ways to informally pursue opportunities for introspection and growth. The specific programs that women described as facilitating their progress in the transition included individual psychotherapy, a milieu-type drug treatment program,[3] a battered women's education support group, parenting classes, and an intensive group-based approach to childhood and adult abuse.

When women related their success in completing these programs, they recalled that it was the programs' facilitators who had the most influence on their ability to benefit from the programs. One woman described the volunteers who conducted the battered women's group as "friends"; she made use of this relationship for both employment and temporary shelter when she was released. Another woman recalled that the facilitators of the drug treatment program enabled her to be honest about ambivalent feelings toward her drug use.

Fletcher et al. (1993) found that drug offenders will return to criminal patterns of behavior after release unless their addiction is addressed while in prison. Seven of the participants were incarcerated on drug charges, yet only three women discussed treatment they had while incarcerated or after their release.

Pollock-Byrne (1990) reported from her survey of prisons that programs that help women learn better parenting skills or increase and better utilize the women's visitation time with children were in high demand by women inmates. Only two participants of the fourteen who had minor children while incarcerated reported involvement with parenting programs, both in state facilities.

In order to avoid what Jose-Kampfner (1990) describes as a sort of existential death, and others have referred to as institutionalization or prisonization, most of the women discussed other means that they used to promote their growth during incarceration. These included reading books, self-directed learning, writing letters, spiritual practices, physical workouts, and developing hobbies and skills.

Finally, participants discovered meaning for their lives that they attributed to the prison experience itself. Whether it was because they could imagine that a worst fate could have happened to them, such as death, or the fact that they had been able to survive traumas they experienced while incarcerated, they described an aspect of growth in which they found meaning for their lives during the transition from prison.

Frankl (1992) describes this type of expression as "tragic optimism." From the stories of concentration camp survivors as well as others who have suffered and survived horrible tragedies, he uses this notion of optimism to describe a view of human potential "which at its best always allows for: (1) turning suffering into a human achievement and accomplishment; (2) deriving from guilt the opportunity to change oneself for the better; and (3) deriving from life's transitoriness an incentive to take responsible action" (140). The fact that formerly incarcerated women, although different from concentration camp survivors in that they were found guilty of a crime against the social order rather than on the basis of being a member of an oppressed group, could recognize the meaning that the incarceration sparked in their lives, speaks to this idea of transformation in the face of sometimes, overwhelming challenges.

4. *What are the specific structural elements that facilitate or inhibit women's processes of reestablishing themselves after release from prison?*

The educational and vocational needs of incarcerated women are urgent, given that work often provides a lifeline for these women and the children they support. Prison programs fall into five major categories: institutional maintenance; education; vocational training; rehabilitative programs; and medical care.

Participants in this study acquired their General Education Diploma (GED), completed classes in clerical work, horticulture, keypunching skills, and computer applications. Women were employed in a range of jobs for both institutional maintenance such as dorm maintenance and food preparation, and vocational skills development such as offset printing and parts assembly. Most of the women who were involved in such activities reported that they had been somewhat helpful in their acquiring employment on release from prison. The most tangible gain that women acquired from employment during incarceration was saving money that could be used for expenses they had when they were released.

The difference between vocational skill-building programs offered to inmates in the state system and those in the federal system was notable; the women described programs offered in the federal system as much more varied and at a higher level of potential compensation. Nan, a federal ex-inmate, related that she worked as a pipe fitter and had been able to acquire her real estate license as well as a nurse's aid certificate during her almost five years of incarceration.[4]

Historically, turn-of-the century reformers in women's prisons were most concerned about returning women to the community as morally fit wives and mothers (Feinman 1994; Rafter 1990). Numerous researchers have indicated that the few programs available to women in prison are still concentrated in sex-stereotyped fields such as cosmetology, food service, laundry, housekeeping, clerical work, and keypunch operation that are compensated at low wages (Glick and Neto 1977; Moyer 1984; Muraskin 1989; Pollock-Byrne 1990).

5. *How do parole or supervision processes and/or conditions affect women's ability to negotiate their reentry after completion of incarceration?*

Women in the study frequently described the parole or supervision process as "doing what I have to do." The process was facilitated by parole officers, most of whom the women described as promoting their transition, despite the intrusion and control that they represented in their everyday lives.

Women wanted to know the rules and expectations of the parole or supervision process. Some women were frustrated because they felt that parole officers sometimes transgressed their privacy in the name of supervision or the overwhelming nature of the expectations placed on them. Mandi, in particular, represented the extreme example of the expectations that some women have to address: in order to both complete parole and meet demands for regaining custody of her children, she had to manage a number of treatment conditions, report to her parole officer regularly, and work two jobs to generate enough income to rent a house large enough for her and her four children. Initially, she did this without a car!

Harris (1993) suggests that the imposition of "needs-based" conditions, which she defines as those that derive from perceptions of women's needy and complex life situations, results in unfair and unequal extension of coercion of women during parole. Erez's (1992) study of parole officers' decision-making found that the more objectively determined areas of needs did not differ between male and female parolees, but identified significant differences in the factors used by parole officers to arrive at their classification and treatment decisions. Erez reported that, for male parolees, the risk level was the more important determinant of "need." In accordance with gender-role expectations, women's needs were seen as being linked to relational indicators such as marital status and associations. In addition, Erez (1992) found that with respect to attitudes, parole officers felt criminal orientation was not an appropriate female role; women, unlike men, were not expected to be hostile or belligerent. Thus, a change in negative attitudes is perceived as important for female parolees but not for males. Some women in my study displayed negative attitudes about parole or supervision expectations that they felt were unfair or inexplicable.

Many of the women also described positive relationships they developed with their parole or supervision officer.

Harris (1993) concludes her critique of "needs-based" sanctioning by suggesting that sanctions or conditions should be parsimoniously applied and only related to expectations that women obey the law. She believes that controlling elements as reflected in other more arbitrary and treatment-type responses are antithetical to an affirmative stance toward women that would facilitate their reintegration after incarceration.

6. *What did women identify as necessary for making it in the free world that could be applied to the benefit of others currently in the transition from prison?*

The major recommendations that women suggested included the following: (a) women need to begin the process of identifying sources of support prior to leaving prison; (b) women need to address issues of abuse and addiction that may prevent them from recognizing their ability to manage the transition; (c) representatives of the correctional system need to treat women with respect and believe in their potential to transform themselves, and provide training for employment at living wages when released; (d) association with other ex-inmates can be a source of support—it should not be an automatic risk for violating a woman on parole or supervision; (e) helping professionals should be educated about the range of needs that women coming out of prison have to face and work with women to define strategies for meeting those needs; (f) the general public, particularly potential employers, should be educated about female offenders and their motivation to succeed, so that they are given an opportunity to (re)establish themselves.

The previous section included a discussion of the findings in the context of other research regarding women's developmental issues and women's recidivism. The following section proposes a conceptual framework for assessing women's transition from prison based on these findings.

AN EMPOWERMENT FRAMEWORK FOR ASSESSING WOMEN'S TRANSITION FROM PRISON

In earlier chapters, I discussed the experience of transition from prison based on the review of related literature. Figure 5.1 presents a framework that also incorporates an understanding of how women in this study describe the external resources and internal resiliencies that the study participants drew on for coping with obstacles during the incarceration and since their release.

In this framework, relationships with parole officers and with family members are also included to reflect the importance of these relationships for assisting women during tough times. The model reflects the overlapping nature of sources of support in the environment as well as the permeability between and among the categories identified as most salient to the transition. The key

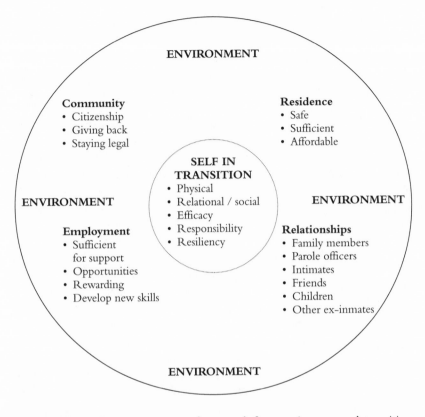

FIGURE 5.1.   An empowerment framework for assessing women's transition from prison.

point is that each woman found a starting point for her transition, sometimes in the way she coped with the incarceration itself, sometimes in the ways she renegotiated family roles and relationships, sometimes in how she managed her obligations of parole or supervision, and sometimes in the way she was able to recreate her role with her children. From that starting point, then, as several of the women described, there was a synergistic effect of other good things happening in their lives that fostered a feeling of hope for the future. Elizabeth captures the image of the snowballing effect of "doing things right" that suggests a readiness for making changes from an internal perspective.

> Once that momentum of doin' things right starts goin' it starts snowballing, and things start coming to you in huge bundles. Really good people just seem to get drawn into your circle. I would like for them to understand there are certain things that you—that I went through, and I'm assuming they're kind of normal feelings: the fear, the anger, and that after

a time, some of those will kind of withdraw, and then, if you can get past the fear and the anger, and if you can start doing things the way they ought to be done . . . after a while things just start rolling so good, and you can stand back and say, "Whoa, I don't even have to do anything, and things good start comin' to me." I wish they could know that, because I know that some of 'em feel like they can never come out of that pit.

If there is a sequential or temporal order to the process of transition, this study indicates that it begins with the woman herself as an active participant in the social world rather than a passive object, acted on by the forces in and around her. Most of the women in the study described how they took responsibility for the decisions they had made, and chose to make use of the incarceration both to bolster their internal strengths and resilience and to amass other external resources they could use after their release.

The reasons women chose more efficacious behavior at the time of their most recent incarceration remain elusive. For some, it may have been a cumulative effect; as one woman put it, she just got "sick and tired of being sick and tired." For others, especially those for whom the incarceration was the first of their lives, the unexpected seriousness and pain of the consequence, especially as indicated by those women incarcerated for federal drug convictions, may have had a lasting effect.

The ways women described managing the prison environment set the stage for how they dealt with the transition. In the institution, basic needs are met and the inmates' schedule for everyday life is fixed. The interaction that women experience in prison constitutes the relationships they build and/or maintain with other inmates, correctional staff, and, to a lesser degree, friends, family members, and intimate partners from the outside world.

As the women noted, when they exited prison, they had to adjust to new responsibilities and a loss of routine. And they were almost immediately faced with the need to find a residence and a way to support themselves by legal means. It is in this interaction between the self and the environment that the transition is situated. How the ex-inmate makes choices for what she can do and where she can be, the types of relationships she brings into her life, and the ways in which they are bounded, and finally, the management of the multiple expectations that she faces, determine her capacity to begin a cycle of efficacy that is self-perpetuating and reinforcing of her desire to assert a noncriminal identity.

Although the process of transition as reflected by the women's experiences indicates that it may begin with the motivational strength of the woman herself, it is generated within an environment that actively promotes or discourages the process by virtue of the resources she can access along the way. The most immediate and necessary physical resources that must be facilitated include those of meeting the need for safe and affordable shelter and securing sufficient and rewarding employment.

The two nonphysical factors, relationships and community, refer to the ways in which women create and maintain supportive relationships and feel connected to the community in which they live. The participants in this study recognized the restorative power of the human bond and sought to connect with people with whom they could have shared goals and a healthy interdependence. In addition, they attempted to address some of the disconnections of previous relationships.

Further, women reported how they had given back or contributed to others, both through their immediate relationships, but also to the community in a more generalized way. Pinderhughes (1994) and Gutiérrez and Lewis (1999) discuss community in terms of power and empowerment that derives from a person's ability to make a home for herself in the world, feel included as a citizen, and have the personal agency to effect change in the immediate environment. These women's perceptions of others' labeling them or stereotyping them due to their criminal record reflected their desire to transcend the "ex" identity (Ebaugh 1984, 1988) to express a noncriminal self through their efforts.

The empowerment framework (Figure 5.1) provides a means for practitioners to assess a woman's progress in the transition by helping her identify intrapersonal, interpersonal, and social sources of efficacy and empowerment that promote reintegration after release from prison.

PRACTICE IMPLICATIONS

As an increasing number of women are separated from society as a consequence of mostly property and drug-related crimes, they will continue to return to a society that has in many ways already given up on them. Social workers, parole officers, and counselors who provide social services on the front lines in prisons, community corrections centers, and probation and parole offices see ex-incarcerated women who may seem, at first glance, overwhelmed and overwhelming, lost in the realities of reestablishing a life from the little that life has given them. The following is a listing of the major implications derived from the women's accounts that provide suggestions for interventions.[5]

1. *"Don't be clinical": finding a safe outlet or source of support for expressing and normalizing feelings about how women experience the transition.*

Despite the current tide toward standardization of practices in the interests of cost containment, the women in this study clearly stated that they wanted to be seen as unique, not like others, with an assortment of particular needs to address and a reservoir of strengths and skills from which they could draw. They needed to be recognized as persons of worth, reflecting more than the label of "ex-inmate" would indicate about their capacity to make it after release from incarceration.

When participants discussed professional helpers who made a difference in their transition, especially in the ways in which they saw the meaning of their experiences, they described individuals who were willing to suspend their "book knowledge" and empathically enter their real-life worlds. Although Elena had served her sentence, it was Mr. G., the ex-inmate drug counselor at Dismas House who most influenced her to stop using drugs. Jeanette spoke of the drug counselors who enabled her while she was in forced sobriety during incarceration to be honest about her struggle regarding her drug addiction and look at its effect in her life. Demi said over and over that it was the people who were "not clinical" who most assisted her, meaning that they related to her in an authentic and caring way. Many of the participants expressed a need to be understood and, as this study demonstrated, listening to the ex-inmate as the expert on her experiences is an important place to begin gaining the empathy necessary for appreciating how best to assist ex-inmates.

The challenge for helping professionals is to play a balancing and co-nurturing role in the reconstruction of the internal self and the development of the external supports for each ex-inmate. In this facilitative role, it may mean that sometimes the helper is more engaged in assisting the woman to find the concrete resources she needs; at other times the helper may play a more reflective role in making visible and affirming unseen strands of growth.

2. *A place of my own: Women in transition from prison require an affordable place to start from where they can exercise autonomy and identify ongoing support and resources for meeting basic needs.*

Having a home—a place to be—is a taken-for-granted part of structuring our daily lives. For women returning to the free world, identifying a place to live provides a starting point of developing an enabling niche (Taylor 1997) from which they can facilitate the transition. In this study, obtaining a residence was also related to identifying and using resources that enabled the woman to maintain shelter for themselves and possibly their children.

Maintaining shelter is a challenge for most women coming directly to the community from the institution because they often have no financial resources to reestablish themselves, and they are faced with multiple and complex expectations about completing parole or supervision and retrieving responsibilities, primarily for the care of their children. Social workers and other helping professionals can work with the correctional system as well as other advocates to establish community-based halfway houses that could provide the kind of "protected environment" that women described as needing on their way out of the institution to the community. The halfway house model will be discussed further under correctional policies, as commitment to its use and support must be made on the policy level.

3. *Healing disconnections: Women in transition from prison both depend on and negotiate their relationships with family members.*

Many of the women in this study, not unlike a high percentage of women in prison nationwide, had lengthy and complex histories of abuse that they experienced as children and as adults in their relationships with family members and intimate partners. In this study, although women discussed some incidence of physical abuse with ex-partners, it was the abuse by family members that they described as having much more of an impact. In addition, several of the women committed the crime for which they were convicted with a family member; others related that they began their substance use in their families as children or adolescents.

Almost all the women, however, discussed the importance of both healing fractured relationships with family members and, if necessary, remaining physically separate from family members until they had regained some emotional well-being. Rene, for example, was certain that her ability to let go of the pain she had experienced from being sexually abused as a child, despite some family discomfort, enabled her to recognize the pattern of choices she had made in her life as an adult.

Social workers and counselors can provide a safe place for women to begin discussing some of the previous issues related to the abuse, but, more important, helping professionals can aid women in understanding the enormity of what they have to address in negotiating their current relationship with family members. In addition, since ex-inmates often have had to depend on family members for care of children during and sometimes since the incarceration, and for financial support in order to meet basic needs, learning how to maintain both autonomy and reciprocity is an important component of deriving efficacy in managing relationships.

4. *Resuming the mothering/parenting role.*

Incarcerated women are far more likely than incarcerated men to be the emotional and financial providers of children prior to incarceration. Thus, one of the greatest differences in stresses for women and men serving time is that the separation from children is generally a much greater hardship for women than for men. In addition, Bloom and Steinhart (1993) found that over half of the mothers in their study of incarcerated women in California reported that their children had never visited them in prison, with the most cited reason being the great distance between the children's home and the prison facility.

The women in this study reported that prison visitation with their children was often blocked by the children's caretaker (usually the woman's mother), due to the difficulty of facilitating the visit and sometimes the caretaker's anger toward the inmate. The federal facilities in which inmates are housed are often located at a great distance from the participant's homes[6] and so, with the exception of Nan who, with her sister's assistance, moved her children to the town in which she was incarcerated, the women reported that they only saw their children once or twice during their incarceration. State ex-inmates reported being able to see their children more often, but this depended on the caretaker's willingness to transport the children to the prison facility for visitation. Continued parenting of children from prison was reportedly mediated by women's unresolved feelings of guilt regarding their relationships with their children prior to their incarceration, the stress that they observed visitation in the institution causes due to the intense surveillance of visitors, and, further, by the woman's own need to detach from events in the family that she couldn't manage or control.

Many women in the study stated that their children were the source of much of their motivation for getting out of prison and their desire to make it in the free world. However, there were several participants who had not yet been able to regain custody of their children or who had made the decision to not regain legal custody of their children. It was important to these women that their children were cared for by someone they trusted, that they had regular visitation, and that they could justify their decision so they did not feel stigmatized for putting the child's best interests over their own or for not meeting societal role expectations.

Practitioners should address both the separation issues of incarcerated mothers and their children and actively identify community resources that will facilitate the incarcerated woman's continued contact with her children so she can regain her parenting role on release in a more gradual process that may be more supportive of both mother and child. Nan, one of the two mothers who delivered an infant while incarcerated, had her children cared for nearby, and she was able to see the infant and her older children regularly. Elena gave up her infant (as well as three other children) to her mother shortly after delivery, and did not see the baby until her release thirteen months later. Elena reported feeling much more stressed about the responsibility of raising her children after her release than did Nan, who had regular visitation with her children that enabled her to develop a bond with her infant and make some parenting decisions while she was incarcerated.

5. *Reaching inside, reaching out: advocating for individual and systemic change.*

Former incarcerated women, from their perspective, often did not have even minimal physiological, safety, and security needs met while they were incarcerated. Maslow (1970) indicated that lower level needs generally have to be met before the higher level needs of belongingness and love, esteem, and self-actualization are met.

In situations when individuals were deprived of health care, isolated from family members and other loved ones, and victimized by efforts to rob them of their dignity, they survived. Throughout the stories, themes of challenge and nourishment abound. It leads one to wonder whether some individuals survive, not because their lower level needs are met, but because their higher needs are met, giving them strength and inner reserves to compensate for basic physiologic and safety reserves needs that are not met. In a time of changing resources for meeting basic needs, it is an important challenge to professional helpers to work toward marshaling external resources, but also support women's internal movement toward growth and reconnection, joining with them during times of disruption and crisis to discover sources for well-being.

Just as it may be difficult for incarcerated women to identify the sources of efficacy within the correctional environment, social workers may also be challenged within this host setting. As Severson (1994) notes, "(T)here are few areas where ideologies are as varied and controversial as in the field of corrections" (452). Social workers generally aspire to recognizing the primacy of the client on the cornerstone value of self-determination, while the correctional system operates under a very different set of priorities and values. Severson argues that social workers must perform a balancing act to meet their ethical obligations to both inmates and the institution.

There is, however, some commonalty in purpose and outcome between social work and corrections. Both systems deliver services that are meant to influence or cause change in behavior that is dysfunctional for the individual and society. The model that guides the delivery of services is very different. However, an expected or hoped-for goal of the intervention is that people be enjoined from violating the law. Social workers can attempt to find ways to enter into the correctional system to identify where common goals can contribute to women's efficacy during incarceration and after release.

Severson (1994) also suggests that "mental health services must be delivered to inmates with the same vigor that other institutional services are delivered" (452). The fact that Mandi, when she was distraught over the loss of her children by virtue of their potential adoption by her mother, could see a counselor who not only talked with her about the crisis, but also called and obtained accurate information for regaining custody calmed Mandi's fears. Crisis intervention and ongoing counseling should also be available and accessible to women during the transition at low cost, and without stigma.

Study participants indicated that they did not believe many social workers understand the enormity of what women face coming out of prison. As social workers become more informed, they can normalize feelings, identify financial and other resources that will assist ex-inmates, work with women to review their readiness for taking on their parenting role, advocate for the extension of mental health resources, and pursue alternatives to incarceration for women offenders.

Social work practices must be designed in concert with correctional policies that are proactively redirected to facilitating women's movement out of the correctional system into legitimate roles in society. Chapin (1995) suggests that a strengths perspective (Saleebey 1997), which recognizes the strengths and resources of people and their environments, can be brought to bear on social policy formulation. One outcome of social workers bringing a theoretical base of practice to correctional policy formulation would be a more inclusive and expanded array of empowering policy options for responding to women in conflict with the law at different junctures of decision-making.

Finally, it is important to consider briefly some possibly unintended consequences of programming and/or the greater intrusion of social work within correctional environments. The control exerted by correctional institutions, and prisons in particular, is overt in nature. Control is also exerted through covert means, for example, via the disciplinary power described by Foucault (1977) and exercised in the process of monitoring and regulating behavior by social service agencies. Social workers must be cautious about building and implementing programs that see the woman offender as the entire source and cure of their problems. Such an approach contradicts the empowerment theory discussed earlier that contextualizes women's actions within multiple and interacting systems of personal efficacy, interpersonal competence, and social access to resources. What is required is to design programs to establish greater equality between providers and participants. Participants, for example, could be encouraged to make program rules and be actively encouraged to formally evaluate the program and program providers. Social workers could also facilitate linking women to free world advocates or support organizations for post-release assistance.

IMPLICATIONS FOR CORRECTIONAL POLICIES

When a woman is incarcerated, her children must be placed with family members or strangers, she may lose her home if she has one, or she loses any legal source of income that she may have. She will usually leave prison with even greater financial liabilities than when she entered, not the least of which is a prison record.

While a woman is in prison, she may rely on her old networks for financial support. Depending on the type of facility, it may not provide for personal hygiene products, postage and writing materials, telephone charges, or snack foods. Women accrue debts to outside friends and family members who support them and their children while they are in prison and they are expected to pay those debts when released. Incarceration may serve only to entrench some women more deeply in a life of abusive relationships, hustling, and violations related to drug use and sales. The following sections describe recommended policies to address the pre-release segment of incarceration, public support for graduated de-institutionalization, and finally, decarceration of nonviolent offenders.

FREE WORLD ATTITUDE

As Sadie noted, formerly incarcerated women are out in the world, as "your neighbors, co-workers, and friends." Women, who commit only a small percentage of violent crimes that require long-term separation for the protection of society, are released from prison after serving an average of less than three years.

Promoting women's reintegration (and rehabilitation) can begin from the day they enter the institution[7] and could be reflected in both attitudes and daily practice. What I call a "free world attitude" should color every programming decision, every interaction with corrections staff, every classification decision, and so on. That attitude would include doing everything possible to assist women to maintain contacts with positive people in their support system or to help them identify and develop new free world contacts. It might include allowing women to wear their own clothes to foster a sense of dignity and pride in appearance especially during the period immediately prior to release. It would include doing everything possible to promote the woman's relationship with her children. It would support women healing relationships with their family members. And it would include the type of role rehearsal that allows women to practice being "ex"-inmates before they exit the institution (Ebaugh 1988).

Policies that further reflect a free world attitude would widen the scope of rehabilitation services to address the multiple and complex needs of incarcerated women. As many of the women indicated, the time they had to reflect in prison was an uncomfortable but profound period for taking stock of their lives. It is also an opportunity for addressing a range of problems that many of the women expressed that they had experienced, and received little treatment for addressing, including substance abuse, previous trauma, and challenges in interpersonal relationships. In addition to more extensive mental health and emotional support services (women reported that they generally could not have access to mental health services until and unless they were exhibiting an extreme set of symptoms), policies need to be implemented to support educational and vocational skill building programs that will enable women to gain employment that will pay living wages.

Women who participated in education courses in prison usually praise them. However, despite the impressive array of subjects provided at some institutions, the majority of women inmates, as reported by some of the women in the study, cannot take advantage of them because of eligibility criteria. Furthermore, due to recently enacted federal legislation,[8] inmates can no longer apply for federal Pell grants or subsidized loans to pay for college classes. Prison administration usually only offer classes to prepare inmates for taking the GED, which three of the study participants obtained.

Policies that address these concerns include both providing an assessment of each woman's vocational and educational skills and interests when she enters the system, and then developing an individualized plan with each woman that would identify resources in the institution and in the community where she will return that could develop her skills for income-producing employment. Further, policies should address the continuing inequity of vocational training opportunities offered to women as compared to men.

Programs that focus specifically on pre-release for women are few and inconsistently offered. The Kansas Department of Corrections, for example, provided a "pre-release reintegration" ten-week program from 1984 to 1989 to women that included modules on the development of specific life skills. A department spokesperson reported that it was a successful program but the administration canceled it when it became too expensive to manage for the smaller number of female releases.

Currently, the job training offerings at the women's facility in Kansas are more limited than they were at the time that most of the study participants were incarcerated. When all female inmates were moved to one location in the state in March 1995, the minimum custody women who had been working at the private prison industry that benefitted Sadie and Susan were transferred to the new site and so lost those jobs. At the new facility, female inmates could work with a smaller private industry but it employed fewer inmates and at less than full-time hours for lower wages.

The Federal Prison Industries (UNICOR) has as its primary mission the "productive employment of inmates" and reportedly provides a variety of job skills and opportunities to gain useful experience that women can draw on for gaining post-prison employment.[9] Nan attributed much of her success, both in coping with the day-to-day frustrations of prison life, and in getting resettled in the free world after more than seven years of incarceration, to the fact that she came out with $8,000 in savings from her employment. Given that so many women enter prison, having been unemployed or underemployed, it is important to examine how employment during incarceration creates opportunities whereby women can contribute to the costs of their incarceration, develop job skills and experience, and save money toward the costs of reintegration.

GRADUATED DEINSTITUTIONALIZATION: THE HALFWAY HOUSE

Consistent with the need for women to have a safe and affordable place to restart their lives, a halfway house offers initial support in the transition. The women of this study had contrasting attitudes, however, about the idea of the halfway house, depending on whether or not the woman had resided at Dismas House prior to her release to the community. Only Denni attributed her progress during the transition to having resided at Dismas House. All of the state ex-inmates discussed the need for a halfway house that would provide women the kind of start-up time purportedly offered by Dismas House

Dismas House participants were more able to meet basic needs in the community because of the time they did not have to assume full responsibilities for themselves or their children, and because they obtained employment shortly after their arrival at the halfway house. Yet five of the six women who had come out to the community from the Dismas House[10] complained about inflexible rules and a controlling structure. A rehabilitative element is built into the structure of the House, and it was the substance abuse program in particular that appealed to the study participants who had resided at Dismas House. Despite what most of the former residents found controlling and difficult to manage, staff at Dismas House reported a very low recidivism rate for women who had resided there (Personal Communication, Nan Lorenz, November 17 1996).

When ex-inmates who had not resided at Dismas House discussed their idea of a halfway house, it was fairly consistent with what the federal ex-inmates described. The major difference seemed to be in who made and enforced the rules. For example, the state-released women thought that there should be rules in the program, but that it would feel more supportive if those rules were enforced by people they could trust because they "had been there" (ex-inmates). Other important aspects of a supportive type of halfway house included staff members who could facilitate job placement and the exclusive use of the house by former women inmates.

There are a number of models for halfway houses for women that have been implemented, sometimes used both as alternative sentencing placements and for women in transition from prison to the community (Austin et al. 1992). Common to these programs is an emphasis on clear goals, consistent admission criteria, diversified financial base, evaluation of client outcomes, and responsiveness to client needs. A former inmate established one of the most successful programs, Our New Beginnings in Portland, Oregon. This program incorporates a balanced mix of ex-inmates and professional staff to deliver comprehensive services designed to meet the diverse needs of women.

Drug abuse among women is a serious problem for the criminal justice system. Without treatment, most of the women currently incarcerated will continue abusing drugs and committing crimes. As some of the women in this study indicated, they were involved in either in-prison treatment or the Dismas House recovery group that enabled them to become free of their addiction. Mandi's relapse demonstrated that maintaining sobriety in the face of overwhelming demands and stresses is very difficult during the transition.

Currently, the availability of treatment for women offenders falls far short of what is needed, and the treatment that is available does not necessarily offer the array of required services. In their nationwide survey of community-based and corrections-based treatment programs, Prendergast and colleagues (1995) emphasize the need for ancillary services that complement drug treatment. Covington's (1999) gender-specific model for recovery offers additional support for treating women's needs in a comprehensive fashion. Although treatment during the time the woman is in custody can be a first step, it is when she is released that it is even more crucial to invest funds in treatment and recovery programs that broadly address women's needs, provide care for infants or children, and coordinate aftercare services.

The women in this study expressed both a desire and an active commitment to making changes in their lives, despite the difficulties of incarceration and the sometimes overwhelming nature of parole/supervision after their release. A recognition by the correctional system of this commitment would be a beginning step toward the development of community-based alternatives to incarceration, as well as exploring the extensive needs of women that they have to address in the transition from prison to the free world.

ALTERNATIVE SENTENCING

The fact that so many women are serving prison sentences for crimes related to drug addiction and property offenses concerns anyone who cares about the human and financial costs of social policies. Most of the women who participated in the study should have been candidates for alternative sentencing programs due to the fact that half did not have a previous incarceration and only four were convicted of a crime against a person. These programs are nonexistent in many states and limited on the federal level by more stringent sentencing guidelines.

Some of the alternative sentences that are currently in use would possibly mean failure for these women. Many alternative sentences involve restitution, paying back the victim or the state for the cost of the crime. Although there was a range of educational and vocational backgrounds among the women in this sample, a good number of them were underemployed or unemployed before their incarceration. They would likely be unable to make restitution.

Another popular form of alternative sentence is the use of house arrest and electronic monitoring. This might be a viable way for some women to serve the time while remaining at home with their children if they have homes and if adequate provisions were made for income maintenance and drug treatment. One of the women in the study served about eight months of her sentence wearing an electronic bracelet by which she could be continuously monitored. She found it embarrassing, but not nearly as controlling as the "boot camp" where she had been incarcerated for eight months. One problem that has been indicated with such policies might be the presence in the home of abusive or addicted partners who could induce a woman to violate her sentencing restrictions and/or threaten her with violence.

Some alternative sentencing programs require a specific amount of time performing community service. Although this could also be an appealing and potentially workable alternative to prison sentences for women, it too has some limitations. Even though the women might benefit from doing community service, particularly where they would be given opportunities for caring for others, such a plan would likely do little to improve a woman's options for resisting illegal activities. Community service work is either unpaid or pays so little that a woman could not support herself and her children; it also would not likely increase her marketable skills for better than minimum wage employment.

The criteria for alternative sentencing policies should be created from examining the typical profile of women offenders and the etiology of their crimes to generate options that could both hold women accountable for their offenses and address some of the social structural issues that many report led to their illegal activities. These options might include: access to safe and affordable housing, temporary income maintenance during a period of intensive job training and apprenticeship, education and job training for employment that will provide sufficient income and benefits for single parents, and support for drug treatment programs that are "gender specific" in their attention to the complexities of women's lives.[11]

The state of Kansas, faced with bulging prison facilities, is currently reviewing options that include reversing some of the recently enacted tougher sentences for those who commit the least serious drug crimes by allowing them possible probation (Dvorak 1996). In a compromise bill, adopted by the Kansas legislature in the 1996 session, tougher prison terms for violent criminals were coupled with changes in drug sentencing that allow some offenders to stay out of prison. Economics may force policy makers to look at options for alternative sentencing simply because it is too expensive to continue building prisons to house inmates at an estimated annual cost of $20,000.

RECOMMENDATIONS STEMMING
FROM THE FINDINGS

Solutions to the issues identified in this study must accommodate both the psychological and social aspects of women's lives. The recommendations that follow have emerged from the study findings and include both broad-brush strokes and specific suggestions.

Women must be freed of the burden of victimization or they will continue to come into conflict with the law. Community agencies must end their isolation from each other and endeavor to work cooperatively for the benefit of women. Continuing efforts must be made by the justice system, social agencies, and educational institutions to expose and eradicate violence against women and children. Governments must redouble efforts to ensure that women are treated equitably in the workplace. A valuing of relationships and of the life-giving and life-affirming functions traditionally assigned to women must be woven into the social fabric.

Staff in correctional settings must learn from the women in their charge and develop appropriate resources and methods of helping them to become integrated into society. Correctional officers and parole/supervision officers can have a profound impact through their regular interactions if they recognize that the individual woman is worthy of respect and has the potential to remake her life. By conceptualizing their tasks around a core of empathy, and the power to effect positive change, the officers as well as the women might become empowered to feel more effective in their worlds.

Another important resource is the women themselves. If an empathic milieu for women's efficacious transition is to be created, women must be able to relate and draw from each other's strengths as they manage the day-to-day struggles of returning to the free world. Rather than disregarding the potential of peer support, the problems in developing an empathic support system should be identified and used as possibilities for uncovering relational issues and generating the means for resolving conflicts.

Given the increasing numbers of drug-addicted women entering prisons, it is important to not only address addictions, but also the multiple issues surrounding drug acquisition, use, and sales, the neglect of children, and women's experiences of exploitation, abuse, and victimization.

Programs must be developed with awareness that women are relational beings. If program designers fail to understand that women do not live in isolation from other people, their programs are likely to resolve nothing. This was particularly evident for those short-term (albeit multiply incarcerated) ex-inmates in the study who rarely benefited from treatment programs while in prison that required time for completion and integration. The movement of women between the prison facility and the community necessitates more comprehensive community links with the prisons to provide continuity of relationships, support, and treatment.

BUILDING KNOWLEDGE FOR WHAT WORKS TO SUPPORT WOMEN MAKING IT

This qualitative study provided an opportunity for formerly incarcerated women to make sense of an individual phenomenon—their incarceration and subsequent release as they sought to rebuild their identities as noncriminal citizens in the free world. Women's stories of transcendence of a criminalized identity have largely been untold and unheard, and female offenders have been part of a construction process in which they are rarely the authors. The structured interview process enabled the women to co-interpret what is socially defined as deviant and shameful. Laird (1989) argues that it is through the telling of the story that a woman may not only better comprehend it, but also compose new stories that can become models for future action.

As described, the study findings also pointed to some unifying themes of developing and using both internally derived strengths and externally discovered resources to craft a cautious path of making it free of both criminal entrapment and institutional surveillance and custody. A study conducted by Koons, Burrow, Morash, and Bynum (1997) identified treatment needs that they related to successful correctional treatment outcomes. These needs included substance abuse education and treatment and the development of parenting and life skills as well as interpersonal and basic education skills. Koons and her colleagues (1997) also indicate that programs that focused on dealing with past victimization issues and targeting self-esteem are promising targets for change for female offenders. These identified treatment needs are consistent with the themes derived from my study.

We cannot generalize these findings to what all women need before or as they exit prison in order to reconstruct their lives. However, they provide a starting point for continued observation and measurement of the factors that contribute to women's reintegration. Finally, meta-analytic reviews of rehabilitation literature have suggested a three-pronged principle of risk, need, and responsivity as necessary components of correctional interventions. These principles concern identifying the clients who should receive the most intensive allocation of correctional treatment, determining the correct targets for change, and ensuring that the characteristics of program delivery are matched to the learning style of the offender (Dowden and Andrews 1999). As correctional systems begin to grapple with the large numbers of women sentenced to incarceration, the need for gender-specific programming contributes an additional element to what constitutes responsivity. There is a corresponding need for systematically examining whether making treatment programs more relation oriented has any impact on post-release success.

APPLYING STUDY FINDINGS— MAKING JUSTICE OTHERWISE

Harris (1987) argues persuasively that a feminist vision of justice would be organized around care and compassion, equal respect for all human life, and the recognition of shared responsibility and interdependence. Themes such as reconciliation, healing, repair of fractured relations, return to community, and forgiveness would characterize a model of justice build around a care/response moral orientation as derived from Gilligan's (1982) work.

Such a feminist vision of justice is still evolving—it does not yet prescribe a specific plan of action for reforming, repairing, or replacing our present system of retributive punishment. A care/response orientation to justice would take into consideration the context within which each of these crimes was committed. A system of justice based on an ethic of care would weigh the context of an action, the intent of the action, the options available to the actor, and what measures could be taken to meet the needs of both parties (the state and defendant or the victim and the perpetrator) and prevent the conditions conducive to further violations.

Harris concludes from her examination of the language and practices of the criminal justice system that the "war on crime" is in essence a domestic civil war of enormous proportion. Dressel (1994) argues a similar point by reviewing the connections between poverty and punishment, with particular emphasis on the scapegoating of people of color. The language of criminal justice is one of objectification: the people processed through the system are offenders, criminals, violators, convicts, deviants, and perpetrators who must be deterred, punished, incarcerated, and executed. Objectification places those objectified in a position of being "the other," not like us, and enables us to banish or execute those who offend "us."

Present criminal justice practices of imprisonment and punishment reflect a vision of justice as a form of retribution. Retribution and revenge do not repair what has been broken or replace what has been lost; rather, they destroy something roughly equal in value to what has already been lost or destroyed. Victims of crime gain little, and generally feel unsatisfied, under the current model of justice. A retribution model of justice diminishes material and human resources by at least as much as was diminished by the original crime, and it diminishes human capacities to repair and forgive.

Punishment implemented by an impersonal and remote criminal justice system means that individuals never have to face directly the human costs of casting out offenders and we never are forced to reach deep within ourselves to find compassion and forgiveness. A feminist vision of justice would view offenders as members of the relational web of the community, for whom and by whom the social contract has been broken in both directions. Responsibility for healing the broken web would rest equally with society and the individual involved, taking care not to hurt or deprive either party needlessly. We can begin using this approach immediately with nonviolent offenders through the creative application of community-based alternative sentencing programs that incorporate models for mediation and reconciliation.

The women who shared their experiences as part of this study have something to teach us about justice too. In the midst of often overwhelming life circumstances, they did not express despair. No one had given up. Each individual was very involved in reconstructing a life based on making different choices about how she could live in conformity with this society's expectations.

There was often acknowledgment of the women's responsibility for the reality of their situations, the difficulty in dealing with the intrusion of control by the criminal justice system in their lives after prison, the multiple challenges in reconstructing their identities in the free world, but there was also a part of them that clung to the possibility of a return to wholeness. Rather than passively waiting for wholeness to emerge, women demonstrated tremendous personal inventiveness in reaching out to others and mobilizing resources from within themselves and from others that enabled them to continue to deal with the disruptions and setbacks that they experienced in the transition.

These women know firsthand that incarceration cannot undo the conditions that led to their illegal actions. If we can welcome these women back into our communities, their voices and their wisdom can help us realize a more compassionate system of justice. This will require a social acceptance of responsibility for the conditions of injustice that brought these women into conflict with the law. Mutual assumption of responsibility—by the women when they break the law and by society when it fails to care and protect—would represent a more just effort to repair the social contract and make it otherwise.

EPILOGUE

Two Years Later

In the fall of 1998, more than two years after I met the women whose stories generated the study from which this book evolved, I wrote a letter to all the participants sharing a summary of the findings and asking them to let me know how they were doing. In the next several weeks, I received phone calls and letters from about half of the group (eight); eventually, I heard from ten of the eighteen women who had participated in the study. Seven of the letters came back to me without a forwarding address; I did not receive a response from Regina, the youngest participant who had a newborn infant and had stated during her interview that she was "ready to put it all behind."

I asked the women to describe their current situation, how they felt about themselves, the kinds of resources that had been helpful to them, goals or hopes, and what they would say to other formerly incarcerated women. The following summarizes what they told me.

DEENI

Deeni was released from federal supervision April 1996. In October 1996, she attended the 8th National Roundtable on Women in Prison in Pasadena, California, and sent me a picture of her and Angela Davis (a formerly incarcerated woman and activist, author of *Women, Race and Class* (1980), and a leader of the campaign to end the prison industrial complex), a keynote speaker at the conference. Deeni was energized by the conference and has since become involved in developing a support group for formerly incarcerated women in the Kansas City area. Deeni has turned the fitness regime that she started in prison as a way of coping into her own business, "teaching various forms of exercise classes, nutrition, and strength training." She continues, "I'm happy, growing, experiencing and loving my life." She believes that for those who want to turn their lives around, "knowing and loving who you are has to be taught, and practiced from the soul." She also says, "I give, give, give and I get so much in return—life is beautiful." She laments that "prisons are constantly being built—it's all about power and politics."

For other incarcerated or transitioning women she believes "the system must offer more to those willing to turn their lives around. Assistance is a must for those wanting a better life." She also offers this bit of advice for other women that reflects so much of who she is and how she has managed her life since her release:

> Keep your head up and not down to the ground. The past must not be forgotten. However, the past must be used to move forward. Associate yourself with those who have what you want, learn from your surroundings, read, save, plan for your future and your children's future, pass on the teachings and the togetherness.

MANDI

I have heard from Mandi several times in the intervening years: she sends me pictures of her children and catches me up on her progress. At the time of the follow-up, she told me she was a volunteer with the STOP Violence program, facilitating a biweekly support group at the state prison facility for women. After a year of completing applications and reference checks, she obtained a full-time job as a postal clerk for the U.S. Postal Service. She too was a participant at the 8th National Women's Roundtable for Women in Prison in 1996 and co-presented a paper about her experiences, especially regarding the mending of her relationship with her mother, at the National Family Corrections Network Conference in 1998 (held in Bethesday, MD). About how she perceived herself, she said, "I love myself. I am okay with who I am. I feel lucky, fortunate and blessed." Her dream is to open a reintegration or transitional living home for women being released from prison. Her advice to other women:

> Raising four kids, single, and clean and sober. I speak often at schools, churches, juvenile centers and on the radio. I feel honored and privileged to be able to share my experiences with others. Don't ever give up. Life does get better once you decide to own your mistakes, accept consequences earned, and then be responsible by doing things different, better, the right "legal" way. Love yourself.

DEMI

Demi's words practically jumped off the page. She said she felt "Excellent!" Recall that she was one of the women who had not been able to financially support full physical custody of her children and worried about how the record of her conviction would affect her future job options. But in her letter she indicated that she not only had custody of her children but that they live "in a very nice townhouse." In addition, she notes, "I have an excellent job that I acquired through hard work and determination. My children are in a loving stable environment and that was the first goal I set for myself. I have a fiancé and he is very loving and supportive." She concludes her report by saying "It took me a long time to get here but I feel all the chaos I experienced prepared me for this time in my life to truly appreciate all I have accomplished. I know how to be happy and it feels good."

At the time she wrote, she indicated that she had five months to go before she completed her term of supervision and expected that at that time she would send her officer a note of thanks for giving her "the respect of not bothering her." She related that she has other goals, first to buy a house and to return to and complete college. She says, "I want to own a home and live in a neighborhood where my kids can ride their bikes up and down the street. I will be getting married in the future and when the kids are a little older, I will return to school at night. I want to obtain a degree for my own personal satisfaction. My biggest goal is to be successful at life. To me that means to be content and happy, which I am. All the rest of it is just new challenges, which make you life fuller." For other women she adds:

> I think the best advice I could give to formerly incarcerated women or anyone else is this: keep a good attitude. Stay positive and focused. Set goals and never lose sight of them. Life is good and everyone deserves to be happy. People will always encounter obstacles, change that to challenges and that is how you will deal with it. You can accomplish anything that you set your mind to. Build a strong support system of family, friends, co-workers and counselors. We all need help and people like to help people. When you come to a place in your life, you can help others. That's how it works. A good attitude will take you anywhere you want to go in this life. I am proof!

ASHLEY

Ashley's responses rang with regret, mostly over her inability to get "the type of job I know I can do which would generate the income I want." She adds that her current job "is fun" and that she'll soon be getting on salary with benefits— "a step up." She remarks, "I still dream of a great paying and exciting job. A husband who will love me unconditionally—even knowing what my past has been like." The issue of feeling stigmatized apparently still haunts her.

As for advice for other women Ashley suggests:

Talk to people, ask a lot of questions. Do not go by what someone tells you—find out for yourself. It's too easy for some silly mistake to get you put back into another difficult situation.

SADIE

Sadie is another of the study participants who has regularly stayed in touch with me. Her advice to other women was that "living well is the best revenge" and by every indication she is living well. Sadie progressed from having an avocation of off-the-road bicycling and working as a crack bicycle mechanic to buying a retail bike shop. She is the sole proprietor and is very happy that she is able to make a good livelihood while doing something she loves.

RENE

Rene wrote that "things are up and down but generally good." At the time she wrote, she had about six and a half months of parole left and was looking forward to becoming a grandmother. She also told me, "I feel better about myself in decision making, but that's all part of new beginning, being able to take charge of your life and make your own decisions on your future and being free of judgment from someone else." She also admitted that she periodically felt "the urge" to use drugs but that she lives "one day at a time to be able to spend time with (her) children and the new grandbaby."

As someone who has had to deal with "arrogant counselors who think they know everything and don't have any idea at all," she suggests to other women, "If you have a counselor, make sure they're right for you; if not, change."

BERNIE

I reached Bernie by phone to find out that her physical health had declined quite a bit in the intervening years, including a broken knee that hadn't healed properly, more heart problems, and kidney failure. She has a homemaker and a new wheelchair that she proclaimed should be bigger, so she could do wheelies in it!

In our conversation she reiterated that the "majority of (formerly incarcerated) women are intelligent, sensitive people—not animals. Acceptance is a big factor in their progress and rehabilitation—it's the multiple forces around them that causes them to fall." Despite her ill health and her goal of "staying alive," she indicated that she was still working with some formerly incarcerated women when she could.

SUZY

Suzy called after she received the letter to tell me that she had been discharged from parole in 1996. She also related how she had taken over Bernie's thrift-store business and was doing well in her marriage and in parenting her son. Her voice exuded confidence and a sense of having found her place in the world.

ELIZABETH

Elizabeth's response to my letter was the most troubling. She acknowledged that "I have dabbled in drugs off and on for nearly twenty years. Just like everyone said, it now had a hold of me. I am an addict. I work and support myself and fulfill my responsibilities but have been unable to stop." I have to wonder how much her experience of incarceration and the attached stigma she perceived contributed to her continued addiction. She said that she was seeking treatment and hoped to "regain control of (her) behavior."

Her advice to others? To remember that "life is ongoing and each breath is good . . . some breaths are better."

I conclude this book with these still evolving but mostly growth-filled, resilient, and hopeful stories from some of the women I originally interviewed. These are women who are contributing to the world around them even as they struggle with the human condition of physical change and emotional challenge.

A final implication from the stories and the continued success communicated by these nonrecidivist women is the notion that, for some women, prison as a correctional intervention seems to work. The women themselves have claimed that prison saved them from death or worse. What is certain is that prison allows time away from outside pressures or easy access to drugs. It provides them with resources they might not otherwise have had, including some programming, drug treatment, and vocational training. Numerous prisoners take the opportunities offered in prison and other correctional facilities and make positive changes despite soul-deadening limitations imposed on them by the prison structure. Many women in this study have survived circumstances far more perilous than a prison term and most will continue to survive, and even thrive, in the new beginnings they are constructing for themselves.

At the cusp of the new century, can we afford to do only what appears to work in retrospect for some when the individual and social costs are so high? This study is an initial attempt to describe and understand women's process of reentry after incarceration. It is a small representation of the thousands of women who enter and exit prison every year in this country. As argued elsewhere, imprisonment affects a disproportionate number of women of color and those marginalized by circumstances of family background, personal abuse, and destructive individual choices. Women in prison represent not only individual mistakes, but also the damage done to women through such shortsighted and detrimental policies as the war on drugs and the overreliance on incarceration as social control.

Former Supreme Court Chief Justice Warren Burger stated in the 1970s that one way to tell the character of a society was in how it treated those who had transgressed against it. It is time to begin a constructive dialogue in our schools of social work, our neighborhoods, and our media that reflects our belief in solutions that challenge women's criminality or their disposability. The description of the lives of women who are making it in the free world offers a starting point for this dialogue and the consequent public policy changes concerning the experiences of women on their own terms.

APPENDIX A

Research Design

The purpose of this study was to describe the experiences of formerly incarcerated women in reconstructing their lives after prison as perceived by the women themselves. I wanted to identify the attitudes, values, behaviors, and environmental factors that facilitate women's completion of parole supervision, as well as avoidance of criminal charges and/or return to custody. Because the study explored highly complex, interactive, and multifaceted phenomena, I adopted a naturalistic design as the essential orientation for investigation (Lincoln and Guba 1985) and a grounded theory approach for analysis (Glaser and Strauss 1967).

RATIONALE FOR A NATURALISTIC INQUIRY

A preeminent issue in research is the "fit" between the research question(s) and design. Heineman Pieper (1989) notes that the "philosophy of research we select determines what questions we let ourselves ask, how we go about answering them, what knowledge we consider valid, and the quality of the knowledge we develop" (10). Because formerly incarcerated women's voices have not been heard describing the unique process of their transition to the free world after incarceration, a naturalistic design provides a good fit by virtue of the following characteristics (Lincoln and Guba 1985, 42–44).

First is the assertion that there is a natural setting to be studied. In this study, the primary interviewing mode of inquiry enabled the women to describe the intricate and changing realities of their experiences following incarceration within their everyday context. The use of self as the primary instrument of data-gathering is another characteristic of the naturalistic paradigm. Since there is no standard that describes the transition, it would be impossible to design *a priori* a survey instrument with enough adaptability to encompass the complexities of this phenomenon. Another characteristic of the naturalistic paradigm is an appreciation for tacit or intuitive knowledge that can be used in the formation of the design as well as in the process of data collection and analysis.

Other characteristics of the naturalistic paradigm that fit with the research purpose include: the use of the qualitative method of interviewing that captures the full range of insights expressed by study participants; the use of theoretical sampling that increases the range of uncovered data among a group, such as formerly incarcerated women who have a variety of backgrounds and experiences; and an inductive data analysis producing grounded theory that is more likely to reflect fully the values, attitudes, and behaviors described by women in transition.

Lincoln and Guba (1985) identified other major characteristics of the naturalistic paradigm as the grounded theory approach to analysis and findings (see also Glaser and Strauss 1967), the use of the case study reporting mode, and the use of different criteria for assessing trustworthiness consistent with the procedures of naturalistic inquiry.

"Grounded theory" follows from data rather than preceding them, and is a logical consequence of the naturalistic paradigm that recognizes multiple realities in the phenomenon under study. This is a multivoiced case study, using in-depth interview procedures to describe the phenomenon of formerly incarcerated women's transition from prison. The selection of the case study approach is consistent with what Lincoln and Guba (1985) indicate is the importance of building "naturalistic generalization" (120, 358) based on the evidence that cumulative case studies provide.

Within the naturalistic paradigm, the appropriate criteria for establishing the trustworthiness of the findings of the inquiry are credibility, dependability, confirmability, and transferability. These are the characteristics that moderate fears about the unreliability of a study that relies on the use of interview material without a control group or base of comparison. I will discuss how I addressed these criteria in a later section.

Finally, the naturalistic paradigm recognizes that the research process is not a neutral activity. Erlandson, Harris, Skipper, and Allen, (1993) argue that "the naturalistic researcher, rather than acquiring power or supporting existing power structures, seeks to *empower* all who participate in the study" (158). This notion of empowerment relates to study methods that minimize status differences between the researcher and the participants and promotes a collaborative approach toward developing findings that will be useful and emancipatory.

STUDY DESIGN

The nature of qualitative methods requires that the researcher view the design as a dynamic process and to regularly evaluate and modify, as needed, elements of the design to make it more congruent with the process of discovery. Although some research procedures were predetermined, interview questions and the framework for analysis and interpretation of themes remained open to modification for the duration of the investigation.

The implementation of the study included three distinct phases: "immersion," "acquisition," and "synthesis and analysis" (Lincoln and Guba 1985). The immersion phase included a review of related literature; identifying contacts within the corrections system; informal meetings with female ex-inmates, prison volunteers, and advocates of women in prison; and facilitation of a support group within a women's prison facility to better understand their daily experiences. This phase also included a reflective focus on my own perspective about research and criminal behaviors.

The acquisition phase included the selection of interview participants and data collection activities. These activities included refinement of the protocol for data collection, administration of the interviews, and a "member check" focus group with study participants to discuss, modify, and affirm tentative themes from the interviews.

The final phase of synthesis and analysis consisted of making meaning of the women's narratives through an iterative process of coding the data to produce patterns in the findings, review and analysis, and production of the findings from the analysis.

DATA COLLECTION

Consistent with the naturalistic approach of this study, the primary source of data was verbatim transcriptions of semistructured, in-person, and audiotaped interviews with eighteen formerly incarcerated women and the member check focus group. Other sources of data included: meeting notes with correctional staff; the information forms that women completed prior to sample selection; observation notes from the interview sessions; extensive post-interview notes, reflexive accounts of nonrecorded conversations, and a methodological log. In addition to the intensive interviews with the selected participants, I interviewed individuals who were involved with the processing or treatment of women on parole or supervision. These interviews of key informants provided factual information about the processing of parolees through the system and confirmed observations about the obstacles women face in reestablishing themselves after having been incarcerated.

Finally, I maintained a methodological log to record personal reflections, a chronological listing of research events, and interpretative "hunches" as the study progressed. This log also served as a means for recording anecdotes and conversations with participants that occurred between interviews.

Study participants were chosen from the eastern Kansas parole region and the Kansas City, Missouri, Federal Office of Probation and Parole. I selected the study participants from the population of women on parole and under federal supervision in these two offices who returned a short "participant information form." One hundred and sixty-five forms were sent to the population of female parolees in the eastern Kansas Parole region and sixty-one forms were sent to women under federal supervision in the Kansas City, Kansas, and Kansas City, Missouri, offices of probation and parole. The information forms provided the participants a confidential method of indicating their interest in the study, descriptive information about their conviction and sentence, and their assessment of their progress since release.

Thirty-eight women returned completed forms. Of those who returned the forms, I selected the final interview sample of eighteen participants according to the criteria that they consented to be interviewed, had been incarcerated as adults in a state or federal facility, had not been interviewed previously about their post-incarceration experiences, and provided a means of contact. In addition to this feasibility criterion, I examined the sample demographic information for a theoretical richness of diversity to maximize the scope of expected data to be collected from participants who had contrasting characteristics and legal histories. After the sample selection was completed, I made phone contacts with the prospective participants to discuss the interview procedures, schedule the interviews, and discuss their rights as study participants, as mandated by institutional research review protocol.

When working with persons under correctional supervision, a crucial issue is to ensure that no coercive influence is brought to bear on potential participants. Such bias has been avoided by presenting notice of the study and the study purpose to the female parole population and asking for voluntary participation independent of their status with the correctional office under which they may have continued supervision. Informed consent was further reinforced by asking each participant to sign a statement that confirmed their voluntary participation in the study. Following each interview, I talked with the participants to assess their feelings about taking part in the interview. Most participants expressed positive feelings about the opportunity to discuss their process of managing their transition, as well as other accomplishments. Participant characteristics are described in Appendix B.

Instruments. The participant information form was pretested by three formerly incarcerated women who reviewed it for ease of comprehension, observed the time it took to complete, and identified any questions that they thought might cause discomfort or put a participant at risk. A colleague reviewed the instrument for ease of readability. The two-page form, consisting of sixteen questions, was then revised for clarity. The items described demographic characteristics, criminal history, and terms of incarceration. One open-ended question enabled the respondent to describe and assess her progress since her release from prison. The form enabled respondents to accept an invitation to participate in an interview about their experiences since prison and provide necessary contact information.

I developed a semistructured interview guide to elicit women's recall of their experiences during the transition from prison. Content in the interview guide was loosely derived from patterns that emerged in prior interviews with formerly incarcerated women,[1] the review of the related literature, the participant information forms, and phone conversations with potential participants. The interview guide was revised for transition statements and clarity after it was pretested. Although the interview guide was used to structure the interview content, questions varied according to the interaction that emerged between each participant and myself consistent with qualitative interviewing methods.

Interview Procedures. The interviews for this study were conducted in 1996 over several months following six "pilot" interviews completed in 1993 to 1994.[2] The pilot study period provided opportunities for me to conduct both one-shot interviews with five women on parole and repeated in-depth interviews with one individual during the three months immediately after her release from prison after serving ten years in prison. These different experiences supported my decision to use a more broad-brush approach wherein I would interview a number of diverse women with a variety of backgrounds and experiences in the transition. This approach did not preclude a more in-depth interview process and, in the case of one participant, I conducted several interviews with her due to the array of insights she had gained in the intervening twelve years since her incarceration.

Interviews took place in various locations. Most respondents chose to meet for the interviews in their homes, two participants came to my office, one woman chose to meet at her office, and one woman elected to meet at a restaurant that was owned by her parents. The interviews averaged one and a half to two and a half hours in length. Follow-up calls were made to the participants to clarify responses to specific questions.

Mishler (1986) notes that interviewing is a method of communication, a common activity with which most of us have a lot of experience. But research interviewing is different from the communicating we do in everyday life. The interviews with formerly incarcerated women were meant to provide an opportunity for the participants to reconstruct a narrative of the process in which they had been engaged as they underwent transition from prison. In other words, the women told the story of their experiences in the free world since they have exited prison and it was my role to facilitate their telling it.

Although it is possible that I did not hear all of what was important to the narrator because of cultural or other differences between the participant and myself (Riessman 1987), fostering a collaborative stance acknowledges the inherently interactive quality of interviewing, and incorporates the empowerment of women as an implicit research principle. As Oakley (1981) points out, when interviewing women from this empowerment standpoint, there is "no intimacy without reciprocity" (49).

Thus, I attempted to develop a collaborative stance by minimizing the traditional hierarchical situation in interviewing, communicating a nonjudgmental acceptance and respect for each of the participants and their knowledge, expressing my own feelings in response to the participant's narration of experiences, and allowing each participant to control the pace of the interview. The interactive relational aspect that developed as a consequence produced rich narratives of women's experiences of reentry.

In each case, after the preliminary discussion about the study and the interview and consent procedures, a broad, open-ended question was used to enable the woman to become comfortable with the interview process and define the starting point and the scope of her reflections. Spradley (1979) stresses the importance of sequencing in interviewing and the notion of a "grand tour" question to begin the interview. Each participant was first asked to "walk me through" the first day or days immediately following their release from prison.

As each interview progressed, the questions became narrower in scope and followed the course of questions outlined in the interview guide, but were tailored to the participant's individual situation. Throughout the interview, I asked probing questions, summarized responses, and requested clarification of meaning. These questions focused on external resources that had been helpful in the transition process, an internal or self-appraisal of progress, examples of obstacles along the way and methods of dealing with them, the impact of the incarceration on the transition, specific perceptions of the parole or supervision process, and, finally, recommendations for the criminal justice system, helping professionals, and the general public.

After several interviews, the guide was refined to eliminate a redundant question and an additional question was included about participants' perception of the interview in order to assess how fully it reflected their experiences and the impact of its telling on them. Following the formal interview, a debriefing period allowed the participant to discuss any concerns the interview stimulated. During this time, participants often shared personal information about their present lives such as showing me family pictures, especially those of children, wedding pictures, pictures of them with friends while incarcerated, official release certificates, and letters from significant mentors or friends. Several participants gave me tours of their homes, pointing out features or sources of pride. I concluded each interview by sharing the next steps in the analysis of the interviews and requesting follow-up phone contact and/or further participation in reviewing the findings. Each participant was given a token gift of appreciation for participating in the study.

Overall, there were few problems with individual interviews. Three participants had to reschedule the interviews due to schedule conflicts. Three women were interviewed in their homes with babies present. This did not tend to impede the interview as much as slow it down and cause some difficulty in understanding the audiotape. Since the interviews took place in fourteen of the participants' homes, the location of the interviews seemed to make it more comfortable for them to discuss what were often emotionally charged topics. Most of the women shared their excitement about participating in the study because, although it was a time in their lives they could not forget, they had had few, if any, opportunities to discuss it or examine its impact in their lives.

DATA ANALYSIS

The primary method of data analysis that I employed was an adaptation of the constant comparative method, as derived from the grounded theory approach of Glaser and Strauss (1967, 101–115). This method involves developing categories, concepts, and broader themes or theory inductively from the interview data and testing them out at each step by returning to the data to evaluate their fit.

In a qualitative investigation, it is common for data analysis to begin simultaneously with the initiation of data collection. In this study, a provisional listing of major themes occurred following each interview. Initial categories were created in phases as data became available and were generated from the emerging conceptual themes repetitively presented across cases. Those themes were then sorted into primary code categories with secondary categories that reflected individual differences among the interview participants.

In the early phase of the interviewing, for example, participants frequently spoke of the stigma they felt and observed when they first were released from prison on parole or under supervision that affected who they were able to talk to about their incarceration as well as employment opportunities. The process of creating general categories and subcategories is visually represented as follows.

PAROLE/SUPERVISION
            ➤ OTHERS' STIGMATIZING PERCEPTION
                        ➤ EMPLOYMENT AVAILABILITY

Categories were added as interviewing and analysis progressed. Ideas emerging from the concurrent data analysis were recorded in the methodological log and were reanalyzed during periods of data analysis following the completion of all the interviews.

These provisional themes were then distributed to all the interview participants for feedback and discussion. Eight of the interview participants and one ex-inmate not included in the study sample attended a focus group member check to review and discuss the themes. The meeting served to confirm the accuracy of three of the major themes (importance of relationships, impact of incarceration, the parole/supervision process) and further refined the importance of association with other peers as a subtheme in the category of recommendations for what would help other women in the immediate period following release from incarceration. The meeting also provided an opportunity to refine some of the meanings of individual categories.

Following the group meeting, I developed a more complete coding instrument by choosing a sample of three transcripts of the interviews based on variations that were built into the participant selection criteria. The majority of coding categories were then created on this sample of transcripts, including both inductively and deductively derived categories as needed, and checked for usefulness against the data. The final coding scheme that emerged from this process was used to consistently code all transcripts from all interview participants.

Coding and comparative analysis of data was accomplished by a combination of manual techniques and the use of a qualitative data analysis software program *Q.S.R. NUD•IST* (Qualitative Solutions and Research Ltd 1995). *NUD•IST* is described by its developers as a system for coding and retrieval, a means of graphic representation of concepts into categories and subcategories, as well as a structure for theory construction of hierarchical linkages among concepts and abstractions (Richards and Richards 1994). Although *NUD•IST* is a sophisticated data management program, its greatest use was in providing a consistent means of indexing the interview transcripts that consisted of 9,316 text units.[3] Indexing included defining codes, organizing them into a structure, and pairing codes with specific parts of the database. In other words, I used the program to *order* the data, not to *interpret* the data, which is a particularly human, manual, and during this study, often messy, enterprise.

A total of 427 categories emerged. By applying the constant-comparative method of analysis that included both within and between case comparison, and by sorting multiple copies of data into the various categories, then refining each of the categories, the major themes and patterns began to emerge. Final coding was done with text, using the categories that best reflected the patterns and themes identified from the interview participants. To manage the mechanical aspects of keeping track of the data, a file was created for each participant (as described earlier) and for each code category across all participants. Within each file, everything a participant said about the topic, that is, "feeling good about myself" (within-case comparison), can be compared to what all other participants said about that topic (between-case comparison).

This process then produced the major themes and patterns within and among the narratives of women's experiences that shaped the findings. The final coding/synthesis process was used to generate a conceptual and conditional model based on theoretical referencing (Yin 1991) by which the findings, inductively grounded in women's accounts of their transition from prison, address the study questions.

ESTABLISHING TRUSTWORTHINESS

Credibility refers to the degree with which findings are derived from the participants' realities and not from the researcher's interests, motivations, and biases.[4] My work with women in prison prior to the study and my informal conversations with women after their release from prison lent credibility to this study. In addition, triangulation of both sources of data (information forms, interviews, focus group, and field notes) and the diversity of women that I interviewed provided multiple slices of the same phenomenon from different perspectives.

Additional components of the research design accommodated opportunities for peer debriefing, negative case analysis, and member checking. Identifying cases that did not fit with previously derived patterns, and reevaluating patterns in light of participants' representations of their own realities, were significant components of the emergent research process.

I conducted a member check focus group after I had completed the interviews and initial coding to produce tentative themes from the narratives. At the focus group meeting, eight of the study participants confirmed these themes and further refined several of the subthemes—for example, peer association and family support.

Dependability refers to whether the findings would be consistently obtained if replicated with the same or similar respondents and context. During the data collection and analysis phases of this study, dependability was assured by first organizing the case study data base that included a file for each participant. Each file held the initial participant information form, the uncoded transcript, a log detailing each contact with the participant, and notes from the interview with each participant. Other files in the system included field notes from interviews with key informants. Files were also established that included all the coded data by case, and then by code category, consistent with the within- and between-case comparison that determined major themes.

A further method for ensuring dependability relates to the sufficiency of detail that is accessible for someone wishing to replicate or extend the current study. The methodological log was used for noting procedural decisions, protocols for methodological decisions, and analytic constructions, as needed throughout the period of study. The methodological log was used to establish the path by which another investigator could, using similar procedures across interviews with a similar mix of questions, and a similar sample of participants, produce a core of consistent data.

Finally, I used two forms of auditing to meet the criterion of dependability. Over the course of data collection, Dr. Edward Canda,[5] a qualitative methodologist, performed three audit checks and a confirmatory final audit to attest to the sufficient detail of the files and the methodological log as described. Further, Dr. Linda Ware,[6] a qualitative researcher with no direct interest in the study, read a sample of five transcripts to examine and affirm the consistency of the coding process.

Confirmability establishes confidence in the truth of the findings considering the context and the participants in the inquiry. By following the same procedures across interviews and by organizing the case study data base, both dependability and confirmability were enhanced and provided an audit trail. The audit trail permits tracing of conclusions back to particular data sources and enables research procedures to be examined in order to determine integrity of methods.

Transferability refers to the conceptual applicability of research findings to other samples and populations or to a body of established theory. By providing detailed and thick descriptions about the research setting, data collection procedures, and the data in the methodological log and the research design and findings, I invite readers to evaluate the degree to which transfer is appropriate. Erlandson et al. (1993) notes that effective thick description refers to the detailing of the data sufficient "to bring the reader vicariously into the context being described" (33). Detailed descriptions enable the potential users of the research findings to make informed judgments about its usefulness and applicability to other settings, as well as identifying implications for further research.

LIMITS TO TRUSTWORTHINESS

A major qualification to the trustworthiness of this study is the possibility of investigator bias. Although there is no pretense to objectivity in the description and interpretation of the data, the previous description of adherence to a set of established criteria provides a system of checks and balances. I have included among these procedures efforts to triangulate sources of data in the analysis by drawing on the literature, interviews with parole officers and other correctional staff, and participants' responses to the initial findings. Data collection techniques were adhered to with rigor. Procedures were carefully documented in the methodological log and through the process of developing an audit trail to facilitate review of research procedures.

Appendix B

Summary of Study Participants

In 1996, I interviewed eighteen women who had been incarcerated in four state facilities and five federal facilities and released in a time span ranging from 1983 to late 1995. Sixteen of the eighteen women resided in a major metropolitan area spanning two Midwestern states. The other two lived in small towns about two hours from the metropolitan area.

Table B.1 provides a summary of participant characteristics by the name they chose to be known for the study.

At the time of the interviews, the women ranged in age from twenty to sixty-seven years old with a median age of thirty-five. Of the eighteen, ten are white; the remainder black (four), Korean/African American (one), Arapaho/ Native American (one), and Hispanic (two). Seven were married or living with an intimate partner, and one of the women self-identified as a lesbian with a partner. Only two of the participants had no children; thirteen of the women were parents of minor children and three were parents of adult children. Three of the women had less than a twelfth-grade education, another three did not graduate from high school but earned a high school equivalency diploma, two had graduated from high school only, and ten (56 percent) of the women had completed some college. Thirteen of the women were employed in either part- or full-time jobs.

Table B.2 compares several selected characteristics of the study participants with the profile of incarcerated women compiled from a national survey of state and federal inmates.

Table B.1

CHARACTERISTICS OF STUDY PARTICIPANTS[1]

Name	Age	Race/ Ethnicity	Marital Status	Number/Sex/Ages of Children	Education[2]	Source of Income
Anita	36	Black	Never married	14-year-old son	10th grade	Employed
Ashley	28	Korean– Black	Never married	9-year-old daughter	Some college	Employed
Bernie	67	White	Widowed	Five adult children	Some college	Self- employed
Deeni	41	Black	Never married	23-year-old son, 25-year-old daughter	College (AA degree)	Employed
Demi	25	White	Never married	4-year-old daughter, 8-year-old son	Some college	Employed
Elena	25	Hispanic	Never married	1-, 6-, 8-, 10-year old daughters, 3-year-old son	Some high school	AFDC
Elizabeth	50	White	Divorced	Two adult daughters, one adult son	Some college	Employed
Jeanette	34	White	Divorced	5-, 7-year-old daughters	Some college	Employed
Mandi	28	White	Divorced	5-year-old daughters, 9-, 11-year-old sons	Some college	Employed

Name	Age	Race/Ethnicity	Marital Status	Number/Sex/Ages of Children	Education[2]	Source of Income
Margi	31	White	Separated	2 months, 4-, 9-year-old-sons	Some college	SSI
Nan	34	Black	Separated	4-, 10-, 12-, 15-year-old daughters, 18-year-old son	GED	Medical leave
Nicole	31	White	Married	No children	GED	Employed
Racque	35	Hispanic	Married	15-year-old daughter	Some high school	Employed
Regina	20	Black	Never married	4-month-old son	High School Diploma	AFDC/Parents
Rene	37	White	Separated	13-year-old daughter, 15-year-old son	GED	Boyfriend
Sadie	37	Arapaho/White	Not married	No children	Some college	Employed
Susan	29	White	Married	4-month-old daughter, 4-year-old son	Some college	Husband
Suzy	35	White	Married	4-year-old son	High School Diploma	Self-employed

[1]At time of interview.
[2]Highest grade completed.

Table B.2

SELECTED CHARACTERISTICS OF A NATIONAL SAMPLE
OF WOMEN PRISONERS COMPARED TO STUDY SAMPLE
(BY PERCENTAGE OF TOTAL)

Characteristics of women	State prisons	Federal prisons	Study sample
Race/Hispanic origin			
White	33%	29%	56%
Black	48	35	28
Hispanic	15	32	11
Other	4	4	.06
Age			
24 or younger	12%	9%	.06
25–34	43	35	50
35–44	34	32	33
45–54	9	18	.06
55 or older	2	6	.06
Median age	33 years	36 years	43 years
Marital status			
Married	17%	29%	33%
Widowed	6	6	.06
Separated	10	21	.06
Divorced	20	10	17
Never married	47	34	39
Education			
8th grade or less	7%	8%	0%
Some high school	37	19	17
High school graduate/GED	39	44	28
Some college or more	17	29	55

SOURCE: Greenfeld, L. A. and Snell, T. L. (1999) *Women Offenders*

As compared to the national samples, this sample had a higher degree of white participants, an older mix of participants, more married women, and a more highly educated selection. This voluntary selection may represent a more stable group of ex-offenders than is typical. However, the range of crimes and variation in criminal history reflects more consistency with the typical "female offender."

Table B.3 summarizes the institutional history of the study participants.

An equal number of women had been incarcerated for property crimes as for drug offenses (seven); four of the participants were convicted for crimes of violence against persons. Seven (39 percent) of the participants had been incarcerated two or more times. Two participants had been previously incarcerated ten times. The women had served sentences that ranged from six months to eight years and had been released from prison anywhere from three months to twelve years. Eleven participants in the interview sample were former state inmates and seven of the sample were former federal inmates. Ten of the participants were still either on parole with the state Department of Corrections or on supervised release under the jurisdiction of the Federal Probation and Parole.

I present further description of the study participants as narrative. This more complete picture enables the reader to know more about the women and their environments and better appreciate the context from which the findings were derived. In addition, the narratives also remind us that the women I interviewed were individually and collectively active *participants* in this study rather than research objects.

Anita. When Anita answered the door of her apartment, it was obvious that she had recently emerged from the shower. She indicated that it had been a hard day at work and I thought that she looked tired and perhaps wouldn't respond fully to my questions. She invited me to sit at her kitchen table in an alcove off the nicely appointed living room and soon we were engaged in conversation. Anita is a thirty-six-year-old African-American woman who works full time at a dry-cleaners. She has a fourteen-year-old son who resides with his father. She served two and a half years in correctional facilities in Kansas, initially on a theft charge and then on a parole violation on a drug possession charge. She was released most recently in December 1994 and is currently on parole in good standing. Anita had indicated on the initial form that she was angry because she had been denied admission to a proprietary business college due to the felony on her record. By the time I met with her, she was already enrolled in another college that was closer to where she lived so she didn't feel as strongly about what she initially identified as discrimination due to her record.

Throughout the interview, Anita discussed her determination to complete classes, stay away from drugs, and develop more reciprocal relationships with potential partners. She discussed the difficulty she had standing up for herself in work situations where she felt like she was sometimes misunderstood as being "mouthy." Anita felt that her competence and experience had been important in helping her get jobs in cleaning establishments. She also felt that she was a good employee. Interestingly, in speaking about her life, she metaphorically stated that women coming out of prison needed "new clothes" in order to succeed.

Table B.3

INSTITUTIONAL HISTORY OF STUDY PARTICIPANTS

Name	Offense[1]	Term of Incarceration	Prior Terms	Time Released
Anita	Theft, drug Violation	3.5 years	2	1.2 years
Ashley	Distribution of cocaine	2 years	1	2.3 years
Bernie	Worthless checks	2 months	10	4.7 years
Deeni	Armed robbery	8 years	3	5.7 years
Demi	Conspiracy to distribute cocaine	30 months	1	2.5 years
Elena	Drug trafficking	2.5 years	1	2 years
Elizabeth	Theft by deception	10 months	1	12 years
Jeanette	Conspiracy to distribute cocaine	30 months	1	11 months
Mandi	Possession of cocaine	9 months	5	1.3 years
Margi	Theft	6 months	1	1.3 years
Nan	Drug sales	4.8 years	1	3 months
Nicole	Aggravated assault	1.5 years	1	1.8 years
Racque	2nd-degree robbery	1.9 years	10	3.4 years
Regina	Auto theft/larceny	6 months	1	8 months
Rene	Aid/abet forgery	1.5 years	4	2 months
Sadie	Aggravated kidnapping	7.5 years	1	7.3 years
Susan	Forgery	1.4 years	2	4.8 years
Suzy	Aggravated incest	2.5 years	1	2.5 years

[1]Offenses resulting in most recent incarceration.

Ashley. Ashley seemed excited about the interview in our initial phone call. She asked me questions about my interest and intent and said that she could tell me enough about her experiences to fill a book. When I said that I wanted to talk to women who were making it since their incarceration, she laughed and said she didn't know that she qualified since she had to work two jobs and still was struggling financially. Ashley is a twenty-eight-year old woman of mixed African-American and Korean parentage. She is the mother of a nine-year-old daughter who has been adopted by Ashley's parents. She offered me coffee and we sat on her living room couch while we talked. The interview was interrupted by phone calls three times. At one point, when she told someone on the phone that she was talking to a "girlfriend," she indicated some discomfort in some people (in this case, a man she had just started dating), knowing about her incarceration. Ashley was a unique member of the study group since she had testified against co-conspirators in a drug-dealing trial and so had won some accommodations within the federal correctional system. For example, she did not have to serve a part of her sentence at the federal community placement (Dismas House) and, to facilitate her reentry, she received some start-up money from the prosecutors involved in her case. The other side of that accommodation is that she was fearful of anyone who had been associated with the case harming her because of her testimony. Consequently, a major issue for her that she discussed in the interview and in the focus group is the matter of "association." By that she meant getting violated by her supervising officer due to her proximity to someone else who is charged in illegal activities. After the interview portion was complete, she gave me a tour of her house, including a wall upstairs covered with artwork created by her daughter. She extensively discussed the problems associated with earning a low income and was thus very proud of her capacity to decorate her house by using thrift-store bargains.

Bernie. Bernie called me about participating in the study as soon as she read about it. She described herself as a sixty-seven-year-old Polish-American with five adult children and eleven grandchildren, who has survived multiple incarcerations in both the California and Kansas correctional systems. She attributed much of her progress to a supportive parole officer. Bernie operates a thrift store and since her most recent release about four years ago had been active in attempting to open a residential center for women coming out of prison. We met at the thrift store where Bernie introduced me to another woman recently released from the municipal jail. We went to her house nearby to complete the interview. The interview was interrupted twice by phone calls and once by a man at the door with a donation for her one-woman social service agency. Bernie operates as part of a network of ex-cons in the area attempting to help other ex-cons find shelter and employment when they come out of prison. Thus, the interview was an interesting blend of her own story of hard drinking, doing time (mostly for bad checks), problems with maintaining custody of her children, her difficult relationship with her mother, and her conflicts with the local governmental forces as she tried to open "Room at the Inn" as a halfway house for formerly incarcerated women. She has had to recently give up these efforts due to medical problems exacerbated by open heart surgery several years ago. We talked for almost three hours in the individual interview and Bernie also attended the group interview where she talked about the importance of "we these people helping we these people."

Deeni. Deeni and I met at her office in a community-based organization for youth. The walls were decorated with posters of Malcolm X and other African-American champions, which reflects Deeni's strong cultural and political identity as an African-American woman and as a practitioner of the Muslim faith. Deeni was one of the more reserved participants during the interview itself, but in other conversations since the interview she has been much more descriptive of her prison experiences and the beliefs she holds about the prison system. Deeni is a forty-one-year-old woman who is the mother of two adult children and grandmother of two grandchildren. She is the primary caretaker of one of her minor-aged grandchildren and a nine-year-old niece. Deeni has been incarcerated three times for a combination of state and federal crimes. She served her most recent sentence of eight years for her participation in an armed bank robbery. She was released from prison in 1990 and continued under federal supervision at the time I met her. Deeni believes that her past experiences have made her a better person because it was while she was in prison the last time that she made use of the system in any way she could so that she could develop skills that would make her employable. The major means to her current career evolved from a fitness regime that she created while she was in prison that included changing her diet and teaching aerobics to other inmates. She took great pride in her job of teaching children and adults about nutrition and fitness and also advocated for a change of rules while she was at Dismas House so that residents now come to the community center where she is employed to take exercise classes. She credits her physical fitness, her spiritual beliefs, and, to some extent, her political ideology as important factors in her success in creating a new life for herself after participating in almost thirteen years of criminal and, in her words, "dangerous" behaviors. In addition to her employment, she has been active in a number of community organizations focused on ending violence in the black community and in AIDS outreach efforts. Deeni attended the focus group meeting where she emphasized inmates building their skills while they are in prison so they would be employable when they came out, and the importance of building social networks outside of prison.

Demi. Demi came to my home/office for the interview in the early evening after she got off work. She was the only participant who had served part of her sentence in a federal "boot camp" (officially called an Intensive Confinement Center) located in Bryant, Texas. Demi is a twenty-five-year-old white woman who is the mother of a daughter, aged four, who resides with her, and a son, eight, who resides with her mother and stepdad. In addition to eight months in the boot camp, she spent eight months at the Dismas House and one year on electronic monitoring/home confinement. At the time of the interview, she remained under federal supervision. Much of our discussion focused on what led to her conviction on a conspiracy charge due to an uncle's use of her phone to make drug deals, her experiences in serving her sentence, and her breakup with her fiancé after she returned to the area after boot camp. Demi indicated that she had accomplished a lot in the past few years as she has gone through the various sanctions for her conviction. She believes the structure of the boot camp provided her an opportunity to learn more about herself and clarify goals for her life. She has attended some classes at a local community college and hopes to continue the education that she began while incarcerated by getting her GED. Although Demi was not able to attend the group meeting, she sent me a card after the interview expressing thanks for the opportunity to tell her story: She said, "It's nice to tell it every once in a while to remember the purpose of it and what I learned."

Elena. Elena is a twenty-five-year-old Hispanic woman who is the mother of five young children (one of whom was born while she was incarcerated and one of whom is not in her custody). She was imprisoned for two and a half years in a federal facility for a drug trafficking offense and released to community placement and federal supervision in March 1994. Elena wrote on her information form that she is a "changed person." When we met for the interview at her apartment, she talked excitedly about the possibilities she saw for herself now that she was going to school to complete her GED and was no longer addicted to drugs. She is most proud of her relationship with her mother and her children, and expressed great satisfaction that she has been able to prove herself to her family. Elena related a goal she has of helping other teenagers turn their lives around as she has been able to do.

Elizabeth. Elizabeth is a fifty-year-old white woman who at the time of her incarceration in 1984 at the women's facility in Lansing, Kansas, for insurance fraud, was the mother of three teenage children, two daughters and a son, who remained with her since-divorced husband during and after her incarceration. Elizabeth has been released from prison and subsequently discharged from parole for more than twelve years and so, of all the women in the sample, was most able to reflect on the long-term effects that her relatively brief incarceration of ten months had on her. Although Elizabeth has been able to put this experience behind her in many ways, the trauma that she recalls experiencing while she was incarcerated and the stigma attached to her status as an ex-offender has had a long-lasting impact. At the time of the interview, Elizabeth was successfully employed in a substance abuse facility as an executive secretary and is buying her lovely home where we met. Even though her record is now legally expunged, she is still worried about her employer finding out about her past, and up until the time of the interview had never discussed her incarceration with her now adult children. In the process of the interview, Elizabeth invited me to talk with one of her daughters about the impact of the incarceration, and later she chose to talk with this daughter about that period of their lives. After the informal conversation I had with the daughter, I interviewed Elizabeth a second time to explore more completely how she negotiated disclosure of her ex-inmate status. Elizabeth attended the group meeting where she emphasized the importance of a "protected environment" and the need for a guidebook to the transition from prison.

Jeanette. Jeanette is a thirty-four-year-old white woman who served two and a half years in two different federal facilities on a drug distribution charge and had been released from custody about a year when we met. Jeanette came out through Dismas House and remained under federal supervision. When Jeanette and I met for the interview at my home after she got off work, she discussed her frustration with not being able to financially support her two daughters, who continue to live with her mother. At the time of the interview, Jeanette was employed as a secretary at a community-based agency that assists people in locating employment. Jeanette expressed her desire to make a better life for her daughters and to that end she is pursuing a college education so that she can get a better paying job. A major issue for her has been long-time addiction to crack cocaine. At the time of her incarceration, she claims that she was not interested in giving up drugs. However, she described the treatment she received while in prison that finally helped her become aware of the impact of the addiction in her life, and other goals that she wanted to pursue. She also observed that many of the women returning to prison had received additional charges because of continuing drug use, which made her anxious about whether and how she would succeed in her own recovery. In addition to her employment and taking night classes at a local community college, Jeanette has been active in several community-wide initiatives for addressing drug abuse.

Mandi. I met Mandi, a twenty-eight-year-old white woman, at her rented house where we sat at the kitchen table and talked for almost three hours. Mandi is the mother of four minor children, two boys and twin girls. During the interview, Mandi was comfortable in talking about her struggles with addiction and her extensive experiences of abuse as an adult in intimate relationships, until she described the effects of her lifestyle on her children. Mandi has been incarcerated five times in jail and state prison facilities in Kansas. She was most recently incarcerated for a drug possession charge for nine months and was released in November 1994. Since then she has been discharged from parole and recently regained legal and physical custody of her children, who had lived with her mother during a period when she was unable to care for them, and then while she was incarcerated and for a year after her release. Mandi's major struggle has been with her dual addiction, first to alcohol and then to crack cocaine. She graphically described the two times she has relapsed even since her release from prison, and then her gradual emergence into recovery. Mandi used the keypunch training she received while in prison to get her first job after her release and then later was offered a manager's position at a fast food restaurant that she frequented. She has done so well in this latter position that she has been promoted several times and has been able to quit her keypunch job. In addition to employment and regular attendance at AA meetings, Mandi is on a bowling league. Mandi attended the focus group meeting where she talked about some of the stigma she experienced while on parole and her financial struggles.

Margi. Margi is a thirty-one-year-old white woman who served her nine-month sentence for theft in a Missouri facility but was transferred to Kansas for parole supervision when she moved back to the town where she had family members. At the time of the interview, Margi had been released for almost a year and a half. We met at the restaurant owned by her parents where she had worked for a while when she had first been released. However, a diagnosed mental disability and a pregnancy and subsequent birth of an infant had prevented her from continuing to work so that she expressed quite a bit of financial worry. In addition to having an infant son from a new relationship since prison, she has three other children, two of whom she has regained legal and physical custody; the other child remains in foster care. An important element that Margi described in her success after incarceration has been terminating her relationship with an abusive partner and beginning a new relationship with someone who believes in her and supports her emotionally.

Nan. Nan is a thirty-four-year-old African-American woman. Nan was a challenging interview to acquire, at first because of a miscommunication about the time and date of the initial appointment, and then because when I showed up again she was in the midst of dressing her youngest child to leave for a doctor's appointment. After some delay (and initial discomfort), we started talking and Nan became very animated as she related some of the experiences she had had while incarcerated and her subsequent accomplishments since her release. Nan served almost five years in one federal facility for a drug trafficking charge. She is the mother of five minor children, with whom she was able to maintain a very close relationship while she was in prison since her youngest sister and her children moved to the town where the prison was located. Her youngest child was born while she was incarcerated. The source of her greatest pride and the focus of her current life is her children. She believes that her previous lifestyle did not reflect the relationship that she now wants to have with her children and has given up the "good life" she had from what she describes as her addiction to the money that drug sales provided.

Nicole. Nicole is a thirty-one-year-old white woman who lives with her husband at her father's trailer in a trailer park where I met her. Nicole works a night job, and so even though it was late afternoon when I met her, it was very soon after she had awakened. Nicole and her husband, whom she met at her first job after she was released from prison, have no children but Nicole talked about their hopes to have a family when they find their own residence. Nicole served time in both a Missouri facility on a theft conviction and in the Kansas system for an aggravated assault conviction. She was released in July 1993 from Kansas custody and remained on parole. Nicole credits her success since her release to help from her family and getting away from the people with whom she had associated prior to her incarceration. She indicated that she is looking forward to the time when she can put her criminal involvement and subsequent incarcerations "behind me."

Racque. Racque called me prior to returning the information form to ask "if this was for real?" After I assured her that it was and that I would travel to the town where she lives in order to find out about her life since her incarceration, she agreed to meet me. When I got to the town in Northeast Kansas where she lives, she met me at a restaurant and then led me to her apartment where we completed the interview. Before we started talking, she showed me a letter from the local housing authority that had rejected her application for subsidized housing based on the fact that she had a felony record. We discussed some options for appealing that determination. Racque is a thirty-five-year-old Hispanic woman who has been incarcerated ten times for a combination of property and street crimes in the California prison system. She was incarcerated most recently for second-degree robbery and served almost two years before she was released in September 1992. She claimed that every time she returned to the streets, she could not make it in a legitimate way and so would receive a parole violation and be reincarcerated very soon after her release; one time she only managed to stay out one night. The turning point for Racque came when a man from Kansas asked her to marry him and she consented so she could get off the streets and out of California. She credits the move to Kansas and regaining physical custody of her now seventeen-year old daughter as well as employment as factors in her success.

Regina. Regina and I met at her parents' house where she has resided since her release from prison about a year before we met. Regina, a twenty-year-old African-American woman, is the youngest participant. When she was eighteen, she was convicted of auto theft and larceny along with a boyfriend at the time and served six months in county jail and the state prison. Since her release, her infant son was born and his care and support have become her major focus. She considers herself lucky for the family support she had during her brush with the law and since her release from prison. By the time of the interview, she had been discharged from parole.

Rene. Rene is a thirty-seven-year-old white woman who, at the time that I interviewed her at the rented house that she shares with a boyfriend, had been released from the Dismas House for only a few months. She had served ten months at a federal prison facility for aiding and abetting in a forgery and then six months at Dismas House. She is the mother of a thirteen-year-old daughter, recently returned to her legal and physical custody, and a fifteen-year-old son still in state custody, who at the time of the interview was residing at a residential treatment center. Rene considers her incarceration a blessing because it propelled her into resolving the pain of multiple victimizations that she had experienced since she was five years old. She is most concerned with rebuilding her relationships with her children and reaching out to others, especially teens, to "help (them) to find a way to deal with things that are hard to exsept [*sic*] or hard to live with."

Sadie. Sadie is a thirty-seven-year-old woman who identifies as white and Native American (Arapaho). She served seven and a half years in a Kansas facility for a conviction of kidnapping and aggravated assault. She has been released from prison since 1988 and was discharged from parole in 1994. Sadie describes herself as successful because she has "made it on my own" and always been able to get employment, which she attributes to her middle-class background, her white skin, and her formal education. We met at her home that is imaginatively adorned with Native American cultural objects and pictures, drums, candles, and crystals. After the interview, Sadie gave me a tour of the large Victorian house, which she is buying, and pointed out the various ways she has renovated it, including a mediation room. Sadie credited her progress in the several years since her release to emotional support from her parents, "free world" friends from the battered women's shelter where she was first employed, a parole officer who requested an early discharge for her, and the fact that she was employed while she was in prison and so came out with a sizable amount of savings. One of her friends is another woman (another study participant, Elizabeth) whom she met while they were both incarcerated.

Susan. Susan is a twenty-nine-year-old white woman who lives in an apartment with her husband, whom she became reacquainted with while they were both incarcerated at the same Kansas facility. Susan has been incarcerated twice on forgery convictions; she served nine months on the most recent conviction and was released in April 1991. Susan attributes her success to having worked out her relationship with her mother, whom she felt abused by as a child, and to the positive relationship she has with her husband. She is the mother of two minor children and is currently in nursing school. She also emphasized the importance of having friends with whom she can be honest about who she is and what she has experienced.

Suzy. Suzy was one of the most emotionally challenging interviews that I did, primarily because she expressed so much loneliness and fear due to the nature of her conviction (aggravated incest). Suzy is a thirty-five-year-old white woman who served two and a half years in a Kansas prison and was released in

1993. One of the conditions of her parole was to obtain continued mental health intervention, which she successfully completed. She has continued to feel stigmatized by her background and fearful of the judgments that might be made of her if her crime became known, especially by co-workers or employers. Consequently she became self-employed as a "junker" where she could work on her own and be flexible in her hours and location. She took pride in her ability to transform junk into earnings, and prior to my leaving her house showed me all the pieces of furniture she had picked up on the streets for free and cleaned up and repaired for their home. She also indicated that her marriage was deteriorating and that she and her husband might divorce now that it was no longer necessary for them to stay together for the sake of retaining custody of their four-year-old son. Suzy spoke with longing of her time in prison, saying that she was "happy and at peace then" because she "knew what to expect." Suzy came to the focus group meeting and expressed her desire for a support group with other women ex-offenders. Several weeks later, I saw her working at the thrift shop that Bernie operates.

Notes

PREFACE

1. Wilmington may bid for women's prison, *Chicago Tribune*, 7/28/1999.
2. Illinois Department of Corrections, Planning and Research, 1998. Unpublished report.

CHAPTER ONE

1. See, for example, Chesney-Lind 1997; Culliver 1993; Faith 1993; Feinman 1994; Heidensohn 1985; Mann 1984; Pollock-Byrne 1990; Smart 1977.

2. See, for example, Carlen 1983; Collins 1997; Dobash, Dobash, and Gutteridge 1986; Fletcher, Shaver, and Moon 1993; Immarigeon and Chesney-Lind 1992; Owen 1998; Simon and Landis 1991; Sommers 1995; Watterson 1996; Zaplin 1998.

3. This was KSA 76.2505; the Act also established the Kansas Department of Corrections.

4. Probation—court ordered community supervision of convicted offenders by a probation agency. In many instances, the supervision requires adherence to specific rules of conduct while in the community.

Jail—confinement in a local jail while pending trial, awaiting sentencing, serving a sentence that is usually less than 1 year, or awaiting transfer to other facilities after conviction.

Prison—confinement in a state or federal correctional facility to serve a sentence of more than 1 year, although in some jurisdictions the length of sentence which results in prison confinement is longer.

Parole—community supervision after a period of incarceration.

5. Based on projections from the first time incarcerated, Bonczar and Beck (1997) estimate the lifetime chance of a black woman going to state or federal prison is three times more likely than that of a white woman and two times more likely than a Hispanic female's.

6. Prison department policies require that all prisoner telephone calls are collect. Since telephone deregulation in 1986, state and federal facilities contract with private phone companies to provide inmate-only services. Investigators have discovered that inmate-only calls have the highest initial rate and per minute rates of all calls. In addition, some providers place a surcharge on each call that is usually limited to a fifteen-minute unit (Information provided by Citizens United for Rehabilitation of Errants, Washington, DC). According to a *Chicago Tribune* article, in the 1998–1999 fiscal year, prison phones earned the State of Illinois nearly $12.3 million. In Florida, they brought in $14.7 million in revenue. In California the take was $23.2 million ("Inmates dial up dollars for Illinois," August 25, 1999).

7. See, for example, Crites 1976; Dobash, Dobash, and Gutteridge 1986; Faith 1993; Heidensohn 1985; Leonard 1982; Steffensmeier 1978.

8. Violent offenses include murder, negligent and nonnegligent manslaughter, rape, sexual assault, robbery, assault, extortion, intimidation, criminal endangerment, and other violent offenses.

Property offenses include burglary, larceny, motor vehicle theft, fraud, possession and selling of stolen property, destruction of property, trespassing, vandalism, criminal tampering, and other property offenses.

Drug offenses include possession, manufacturing, trafficking, and other drug offenses.

Public-order offenses include weapons, drunk driving, escape/flight to avoid prosecution, court offenses, obstruction, commercialized vice, morals and decency charges, liquor law violations, and other public-order offenses.

9. I will generally use the concept of self-efficacy as developed by Bandura (1982, 1989, 1992) to represent the internalized process of becoming empowered, or recognizing one's own agency to make decisions in one's own life and manage adverse circumstances—this will be discussed more in chapter 4.

10. In an evaluation of recidivism models from eleven states, Maltz (1984, 62–63) found nine distinct categories for determining an outcome of "failure." These include: arrest, reconviction, reincarceration, parole violation, parole suspension, parole revocation, offense type, absconding, and probation violation. Each of these categories could then be further qualified (and complicated) by the number of incidents, seriousness of incidents, and jurisdictional issues.

CHAPTER TWO

1. There are many sources for "the personal is political," a basic feminist principle that emerged from the consciousness of the second wave of feminism during the mid- to late 1970s. See, for example, writings by Friedan (1963) and Freeman (1995).

2. The Dismas House is a not-for-profit agency founded in 1972 by a group of community-minded people under the leadership of a Catholic priest and a few Protestant men and women from several local churches. Dismas House first housed municipal and state ex-inmates, and in 1983 obtained the contract to house men and women referred from the Federal Bureau of Prisons. The facility has a capacity for twenty women and seventy-two men (Dismas House Employee Handbook, June 24, 1993).

CHAPTER THREE

1. Weisstein has written about the classic Milgram study in which 62.5 percent of the study subjects, when directed to do so, administered a series of shocks to a study confederate up to a level that the subjects believed could be fatal.

2. These randomly selected students showed real and dramatic increases in their intelligence scores as compared to the rest of the students. Something in the behavior of the teacher demonstrated to the selected students that they expected high results and student test scores rose accordingly.

3. Women who have been separated from the experience of parenting during incarceration, for example, could strengthen their post-prison effectiveness pertaining to that role if they had gradual periods of extended interaction with their children, during which they could practice and begin to reassume their parenting role.

4. Resuming the housewife role was pivotal to the perception of restoration, while leaving housework undone was considered a signal of emotional trouble.

5. A pseudonym.

CHAPTER FOUR

1. See the account of the expanded use of the battered women's syndrome in *More than victims: Battered women, the syndrome society, and the law* by D.A. Downs (1996).

2. The national incidence study of violence against women has been widely criticized by feminist researchers on the grounds that the findings of an almost equal use of force by women against men did not take into account previous violence to the woman by the man. See Saunders 1988, for example.

3. This member was not interviewed separately but had been interviewed before the current study and came to the focus group meeting to respond to the initial findings.

4. This notion of bounded separation as a means of active choice-making regarding unhealthy or harmful relationships derives from the discussion of the relational model for women's development espoused by Jordan 1997 and others.

CHAPTER FIVE

1. My thanks to Dennis Saleebey for the use of his phrase, "it could be otherwise" to express the possibilities inherent in exploring alternative methods and frameworks for human and social betterment.

2. Now known since the Personal Responsibility and Work Opportunity Reconciliation Act of 1996 as Temporary Assistance for Needy Families (TANF).

3. An evaluation of this federal residential drug abuse treatment program indicated that inmates who completed the program were 73 percent less likely to be rearrested in the first six months after release than untreated inmates. Further, inmates who had completed the treatment were 44 percent less likely than those who had not received treatment to be detected for drug use within the first six months of their release. Women constituted 18 percent of the sample (342 out of 1,866). See Bureau of Prisons report "Trial drug treatment evaluation—six month report" published February 1998.

4. The Federal Bureau of Prisons report, "A profile of female offenders" published May 1998, describes the current array of occupational training programs, UNICOR industries, parenting programs, and psychological and drug treatment offered at the various facilities.

5. In this section, I am suggesting advances in direct interventions that may be addressed by anyone in a helping capacity, but challenge social workers in particular to become aware of these issues in the multiple settings in which they may encounter former inmates.

6. The federal participants in the study had been incarcerated in Alderson, West Virginia, Lexington, KY, Pleasanton, CA, and at the Intensive Confinement Center (boot camp) at Bryan, TX. According to the Bureau of Prisons homepage (www.bop.gov) women (comprising 7.5 percent of the federal inmate population) are currently housed in twenty federal facilities including prison camps, correctional institutions, a medical center, and metropolitan correctional center.

7. The Colorado Department of Corrections is currently constructing a new facility for women that by its completion in 2002 will have a capacity for 900 women. The "integrated model for female incarceration" they use draws on a "reintegration model" that, according to Joanie Shoemaker, Clinical Administrator, will involve staff in all areas of the facility—custody/control, medical, mental health, and program staff.

8. Subtitle S of the Violent Crime Control and Law Enforcement Act of 1994 amended the Higher Education Act of 1965 to prohibit the award of a Pell grant to any individual who is incarcerated in a federal or state penal institution.

9. According to the Federal Bureau of Prisons report, "A profile of female offenders," as of May 21, 1998, 15 percent of all female inmates worked in Federal Prison Industries (UNICOR). The survivability rate (time crime-free after release) is 36 percent longer for female inmates who participated in UNICOR and vocational training programs than for those who did not.

10. Dismas House is not a halfway house, but rather a Community Corrections Center where the inmate completes the remainder of her custodial incarceration. The inmate must apply for and earn this option by good behavior while incarcerated in a prison facility.

11. Stephanie Covington (1999) has created a program that she calls a comprehensive model for treating women's addiction within the criminal justice system. The model draws on a holistic theory of women's addiction, the theory of women's psychological development (Jordan et al. 1991; Jordan 1997), and the three-stage model of trauma constructed by Herman (1992).

APPENDIX A

1. See O'Brien 1994.

2. These initial conversations helped me establish the initial categories for questions and procedures that I used in the current study.

3. A text unit can be a sentence or a paragraph of responses to a question or a statement about a particular issue.

4. These terms, as well as the term "establishing trustworthiness," are derived from Lincoln and Guba, 1985.

5. University of Kansas-School of Social Welfare.

6. University of Rochester-Margaret Warner Graduate School of Education and Human Development.

References

ACE Program Members. 1998. *Breaking the walls of silence.* New York: Overlook Press.

Adams, D., and J. Fischer. 1976. The effects of prison residents' community contacts on recidivism rates. *Corrective & Social Psychiatry & Journal of Behavior Technology* 22(4): 21–27.

Adams, T. C. 1979. Some MMPI differences between first and multiple admissions with a state prison population. *Journal of Clinical Psychology* 32(3): 555–558.

Adler, F. 1975. *Sisters in crime: The rise of the new female criminal.* New York: McGraw-Hill.

Adler, P. 1992. The "post" phase of deviant careers: Reintegrating drug traffickers. *Deviant Behavior* 13: 103–26.

Alleman, T. 1993. Varieties of feminist thought and their application to crime and criminal justice. In *It's a crime: Women and justice,* eds. R. Muraskin and T. Alleman, 3–42. Englewood Cliffs, NJ: Regents/Prentice-Hall.

American Correctional Association. 1990. *The female offender: What does the future hold?* Washington, DC: St. Mary's Press.

Aptheker, B. 1989. *Tapestries of life: Women's work, women's consciousness, and the meaning of daily experience.* Amherst: The University of Massachusetts Press.

Arnold, R. A. 1990. Processes of victimization and criminalization of black women. *Social Justice* 17(3): 153–66.

Arvantes, T. M. 1994. *Female drug use and crime.* Paper presented at the annual program meeting of the American Society of Criminology, Miami, FL.

Austin, J., Bloom, B., and T. Donahue. 1992. *Female offenders in the community: An analysis of innovative strategies and programs.* Washington, DC: U.S. Government Printing Office.

Bachman, R. 1994. *Violence against women: A national crime victimization survey report* (NCJ-145325). Washington, DC: U.S. Government Printing Office.

Bandura, A. 1982. Self-efficacy mechanism in human agency. *American Psychologist* 37: 122–147.

———. 1989. Human agency in social cognitive theory. *American Psychologist* 44(9): 1175–1184.

———. 1992. Exercise of personal agency through the self-efficacy mechanism. In *Self-efficacy: Thought Control of Action*, ed. R. Schwarzer, 3–38. Washington, DC: Hemisphere Publishing Corporation.

Banks, M. E., and R. J. Ackerman. 1983. *Women prisoners: Reintegration into family and community.* Paper presented at the 91st annual convention of the American Psychological Association, Anaheim, CA.

Baruch, G., R. Barnett, and L. Rivers. 1983. *Lifeprints; New patterns of love and work for today's woman.* New York: McGraw-Hill.

Baum, F.L. 1984. *The wonderful wizard of oz.* New York: Ballatine Books.

Baunach, P. 1985. *Mothers in prison.* New Brunswick, NJ: Transaction Books.

Beck, A. J. 2000. *Prison and jail inmates at midyear 1999.* Washington, DC: U.S. Government Printing Office.

Beck, A. J., and B. E. Shipley. 1989. *Recidivism of prisoners released in 1983.* Washington, DC: U.S. Government Printing Office.

Beck, A. J., and C. J. Mumola. 1999. *Prisoners in 1998.* Washington, DC: U.S. Government Printing Office.

Becker, H. 1963. *Outsiders: Studies in the sociology of deviance.* New York: Free Press.

Beckerman, A. 1989. Incarcerated mothers and their children in foster care: The dilemma of visitation. *Children and Youth Services Review* 11(2): 175–183.

Belenky, M. F., B. M. Clinchy, N. R. Goldberger, and J. M. Tarule. 1986. *Women's ways of knowing.* New York: Basic Books.

Belknap, J. 1996. *The invisible woman: Gender, crime, and justice.* Belmont, CA: Wadsworth.

Benard, B. 1999. Applications of resilience: Possibilities and promise. In *Resilience and development: Positive life adaptations*, eds. D. M. Glantz and J. L. Johnson, 269–277. New York: Kluwer Academic/Plenum Publishers.

Bepko, C. 1989. Disorders of power: Women and addiction in the family. In *Women in families: A framework for family therapy*, eds. M. McGoldrick, M. Anderson, and F. Walsh, 406–426. New York: W.W. Norton.

Berger, P. L., and T. Luckmann. 1967. *The social construction of reality: A treatise in the sociology of knowledge.* New York: Anchor Books.

Black, W. A., and R. A. Gregson. 1973. Time perspective, purpose in life, extroversion & neuroticism in New Zealand prisoners. *British Journal of Social and Clinical Psychology* 12 (1): 50–60.

Blackler, C. 1968. Primary recidivism in adult men: Differences between men on first and second prison sentence. *British Journal of Criminology* 8(2): 130–169.

Bloom, B. 1987. *Families of prisoners: A valuable resource.* Paper presented at the annual meeting of the Academy of Criminal Justice Sciences. St. Louis, MO.

Bloom, B., and D. Steinhart. 1993. *Why punish the children? A reappraisal of the children of incarcerated mothers in America.* San Francisco: National Council on Crime and Delinquency.

Bloom, B., M. Chesney-Lind, and B. Owen. 1994. *Women in California prisons: The hidden victims of the war on drugs.* San Francisco: Center of Juvenile and Criminal Justice.

Bloom, B., E. Leonard, and B. Owen. 1994. *Profiling the needs of California's female prisoners: An overview of prison programs.* Paper presented at the annual program meeting of the American Society of Criminology, Miami, FL.

Bloom, B., and S. Covington. 1998. Gender-specific programming for female offenders: What is it and why is it important? Paper presented at the 50th annual meeting of the American Society of Criminology, November 11–14. Washington, D.C.

Blumstein, A., J. Cohen, J. Roth, and D. Visher, eds. 1989. *Criminal careers and career criminals,* Vol. 1. Washington, DC: National Academy Press.

Bonczar, T. P., and A. J. Beck. 1997. *Lifetime likelihood of going to state or federal prison.* Washington, DC: U.S. Government Printing Office.

Bonczar, T. P., and L. E. Glaze. 1999. *Probation and parole in the United States, 1998.* Washington, DC: U.S. Government Printing Office.

Bonta, J., B. Pang, and S. Wallace-Capretta. 1995. Predictors of recidivism among incarcerated female offenders. *The Prison Journal* 75(3): 277–294.

Boudouris, J. 1984. Recidivism as a process. *Journal of Offender Counseling, Services, and Rehabilitation* 8(3): 41–51.

Bowler, M. December 1999. Women's earnings: An overview. *Monthly Labor Review,* pp. 13–21.

Braithwaite, J. 1989. *Crime, shame and reintegration.* Cambridge: Cambridge University Press.

Bricker-Jenkins, M., and N. R. Hooyman, eds. 1986. *Not for women only: Social work practice for a feminist future.* Silver Springs, MD: National Association of Social Workers.

Brien, P. M., and A. J. Beck. 1996. *HIV in Prisons 1994.* Washington, DC: U.S. Government Printing Office.

Brown, J. A. 1990. *Justice Denied.* Chicago: The Noble Press.

Brown, J. D. 1991. The professional ex-: An alternative for exiting the deviant world. *Sociological Quarterly* 32: 219–230.

Browne, A. 1987. *When battered women kill.* New York: Free Press.

Burkhart, K.1973. *Women in prison*. Garden City, NY: Doubleday.

Burstein, J. 1977. *Conjugal visits in prison*. Lexington, MA: Lexington Books.

Buttram, J. L., and R. A. Dusewicz. 1977. *Effectiveness of educational programs in state correctional institutions: A follow-up study of ex-offenders. Final report*. Philadelphia: Research for Better Schools, Inc.

Carlen, P. 1983. *Women's imprisonment*. London: Routledge and Kegan Paul.

———. 1988. *Women, crime and poverty*. Philadelphia: Open University Press.

Carlen, P., and A. Worrall, eds. 1987. *Gender, crime and justice*. Philadelphia: Open University Press.

Carney, F. J. 1967. Predicting recidivism in a medium security correctional institution. *Journal of Criminal Law, Criminology & Police Science* 58(3): 338–348.

———. 1971. Evaluation of psychotherapy in a maximum-security correctional institution. *Journal of Criminal Law, Criminology, and Police Science* 58(3):338–348.

Chambliss, W. J. 1984. *Harry King: A professional thief's journey*. New York: Wiley.

Chapin, R. K. 1995. Social policy development: The strengths perspective. *Social Work* 40(4):506–514.

Chapman, J. R. 1980. *Economic realities and the female offender*. Lexington, MA: Lexington Books.

Chesney-Lind, M. 1989. Girls' crime and woman's place: Toward a feminist model of female delinquency. *Crime and Delinquency* 35:5–30.

———. 1991. Patriarchy, prisons, and jails: A critical look at trends in women's incarceration. *The Prison Journal* 71(1):51–67.

———. 1992. Putting the brakes on the building binge. *Corrections Today* 54:30–34.

———. 1997. *The female offender: Girls, women and crime*. Thousand Oaks, CA: Sage.

Chesney-Lind, M., and N. Rodriguez. 1983. Women under lock and key: A view from the inside. *The Prison Journal* 63(2):47–65.

Chodorow, N. 1978. *The reproduction of mothering: Psychoanalysis and the sociology of gender*. Berkeley: University of California Press.

———. 1989. *Feminism and psychoanalytic theory*. New Haven, CT: Yale University Press.

Clarke, S. H., and L. Crum. 1985. *Returns to prison in North Carolina*. Chapel Hill: Institute of Government, University of North Carolina at Chapel Hill.

Clarke, S. H., and A. L. Harrison. 1992. Criminal recidivism: How is it affected by community correctional programs and imprisonment? *Popular Government* 58(1):19–28.

Cogburn, H. E. 1988. *Recidivism study: Positive terminations from J. F. Ingram State Technical College, 1976–1986*. Deatsville, AL: J. F. Ingram State Technical College.

Collins, B.G. 1993. Reconstructing codependency using a self-in-relation theory: A feminist perspective. *Social Work* 38(4):470–476.

Collins, C. F. 1997. *The Imprisonment of African American women.* Jefferson, NC: McFarland and Company

Collins, P. H. 1991. *Black feminist thought: Knowledge, consciousness, and the politics of empowerment.* Boston: Unwin Hyman.

Comack, E. 1993. *Women offenders' experiences with physical and sexual abuse: A preliminary report.* University of Manitoba: Criminology Research Centre.

Covington, S. 1998. The relational theory of women's psychological development: Implications for the criminal justice system. In *Female Offenders,* ed. R. T. Zaplin, 113–128. Gaithersburg, MD: Aspen.

———. 1999. *Helping women recover: A program for treating substance abuse addiction.* San Francisco, CA: Jossey-Boss.

Cowie, J., V. Cowie, and E. Slater. 1968. *Delinquency in girls.* London: Heinemann.

Crites, L. 1976. Women offenders: Myth vs. reality. In *The female offender,* ed. L. Crites, 33–44. Lexington, MA: Lexington Books.

Culliver, C. ed. 1993. *Female criminality: The state of the art.* New York: Garland.

Curtis, R. L., and S. Schulman. 1984. Ex-offenders, family relations, and economic supports: The "significant women" study of the TARP project. *Crime and Delinquency* 30(4):507–528.

Daly, K. 1994. *Gender, crime, and punishment.* New Haven, CT: Yale University Press.

Daly, K., and M. Chesney-Lind. 1988. Feminism and criminology. *Justice Quarterly* 5(4):497–538.

Daly, K., and D. J. Stephens. 1995. The "Dark Figure" of criminology: Toward a black and multi-ethnic feminist agenda for theory and research. In *International feminist perspectives in criminology: Engendering discipline,* eds. F. Heidensohn and N. H. Rafter, 189–215. Bristol, PA: Open University Press.

Danner, T. A., W. R. Blount, I. J. Silverman, and M. Vega. 1995. The female chronic offender: Exploring life contingency and offense history dimensions for incarcerated female offenders. *Women and Criminal Justice* 6(2):45–66.

Davis, L. V. 1994. Why we still need a woman's agenda for social work. In *Building on Women's Strengths: A social work agenda for the twenty-first century,* ed. L. V. Davis. New York: Haworth.

Denver Anti-Crime Council. 1974. Adult recidivism. Denver, CO: Author.

DeVine, M. D. 1974. *The Environmental Deprivation Scale (EDS): The role of environmental factors in the analysis and prediction of criminal behavior and recidivism.* Montgomery, AL: Rehabilitation Research Foundation.

Dismas House Employee Handbook. June 24, 1993. Kansas City, MO: Author.

Ditton, P. M. 1999. *Mental health and treatment of inmates and probationers.* Washington, DC: U.S. Government Printing Office.

Dobash, R. P., R. E. Dobash, and S. Gutteridge. 1986. *The imprisonment of women.* New York: Basil Blackwood.

Dougherty, J. 1998. Power-belief theory: Female criminality and the dynamics of oppression. In *Female offenders: Critical perspectives and effective interventions,* ed. R. T. Zaplin, 134–159. Gaithersburg, MD: Aspen Publishers.

Dowden, C., and D. A. Andrews. 1999. What works for female offenders: A meta-analytic review. *Crime & Delinquency* 45(4):438–453.

Downs D. A. 1996. More than Victims: Battered women, the syndrome society, and the law. Chicago: University of Chicago Press.

Dressel, P. L. 1994. . . . and We keep on building prisons: Racism, poverty, and challenges to the welfare state. *Journal of Sociology & Social Welfare* 21(3):7–30.

Dressel, P., J. Porterfield, and S. K. Barnhill. 1998. Mothers behind bars. *Corrections Today* 60(7):90–94.

Ducan, V. 1977. On the cutting edge: A unique barber styling school boasts excellent record. *Corrections Today* 59:120–121.

Durant, T. J. 1993. The changing complexion of female crimes: A sex and race comparison, 1960–1990. In *Female criminality: The state of the art,* ed. C.C. Culliver, 43–61. New York: Garland Publishing.

Dvorak, J. A. 1996. '96 law cuts jail stays for inmates. *The Kansas City Star,* August 25, A-1–A-21.

Eagly, A. H. 1987. *Sex differences in social behavior: A social-role interpretation.* Hillsdale, NJ: Erlbaum.

Ebaugh, H.R.F. 1984. Leaving the convent: Role exit and self-transformation. In *The existential self in society,* eds. J.A. Kotarba and A. Fontana, 156–176. Chicago: University of Chicago Press.

———. 1988. *Becoming an Ex.* Chicago: University of Chicago Press.

Erez, E. 1992. Dangerous men, evil women: Gender and parole decision making, *Justice Quarterly* 9(1):105–126.

Erlandson, D. A., E. L. Harris, B. L. Skipper, and S. D. Allen. 1993. *Doing naturalistic inquiry: A guide to methods.* Newbury Park, CA: Sage.

Faith, K. 1993. *Unruly women.* Vancouver, Canada: Press Gang Publishers.

Fear of Crime. *Current Events,* 98(6):1–3.

Feinman, C. 1994. *Women in the criminal justice system.* (3rd ed.). Westport, CT: Praeger.

Fessler, S. R. 1991. *Mothers in the correctional system: Separation from children and reunification after incarceration.* Unpublished doctoral dissertation, State University of New York at Albany.

Field, G. 1989. The effects of intensive treatment on reducing the criminal recidivism of addicted offenders. *Federal Probation* 49(2):50–55.

Fishman, L. 1986. Repeating the cycle of hard living and crime: Wives' accommodations to husbands' parole performance. *Federal Probation* 2(1):44–54.

Fletcher, B. R., L. D. Shaver, and D. G. Moon, eds. 1993. *Women prisoners: A forgotten population*. Westport, CT: Praeger.

Foucault, M. 1977. *Discipline and punish: The birth of the prison*. London: Penguin.

Frankl, V. E. 1992. *Man's search for meaning*. Boston, MA: Beacon Press. (Original work published 1959).

"Free?" *Tightwire*, 27. Kingston: Prison for Women.

Freedman, E. B. 1981. *Their sisters' keepers: Women's prison reform in America, 1830–1930*. Ann Arbor: University of Michigan Press.

Freeman, J. 1995. The women's liberation movement: Its origins, organizations, activities, and ideas. In *Women: A feminist perspective* (5th ed.), ed. J. Freeman. Palo Alto, CA: Mayfield Publishing.

Friedan, B. 1963. *The feminine mystique*. New York: Norton.

Friedman, L. M. 1993. *Crime and punishment in American history*. New York: Basic Books.

Gaudin, J. M. 1984. Social work roles and tasks with incarcerated mothers. *Social Casework: The Journal of Contemporary Social Work* 65(5):279–286.

Gelles, R. J. 1987. *Family violence*. Beverly Hills: Sage

Gendreau, P. 1996. Offender rehabilitation: What we know and what needs to be done. *Criminal Justice and Behavior* 23(1):144–161.

Gendreau, P., B. A. Grant, and M. Leipciger. 1979. Self esteem, incarceration, and recidivism. *Criminal Justice and Behavior* 6(1):67–75.

General Accounting Office. 1979. *Female offenders*. (GGD-79-73). Washington, DC: U.S. Government Printing Office.

Giallombardo, R. 1966. *Society of women: A study of a woman's prison*. New York: Wiley.

Gilfus, M. 1988. *Seasoned by violence/tempered by love: A qualitative study of women and crime*. Unpublished doctoral dissertation, Brandeis University.

———. 1992. From victims to survivors to offenders: Women's routes of entry and immersion into street crime. *Women & Criminal Justice* 4:63–89.

Gilliard, D. K., and A. J. Beck. 1998. *Prison and jail inmates at midyear 1997*. Washington, DC: U.S. Government Printing Office.

Gilligan, C. 1982. *In a different voice: Psychological theory and women's development*. Cambridge, MA: Harvard University Press.

Glaser, B., and A. Strauss. 1967. *The discovery of grounded theory*. Chicago: Aldine.

Glaser, D. 1969. *The effectiveness of a prison and parole system*. Indianapolis, IN: Bobbs-Merrill Educational Publishing.

Glick, R. M., and V. V. Neto. 1977. *National study of women's correctional programs*. Washington, DC: U.S. Government Printing Office.

Glueck, S., and E. T. Glueck. 1934. *Five hundred delinquent women.* New York: Alfred A. Knopf.

Goffman, E. 1961. *Asylums.* Garden City, NY: Anchor Books.

———. 1963. *Stigma: Notes on the management of spoiled identity.* New York: Simon and Schuster.

Gorey, K. M., and D. R. Leslie. 1997. The prevalence of child sexual abuse: Integrative review adjustment for potential response and measurement biases. *Child Abuse and Neglect* 21: 391–398.

Greenfeld, L. A., and T. L. Snell. 1999. *Women offenders.* Washington, DC: U.S. Government Printing Office.

Gunn, J., R. Nicol, J. Gristwoon, and R. Foggitt. 1973. Long-term prisoners. *British Journal of Criminology* 13(4):331–340.

Gutiérrez, L. M., and E. A. Lewis. 1999. *Empowering women of color.* New York: Columbia University.

Hairston, C. F. 1991. Mothers in jail: Parent-child separation and jail visitation. *Affilia* 6(2):9–27.

Hamparian, D. M., J. M. Davis, J. Jacobsen, and R. McGraw. 1985. *The young criminal careers of the violent few.* Washington, DC: U.S. Government Printing Office.

Hardesty, C., P. G. Hardwick, and R. Thompson. 1993. Self-esteem and the woman prisoner. In *Women prisoners: A forgotten population,* eds. B. R. Fletcher, L. D. Shaver, and D. G. Moon, 27–44. Westport, CT: Praeger.

Harlow, C. W. April 1999. *Prior abuse reported by inmates and probationers.* Washington, DC: U.S. Government Printing Office.

Harris, M. K. 1987. Moving into the new millennium: Toward a feminist vision of justice. *The Prison Journal,* 67(2):27–38.

———. 1993. *In her best interests: Needs-based sanctions on female offenders.* Presentation at Summit on Female Offenders May 27, Johnson County, Kansas.

Hassel, L. W. 1988. Keeping them from coming back to prison in Arkansas. *Vocational Education Journal* 63(1):28–29, 70.

Heffernan, E. 1972. *Making it in prison: The square, the cool, and the life.* New York: Wiley.

Heidensohn, F. 1985. *Women and crime.* New York: University Press.

Heineman Pieper, M. 1989. The heuristic paradigm: A unifying and comprehensive approach to social work research. *Smith College Studies in Social Work* 60:8–34.

Herman, J. L. 1992. *Trauma and recovery.* New York: Basic Books.

Herman, N. J. 1993. Return to sender: Reintegrative stigma-management strategies of ex-psychiatric patients. *Journal of Contemporary Ethnography* 22(3):295–330.

Higgins, G. O. 1994. *Resilient adults: Overcoming a cruel past.* San Francisco: Jossey-Bass.

Hill, G. D., and E. M. Crawford. 1990. Women, race, and crime. *Criminology* 28(4):601–626.

Hoffman, K. S. 1983. Women offenders and social work practice. In *Social work in juvenile and criminal justice settings,* ed. A.R. Roberts, 329–347. Springfield, IL: Charles C Thomas.

Hoffman, P. B., and J. L. Beck. 1984. Burnout: Age at release from prison and recidivism. *Journal of Criminal Justice* 12(6):617–623.

Holloway, J., and P. Moke. 1986. *Post secondary correctional education: An evaluation of parolee performance.* Wilmington, OH :Wilmington College.

Holt, L. 1986. *Statistical tables describing the background characteristics and recidivism rates for releases from Massachusetts pre-release facilities during 1983.* Boston: Massachusetts Department of Corrections.

Holt, N., and D. Miller. 1972. *Explorations in inmate-family relationships.* (Research report no. 46). Sacramento: California Department of Corrections.

Illinois Criminal Justice Information Authority. 1985. *Repeat Offenders in Illinois.* Chicago, IL: Author.

Illinois Department of Corrections, Planning and Research. 1998. Unpublished report.

Immarigeon, R. and M. Chesney-Lind. 1992. *Women's prisons: Overcrowded and overused.* San Francisco, CA: National Council on Crime and Delinquency.

Inciardi, J. A., D. Lockwood, and A. E. Pottieger. 1993. *Women and crack-cocaine.* New York: Macmillan.

Inciardi, J. A., and A. E. Pottieger. 1986. Drug use and crime among two cohorts of women narcotic users: An empirical assessment. *The Journal of Drug Issues* 16: 91–106.

Inmates Dial up Dollars for Illinois. 1999 *Chicago Tribune,* 25 August.

Johnson, D. C., R. W. Shearon, and G. M. Britton. 1974. Correctional education and recidivism in a woman's correctional center. *Adult Education* 24(2):121–129.

Johnston, D. 1995. Child custody issues of women prisoners: A preliminary report from the CHICAS Project. *The Prison Journal* 75(2):222–239.

Jones, A. 1980. *Women who kill.* New York: Holt, Rinehart, and Winston.

Jordan, J. V. 1997 (ed). *Women's growth in diversity.* New York: Guilford Press.

Jordan, J. V., A. G. Kaplan, J. B Miller, I. P. Stiver, and J. L. Surrey. 1991. *Women's growth in connection: Writings from the Stone Center.* New York: The Guilford Press.

Jose-Kampfner, C. 1990. Coming to terms with existential death: An analysis of women's adaptation to life in prison. *Social Justice* 17(2):110–125.

Jurik, N. C. 1983. The economics of female recidivism. *Criminology* 21(4):603–622.

Kagay, M. 1994. Top woe: Health or crime. *New York Times,* 7 August.

Katz, P. A., A. Boggiano, and L. Silvern. 1993. Theories of female personality. In *Psychology of women: A handbook of issues and theories,* eds. F. L. Denmark and M. A. Paludi, 247–280. Westport, CT: Greenwood Press.

Klein, D. Fall, 1973. The etiology of female crime: A review of the literature. *Issues in Criminology* 8(2):3–30.

———. 1995. Crime through gender's prism: Feminist criminology in the United States. In *International feminist perspectives in criminology: Engendering a discipline,* eds. N. H. Rafter and F. Heidensohn, 216–240. Bristol, PA: Open University Press.

Kohlberg, L. 1969. *Stages in the development of moral thought and action.* New York: Holt, Rinehart, and Winston.

Kondrat, M. E. 1995. Concept, act, and interest in professional practice: Implications of an empowerment perspective. *Social Service Review* 69(3):405–428.

Konopka, G. 1966. *The adolescent girl in conflict.* Englewood Cliffs, NJ: Prentice-Hall.

Koons, B. A., J. D. Burrow, M. Morash, and T. Bynum. 1997. Expert and offender perceptions of program elements linked to successful outcomes for incarcerated women. *Crime & Delinquency* 43:512–532.

Kubler-Ross, E. 1969. *On death and dying.* New York: Macmillan.

Laird, J. 1989. Women and stories: Restorying women's self-constructions. In *Women in families,* eds. M. McGoldrick, C. Anderson, and F. Walsh, 428–449. New York: Norton.

Lambert, L. R., and P. G. Madden. 1976. The adult female offender: The road from institution to community life. *Canadian Journal of Criminology and Corrections* 18(4):319–331.

Larson, J. H., and J. Nelson. 1984. Women's friendship and adaptation to prison. *Journal of Criminal Justice* 12(4):601–615.

Leonard, E. B. 1982. *Women, crime and society: A critique of theoretical criminology.* New York: Longman.

Lincoln, Y. S., and E. G. Guba. 1985. *Naturalistic inquiry.* Beverly Hills, CA: Sage.

Linden, R., L. Perry, D. Ayers, and T. A. Parlett. 1984. An evaluation of a prison education program. *Canadian Journal of Criminology* 26(1):65–73.

Lindforss, L., and D. Magnussen. 1997. Solution-focused therapy in prison. *Contemporary Family Therapy* 19(1):89–103.

Lindstrom, N., and K. Hallett. 1992. *Executive summary: A study of female recidivists at Minnesota Correctional Facility at Shakopee.* Unpublished report, Minnesota Department of Corrections.

Lombroso, C. 1903, 1916. *The female offender.* New York: D. Appleton.

Long, G.T., F. E. Sultan, S. A. Kiefer, and D. M. Schrum. 1984. The psychological profile of the first offender and the recidivist: A comparison. Special issue: Gender issues, sex offenses, and criminal justice. Current trends. *Journal of Offender Counseling, Services, and Rehabilitation* 9(1–2):119–123.

Mahan, S. 1996. *Crack cocaine, crime, and women: Legal, social and treatment issues.* Thousand Oaks, CA: Sage.

Maltz, M. D. 1984. *Recidivism.* Orlando, FL: Academic Press.

Mann, C. R. 1984. *Female crime and delinquency.* University: University of Alabama Press.

Martin, R. L., C. R. Cloninger, and S. B. Guze. 1978. Female criminality and the prediction of recidivism: A prospective six-year follow-up. *Archives General Psychiatry* 35:207–214.

Maslow, A. H. 1970. *Toward a psychology of being.* New York: Van Nostrand.

McCarthy, B. R. 1980. Inmate mothers: The problems of separation and reintegration. *Journal of Offender Counseling, Services & Rehabilitation* 4(3):199–212.

McHugh, M. C., I. H. Frieze, and A. Browne. 1993. Research on battered women and their assailants. In *Psychology of women: A handbook of issues and theories,* eds. F. L. Denmark and M. A. Paludi, 247–280. Westport, CT. Greenwood Press.

Meranze, M. 1996. *Laboratories of virtue: Punishment, revolution and authority in Philadelphia, 1760–1835.* Chapel Hill: The University of North Carolina Press.

Merton, R. 1956. *Social theory and social structure.* New York: Free Press.

Miller, J. B. 1976. *Towards a new psychology of women.* Boston: Beacon Press.

———. 1982. Women and power. Work in progress. Stone Center Working Papers Series. Wellesley, MA: Stone Center.

Minnich, E. K. 1990. *Transforming Knowledge.* Philadelphia: Temple University Press.

Mishler, E. G. 1986. *Research interviewing: Context and narrative.* Cambridge, MA: Harvard University Press.

Moyer, I. 1984. Deceptions and realities of life in women's prisons. *The Prison Journal* 64(1):45–56.

Muraskin, R. 1989. *Measuring disparate treatment in correctional facilities: Male inmates vs. female inmates.* Unpublished manuscript, Long Island University.

Oakley, A. 1981. Interviewing women: A contradiction in terms. In *Doing feminist research,* ed. H. Roberts, 30–61. London: Routledge & Kegan Paul.

O'Brien, P. 1994. *Exit from prison: One woman's experience.* Paper presented at the annual meeting of the American Society of Criminology, Miami, FL.

———. 1995a. *Reconceptualizing the role of social workers with ex-incarcerated women: Reweaving the web of connection.* Unpublished manuscript. University of Kansas School of Social Welfare, Lawrence.

———. 1995b. From surviving to thriving: The complex experience of living in public housing. *Affilia* 10(2):155–178.

Odubekun, L. 1992. A structural approach to differential gender sentencing. *Criminal Justice Abstracts* 24(2):343–360.

Owen, B. 1998. *In the mix: Struggle and survival in a women's prison.* Albany: State University of New York Press.

Ozawa, K. 1994. Follow-up studies of Class B male prisoners (1): Personal and socio-economic factors on recidivism. *Japanese Journal of Criminal Psychology* 32 (1):37–50.

Petersilia, J., P. W. Greenwood, and M. Lavin. 1978. *Criminal careers of habitual felons.* Washington, DC: U.S. Government Printing Office.

Phillips, L., and H. L. Votey 1984. Black women, economic disadvantage and incentives to crime. *American Economic Association Papers and Proceedings* 74: 293–297.

Pinderhughes, E. 1983. Empowerment for our clients and for ourselves. *Social Casework* 64(6):331–338.

———. 1994. Empowerment as an intervention goal. In *Education and research for empowerment practice,* eds. L. Gutierrez and P. Nurius, 17–30. Seattle, WA: Center for Policy and Practice Research.

Piper, E. 1985. Violent recidivism and chronicity in the 1958 Philadelphia cohort. *Journal of Quantitative Criminology* 4:93–121.

Pollak, O. 1950. *The criminality of women.* New York: A. S. Barnes.

Pollock-Byrne, J. M. 1990. *Women, prison, and crime.* Belmont, CA: Brooks/Cole.

Prendergast, M. L., J. Wellisch, and G. Falkin. 1995. Assessment of and services for substance-abusing women offenders in community and correctional settings. *The Prison Journal* 75(2):240–256.

Qualitative Solutions and Research Ltd. 1995. *QSR NUD•IST.* Thousand Oaks, CA: Scolari.

Raeder, M. S. 1993. Gender and sentencing: Single moms, battered women and other sex based anomalies in the gender-free world of the federal sentencing guidelines. *Pepperdine Law Review* 20(3):905–990.

Rafter, N. H. 1990. *Partial justice: Women in state prisons 1800–1935.* (2nd ed.). Boston: Northeastern University Press.

Rennison, C. M. 1999. *Criminal victimization 1998. Changes 1997–98 with Trends 1993–98.* Washington, DC: U.S. Government Printing Office.

Richards, T. J., and L. Richards. 1994. Using computers in qualtitative research. In *Handbook of qualitative research,* eds. N. K. Denzin and Y. S. Lincoln, 73–94. Thousand Oaks, CA. Sage.

Richie, B. E. 1996. *Compelled to crime. The gender entrapment of battered women.* New York: Routledge.

Riessman, C. K. 1987. When gender is not enough: Women interviewing women. *Gender and Society* 1(2):172–207.

Robinson, E. B. 1971. *Women on parole: Reintegration of the female offender.* Unpublished doctoral dissertation, Ohio State University.

Robinson, R. A. 1992. Intermediate sanctions and the female offender. In *Smart sentencing: The emergence of intermediate sanctions,* eds. J. B. Byrne, A. J. Lurigio, and J. Petersilia, 245–260. Newbury Park, CA: Sage.

————. 1994. Private pain and public behaviors: Sexual abuse and delinquent girls. In *Qualitative studies in social work research,* ed. K. Riessman, 73–94. Thousand Oaks, CA: Sage.

Robson, R. 1992. *Lesbian (out)law: Survival under the rule of law.* Ithaca, NY: Firebrand.

Rosaldo, M. Z. 1974. *Women, culture & society.* Stanford, CA: University Press.

Rose, S. M. 1994. Reclaiming empowerment: A paradigm for social work. In *Education and research for empowerment practice,* eds. L. Gutierrez and P. Nurius, 31–36. Seattle, WA: Center for Policy and Practice Research.

Rose, S. M., and B. L. Black.1985. *Advocacy and empowerment: Mental health care in the community.* Boston: Routledge and Kegan Paul.

Rouse, J. J. 1991. Evaluation research on prison-based drug treatment programs and some policy implications. *International Journal of the Addictions* 26(1):29–44.

Ruble, D. N. 1988. Sex-role development. In *Developmental psychology: An advanced textbook,* M. H. Bornstein and M. E. Lamb, 411–460. Hillsdale, NJ: Erlbaum.

Sabol, W. J., and J. McGready. 1999. *Time served in prison by federal offenders, 1986–97.* Washington, DC: U.S. Government Printing Office.

Saleebey, D. (ed.). 1997. *The strengths perspective in social work practice* (2nd ed.). New York: Longman.

Saunders, D. G. 1988. Wife abuse, husband abuse, or mutual combat? In *Feminist perspectives on wife abuse,* eds. K. Yllo and M. Bograd, 90–113. Newbury Park, CA: Sage.

Schaef, A. W. 1992. *Women's reality: An emerging female system in a white male society* (3rd ed.). San Francisco: Harper.

Schulke, B. B. 1993. *Women and criminal recidivism: A study of social constraints.* Unpublished doctoral dissertation, George Washington University.

Sears, K. 1989. *The significance of relationship with important male "others" in the first conviction of female offenders.* Unpublished doctoral dissertation. Fielding Institute.

Severson, M. M. 1994. Adapting social work values to the corrections environment. *Social Work* 39(4):451–456.

Shover, N. 1983. The later stages of ordinary property offenders' careers. *Social Problems* 31: 208–218.

Simon, B. L. 1995. *The empowerment tradition in American social work: A history.* New York: Columbia University Press.

Simon, R. 1975. *Women and crime.* Lexington, MA: Lexington Books.

Simon, R., and J. Landis. 1991. *The crimes women commit, the punishments they receive.* Lexington, MA: Lexington Books.

Singer, M. I., J. Bussey, L. Song, and L. Lunghofer. 1995. The psychosocial issues of women serving time in jail. *Social Work* 40(1):103–113.

Smart, C. 1977. *Women, crime and criminology: A feminist critique.* London: Routledge and Kegan Paul.

Smith, B. V., and C. Dailard. Summer, 1994. Female prisoners and AIDS: On the margins of public health and social justice. *AIDS and Public Policy Journal* 9(2):78–85.

Snell, T. L. 1994. *Women in prison: Survey of state prison inmates, 1991.* Washington, DC: U.S. Government Printing Office.

Snodgrass, J. 1982. *The jack-roller at seventy: A fifty-year follow-up study.* Lexington, MA: Lexington.

Sobel, S. B. Winter 1982. Difficulties experienced by women in prison. *Psychology of Women Quarterly* 7(2):107–117.

Solomon, B. 1976. *Black empowerment: Social work in oppressed communities.* New York: Columbia University Press.

———. 1982. Empowering women: A matter of values. In *Women, power, and change,* eds. A. Weick and S. Vandiver, 206–214. Silver Springs, MD: National Association of Social Workers.

Sommers, E. K. 1995. *Voices from within: Women in conflict with the law.* York, Ontario: University of Toronto Press.

Spradley, J. P. 1979. *The ethnographic interview.* New York: Holt, Rinehart and Winston.

State v. Heitman, 105 Kan 139, 181 P. 630 (1919).

Steffensmeier, D. J. 1978. Crime and the contemporary woman. *Social Forces* 572:566–84.

Steffensmeier, D. J., and E. Allan. 1998. The nature of female offending: Patterns and explanation. In *Female Offenders,* ed. R. T. Zaplin, 5–29. Gaithersburg, MD: Aspen.

Steffensmeier, D. J., and C. Streifel. 1993. Trends in Female Crime, 1960–1990. In *Female Criminality: The state of the art,* ed. C. C. Culliver, 63–101. New York: Garland.

Straus, M., and R. J. Gelles. 1986. Societal change and change in family violence from 1975 to 1985 as revealed by two national surveys. *Journal of Marriage and the Family* 48:465–479.

Straus, M., R. J. Gelles, and S. K. Steinmetz. 1980. *Behind closed doors: Violence in the American Family.* Garden City, NY: Anchor/Doubleday.

Sutherland, E. 1934. *Principles of criminology.* Chicago: J. B. Lippincott.

Sykes, G. 1958. *A society of captives.* Princeton, NJ: Princeton University Press.

Taylor, J. 1997. Niches and practice: Extending the ecological perspective. In *The Strengths Perspective in Social Work* (2nd ed.), ed. D. Saleebey. New York: Longman.

Teplin, L. A. 1994. Psychiatric and substance abuse disorders among male urban jail detainees. *American Journal of Public Health* 84:290–293.

Teplin, L. A., K. M. Abram, and G. M. McClelland. 1996. The prevalence of psychiatric disorder among incarcerated women: I. Pretrial jail detainees. *Archives of General Psychiatry* 53(6):505–512.

Thomas, J. 1995. New trial granted as woman invokes battered wife claim. *Kansas City Star,* 30 November.

Thomas, W. I. 1907. *Sex and society.* Boston: Little Brown.

———. 1923. *The unadjusted girl.* Boston: Little Brown.

Tjaden, P. and N. Thoennes (2000). *Extent, Nature, and Consequences of Intimate Partner Violence: Findings from the National Violence against Women Survey.* Washington, DC: U.S. Government Printing Office.

Vedder, C. B., and D. B. Sommerville. 1970. *The delinquent girl.* Springfield, IL: Charles C Thomas.

Visher, C. 1983. Gender, police arrest decisions, and notions of chivalry. *Criminology* 21:22–23.

Ward, D. A., and G. G. Kassebaum. 1965. *Women's prison: Sex and social structure.* Chicago: Aldine Publishing Company.

Warren, C. A. B. 1980. Destigmatization of identity: From deviant to charismatic. *Qualitative Sociology* 3(1):59–72.

———. 1991. *Madwives: Schizophrenic women in the 1950s.* New Brunswick, NJ: Rutgers University Press.

Warren, M. Q., and J. L. Rosenbaum. 1986. Criminal careers of female offenders. *Criminal Justice and Behavior* 13(4):393–418.

Watterson, K. 1996. *Women in prison: Inside the concrete womb* (Rev.ed.). Boston: Northeastern University Press.

Weisstein, N. 1970. "Kinde, Kuche, Kirche" as scientific law: Psychology constructs the female. *In Sisterhood is powerful,* ed. R. Morgan, 228–245. New York: Vintage.

Widom, C. S. 1979. Female offenders: Three assumptions about self-esteem, sex-role identity, and feminism. *Criminal Justice and Behavior* 6(4):365–382.

———. 1989. Child abuse, neglect, and violent criminal behavior. *Criminology* 27: 251–271.

Wilmington May Bid for Women's Prison. 1999. *Chicago Tribune,* 28 July.

Wilson, N. K. 1993. Stealing and dealing: The drug war and gendered criminal opportunity. In *Female Criminality: The state of the art,* ed. C. C. Culliver, 169–194. New York: Garland.

Wolin, S. J., and S. Wolin.1993. *The resilient self: How survivors of troubled families rise above adversity.* New York: Villard Books.

Wooldredge, F. D., and K. Masters. 1993. Confronting problems faced by pregnant inmates in state prisons. *Crime & Delinquency* 39(2):195–203.

Yin, R. 1991. *Case study research: Design and methods.* Newbury Park, CA: Sage.

Yllo, K. 1984. The impact of structural inequality and sexist family norms on rates of wife-beating. *Journal of International and Comparative Social Welfare* 1:1–29.

Young, D. S. 1996. Contributing factors to poor health among incarcerated women: A conceptual model. *Affilia* 11(4):440–461.

Young, D. S., and C. J. Smith. 2000. When moms are incarcerated: The needs of children, mothers, and caregivers. *Families in Society* 81(2): 130–141.

Young, I. M. 1994. Punishment, treatment, empowerment: Three approaches to policy for pregnant addicts. *Feminist Studies* 20(1):33–57.

Zalba, S.R. 1964. *Women prisoners and their families.* Los Angeles: Delmar.

Zaplin, R. 1998. *Female offenders: critical perspectives and effective interventions.* Gaithersburg, MD: Aspen.

INDEX

VERMONT COLLEGE LIBRARY

0 0036 00002892

Please remember that this is a library book,
and that it belongs only temporarily to each
person who uses it. Be considerate. Do
not write in this, or any, library book.

DATE DUE

NO 14 '03			
MR 13 '04			
DE 15 '05			
		WITHDRAWN	